BROOKINGS TRADE FORUM

2002

Susan M. Collins
Dani Rodrik

Editors

BROOKINGS INSTITUTION PRESS
Washington, D.C.

ISSN 1520-5479
ISBN 0-8157-1285-5

Subscription Rates
Individuals and institutions $26.95
Standing order plans are available by calling 1-800/275-1447 or 202/797-6258.
For foreign orders add $6.00 surface mail and $14.00 airmail.

Send subscription orders to the Brookings Institution, Department 037, Washington, D.C. 20042-0037. Or call 202/797-6258, toll-free 1-800/275-1447, or fax 202/797-2960.

Visit Brookings online at www.brookings.edu.

Brookings periodicals are available online through both Online Computer Library Center (contact OCLC subscriptions department at 1-800/848-5878, ext.6251) and Project Muse (http://muse.jhu.edu).

Brookings Trade Forum

2002

Editors' Summary   *ix*

ANDREW POWELL
Argentina's Avoidable Crisis: Bad Luck, Bad Economics,   *1*
  Bad Politics, Bad Advice

RICARDO HAUSMANN *and* ANDRÉS VELASCO
Hard Money's Soft Underbelly: *59*
  Understanding the Argentine Crisis
Comments on the Argentina Papers by Joyce Chang and Liliana Rojas-Suarez   *105*
Discussion   117

FATIH ÖZATAY *and* GÜVEN SAK
Banking Sector Fragility and Turkey's 2000–01 Financial Crisis   *121*
Comments by Peter Garber and Atish Ghosh   161
Discussion   169

Panel: Views on Currency Crises
MORRIS GOLDSTEIN
Lessons of Recent Currency Crises   *173*

JOSE LUIS MACHINEA
Currency Crises: A Practitioner's View   *183*

YUNG CHUL PARK
Does East Asia Need a New Development Paradigm?   *211*
Discussion   227

₿ THE BROOKINGS INSTITUTION

The Brookings Institution is an independent organization devoted to nonpartisan research, education, and publication in economics, government, foreign policy, and the social sciences generally. Its principal purposes are to aid in the development of sound public policies and to promote public understanding of issues of national importance.

The Institution was founded on December 8, 1927, to merge the activities of the Institute for Government Research, founded in 1916, the Institute of Economics, founded in 1922, and the Robert Brookings Graduate School of Economics and Government, founded in 1924.

The general administration of the Institution is the responsibility of a Board of Trustees charged with safeguarding the independence of the staff and fostering the most favorable conditions for scientific research and publication. The immediate direction of the policies, program, and staff is vested in the president, assisted by an advisory committee of the officers and staff.

In publishing a study, the Institution presents it as a competent treatment of a subject worthy of public consideration. The interpretations or conclusions in such publications are those of the author or authors and do not necessarily reflect the views of the other staff members, officers, or trustees of the Brookings Institution.

BROOKINGS TRADE FORUM is a series of annual volumes that provide authoritative and in-depth analysis on current and emerging issues in international economics. The series aims to explore questions on international trade and macroeconomics in an interdisciplinary fashion with both practitioners and academics and seeks to gather in one place papers that provide a thorough look at a particular topic affecting international economic policy. Leading experts in the field will contribute to each volume. This fifth issue examines the recent currency crises, with edited versions of the papers and comments presented at a conference held at the Brookings Institution, May 2, 2002.

The conference and journal have been supported by the New Century Chair in International Trade and Economics at the Brookings Institution.

SUSAN M. COLLINS
DANI RODRIK

Editors' Summary

Currency crises are paramount but extremely perplexing problems in today's international economy. Initially erupting in a country's financial markets, these crises typically spread throughout a country's economy and beyond—often with devastating consequences for real economic activity. The resultant reductions in domestic living standards can be severe and long lasting. Why do such crises continue to erupt? Can the growing number of past experiences enable us to better understand current crises, mitigate their impact, and prevent additional crises from occurring in the future?

Brookings Trade Forum 2002 brought together experts on the two most recent crises—in Argentina and Turkey—as well as economists and policymakers who have studied currency crises more broadly. The result was a lively and informed debate, conducted in three sessions. One session focused on the ongoing crisis in Argentina. The two papers presented in this session provide quite different assessments of what went wrong and what might have been done differently to prevent the crisis. A second session focused on the recent experience in Turkey. The third session, a discussion launched by three panelists, provided an open-ended discussion of the lessons to be drawn for the future.

The fifth annual conference of the Brookings Trade Forum was held in Washington on May 2, 2002. This volume contains the papers, panelist remarks, invited commentary, and general discussions from that conference.

In the first paper, Andrew Powell argues that the Argentine crisis was not inevitable and could have been avoided. While the currency was overvalued by conventional measures, especially after the devaluation of the Brazilian real, he finds that Argentina's current account had more or less adjusted by the end of 2000. And while Argentina did need a fiscal adjustment, he argues that until the end of 2000, and perhaps even until the second quarter of 2001, the magnitude of the required adjustment was relatively small. In actuality Argentina accomplished virtually no fiscal adjustment whatsoever.

Powell argues that the root of Argentina's crisis was, therefore, the interaction of four factors. First, the country suffered from bad luck, including a significant decline in its terms of trade and a recession in Brazil, its main trading partner. Second, fiscal adjustment, though moderate, was required. Third, the current account adjustment process was very slow, involving both deflation and recession. Finally, and very important, Argentina's politics were extremely messy—hence its inability to reduce national spending without creating enormous political uncertainty. Powell presents the interaction of these factors as a vicious, self-enforcing cycle, potentially implying multiple equilibria, both for the economic variables and between the economic and political outcomes.

Powell's paper opens with a brief description of the events beginning in the late 1990s. The paper then uses vector autoregression (VAR) analysis to study the linkages between these variables. Powell finds significant interrelations between key economic and political indicators. In particular, political risk fed through to worsened economic fundamentals, and these fed back to increased political risk. Low fiscal revenues and lower imports fed through to higher spreads on Argentina's international bonds, which in turn fed back to both lower imports and budgetary difficulties instead of fiscal revenues. The results support the view that politics and fiscal variables were key drivers of Argentina's problems.

Different authors have criticized the role of the International Monetary Fund (IMF) in Argentina. Powell argues that the International Monetary Fund was in an impossible position. Although the IMF became increasingly uncomfortable with Argentina's policies, it also recognized that withdrawal of its support would likely create the conditions for a private sector run that would end in default and probable devaluation. The IMF was thus caught between its growing concern about moral hazard and the possibility of a run. Powell argues that this dilemma is likely to characterize future IMF relations with countries in a crisis.

The lack of support for the March 2001 Lopez-Murphy plan marked a watershed, which can be seen as identifying the limits of the adjustment in government spending that was politically feasible under the de la Rua government. With bond spreads over 1,000 basis points, it can be argued that the IMF had to make a decision to either assist Argentina strongly or withdraw. However, the IMF did neither. Powell develops a more formal game theoretic analysis to study the behavior of both sides in this episode. Perhaps surprisingly, this model suggests that Argentina's action ("deviation to more risky play") and the IMF's vacillation may in fact be part of rational "equilibrium" play.

In summarizing the situation as of July 2002, Powell notes that the tension between moral hazard and private sector confidence continues. Unfortunately, the "cooperative solution" may only become available when the IMF's threat of removing support again becomes meaningful. He concludes that under its current modus operandi, the IMF becomes largely irrelevant to a country in a crisis as deep as Argentina's.

Powell also uses his model of Argentina-IMF relations to motivate a broader discussion about the need for a more efficient crisis resolution process—what is now typically called reforms to the international financial architecture. In particular, Powell stresses the need to reduce the incentives for countries to pursue riskier policies as default becomes more likely. He suggests that a bankruptcy procedure for sovereigns might provide a solution. He also suggests that his analysis may help to put some bounds on how attractive or painful such a procedure may need to be so as to provide more appropriate incentives.

Ricardo Hausmann and Andrés Velasco present an analysis of Argentina's crisis that is quite similar to Powell's in some respects, but strikingly different in others. They begin by pointing out that Argentina's was not a crisis that caught people by surprise. Instead it was a protracted affair, attracting the attention of some of the best minds in Washington, Wall Street, and Buenos Aires. Many well-trained economists proposed various diagnostics and innovative policy initiatives. The country's much-maligned politicians and parties supported austerity policies. And, until late in the game, the international community provided financial support. Yet the catastrophe proved "impossible to avoid."

Hausmann and Velasco examine what they see as the three main theories put forward as the crisis deepened. First, some analysts have argued that the problem had a fiscal origin and required a fiscal response. For others, it was a multiple equilibria story, in which self-fulfilling pessimism kept interest rates too high and growth too low for the numbers to add up. The third group of analysts blamed the exchange rate, arguing that the real value of the currency had moved in the wrong direction.

Hausmann and Velasco then argue that none of these stories on its own makes sense. In spite of the strong temptation to blame everything on irresponsible politicians, they argue that a simple fiscal explanation is inadequate. They find no evidence of a spending boom in Argentina—as a share of GDP, primary government expenditures remained roughly constant in the 1993–2001 period. Public debt did grow rapidly. But they argue that this debt accumulation was not driven by a lack of adjustment effort, but instead to a significant extent by the transition costs of the Social Security system, the recession, and the recognition of preexisting debts.

Although Hausmann and Velasco agree that there were elements of self-fulfilling pessimism in the Argentine debacle, they find it hard to make the case that multiple equilibria alone were to blame. Given the difficulties of changing relative prices, they find that reestablishing enough confidence to assure moderate growth would have required maintaining a current account deficit in excess of 5 percent of GDP and accumulating an additional $20 billion in external debt between 1998 and 2001. While possibly feasible in an idealized world with perfect capital markets, they conclude that such a path was an extremely unlikely bet in a more realistic setting with sovereign risk and imperfect commitment to repay.

In contrast, they argue that to make sense of what went wrong one must focus on the interaction between two factors: Argentina's misaligned real exchange rate and its capacity to borrow abroad, which went from ample in the early 1990s to nil by 2001. To highlight these issues, Hausmann and Velasco develop a framework in which export prospects determine the access of financially constrained countries to external resources. Starting in 1999, expectations of Argentina's future export growth arguably declined sharply: expected returns to capital in this sector fell, along with low export prices and an appreciating real multilateral exchange rate. The drastic tightening of the financing constraint explains the onset of Argentina's investment decline and recession. Thereafter negative factors fed on each other: higher risk premiums and smaller capital flows meant less demand for domestic investment, which in turn depressed aggregate demand and output, further curtailing creditworthiness and Argentina's ability to borrow.

The authors note that other countries in the region suffered similar capital account shocks and were forced to undertake rapid current account reversals. But those countries, especially Chile and Brazil, could rely on sharp changes in relative prices to help speed up the adjustment. Those countries were also much less dollarized than Argentina, reducing the negative balance sheet effects. Since relative prices could not adjust quickly in Argentina (deflation did its painful job, but very slowly), quantities had to. The economy began contracting sharply in 1999 and has remained on that course ever since. In this sense, Argentina's financial crisis was a growth crisis: if incomes keep dropping, at some point debts become impossible to pay.

Hausmann and Velasco conclude that this situation presented policymakers with an unusually nasty menu of options. Standard fiscal contraction ran the risk of further contracting an already depressed economy, while having a highly uncertain impact on expectations, investment, and future growth. Using the exchange rate, as textbooks recommend, was no easier. Argentina clearly suffered from exchange rate overvaluation. But given the large stock of dollar-denominated debt, both private and public, devaluation by itself would have most likely made matters worse. Arguably a devaluation accompanied by a symmetric pesification of financial claims might have resolved the overvaluation while minimizing the negative balance sheet effect.

An extensive discussion about Argentina followed presentation of these two papers. Many participants, including the invited discussants, argued that Hausmann and Velasco's analysis underestimated the size and relevance of Argentina's fiscal problem. The participants emphasized the importance of the provinces, and the need for fuller analysis of the budgetary implications of both Social Security reform and privatization. Some speakers stressed the view that Argentina's deflation is an important factor that has received insufficient attention. There was also discussion of the extent to which Argentina's economic performance had differed from that of other economies in the region since 1999, and why its crisis became so severe after mid-2001.

In the third paper, Fatih Özatay and Güven Sak examine the 2000–01 crisis in Turkey. This experience is perhaps less well known, but also raises both puzzling issues and some potential lessons. They point out that the Turkish economy has been hit by two crises in the past decade. The first one occurred at the beginning of 1994, when the country was maintaining a managed float. The second and more severe crisis was preceded by turmoil in domestic financial markets that burst in the second half of November 2000—in the midst of an IMF-supported exchange rate–based stabilization program. Under this plan, the Turkish central bank implemented a crawling peg exchange rate regime under strict currency board rules. Not only was the rate of crawl predetermined, but the timing and method for transitioning to a floating exchange rate were publicly announced at the outset.

In fact, the regime collapsed four months before the planned exit date. At the end of December 2000, average interest rates were almost four times higher than they had been at the beginning of November and more than five times higher than the preannounced year-end depreciation rate of the Turkish lira. This unsustainable situation ended on February 19, 2001, when the prime minister announced that there was a severe political crisis. Three days later the exchange rate system collapsed, and Turkey declared that it would implement a floating exchange rate.

In this paper, Özatay and Sak analyze the reasons behind this second crisis. In the process, they provide a wealth of facts and figures about economic policy and performance during the relevant period. Their main conclusion is that the root cause of the crisis was an increasingly fragile banking sector and a set of triggering factors that made this fragility very evident.

The authors begin by examining the evolution of key economic variables. They show that Turkey's macroeconomic fundamentals were quite weak during the 1999–2000 period (including budget and current account deficits and an overvalued exchange rate). However, they argue that this episode does not fit the pattern of what has been called a first-generation crisis. Specifically, the budget was financed by issuance of domestic debt, not money creation. And perhaps because of the IMF standby agreement signed in December 1999, the situation was improving in 2000, not deteriorating. There was no gradual depletion of foreign exchange reserves, nor was there a gradual rise in interest rates. Instead, these changes occurred suddenly and dramatically when the crisis erupted.

Özatay and Sak argue that the Turkish experience also does not fit the story underlying a so-called second-generation crisis, in which speculation arises from expectations regarding government policy in the aftermath of a crisis. They point out that postcrisis policies have not, in fact, been expansionary. A new IMF agreement was signed, and the primary budget surplus was substantially increased.

Instead, Özatay and Sak build the case that the main underlying problem revolved around the interaction between debt finance and Turkish banks. They argue that the banking system fragility was caused by Turkey's high public sector borrowing requirement and the way it was financed. To support this view, they analyze the structural characteristics of the Turkish banking system and provide a detailed discussion of the mechanics of the crisis process that unfolded. They provide evidence regarding the accumulation of risk in the banking system in the period preceding the crisis, including the increasing mismatches in currency and maturity and the rising volume of nonperforming loans. The authors show that the source of risk differed significantly between private and state banks. They also document substantial variation in exposure among private banks.

Hence the banking system was highly vulnerable to capital reversals. Delays in implementing structural reforms (especially related to banking supervision), as well as political uncertainties, contributed to the vulnerable financial environment. The crisis exploded after key banks lost their credit lines, making it difficult for the government to roll over debt instruments, thus raising interest rates and prompting concerns about the sustainability of the debt.

There was considerable interest in the details of what happened in Turkey's financial system prior to the collapse. However, Peter Garber argued that the paper makes too much of the differences among the alternative models of a currency crisis. In his view, the underlying issue is how to cover the financial hole in the government. He also discussed the reasons why external banks continued to lend actively to Turkey. Atish Ghosh suggested that the authors should pay more attention to an alternative explanation of what happened. He argued that Turkey's crisis may simply be another example of a failed exchange rate–based program to stabilize inflation. This generated some discussion of whether the stabilization program, with its preannounced exit date, had been a credible and sensible strategy at the outset.

The third session of the Trade Forum was a panel discussion. Three experts were invited to discuss their views regarding currency crises more generally, including causes and appropriate policy responses.

Morris Goldstein focused his remarks on the lessons to be learned regarding currency regimes and debt problems in emerging economies. He argued that a country's currency regime matters a lot, both for reducing vulnerability to crises and for improving macroeconomic performance. Based on his reading of the evidence, he concludes that adjustable and crawling pegs are prone to currency mismatch and particularly vulnerable to crises. Further, it appears very difficult to engineer a noncrisis transition to more flexibility. Currency boards, while perhaps less fragile, are still vulnerable to speculative attack and significantly limit policy responses to recession. And nonindustrial economies appear to have a "fear of floating," so that most floats are more *de jure* than *de facto*. In this context, he makes the case of an exchange rate regime he calls managed floating plus. This enables countries to maintain some monetary independence while actively targeting inflation and taking measures to reduce currency mismatch. He cites Chile, Brazil, and Mexico as examples of countries that have recently done well pursuing this type of regime. However, he cautions that no exchange rate regime should be viewed as a panacea.

Goldstein also argued that standard analyses of debt sustainability are likely to be overly optimistic. In his view, these analyses typically pay inadequate attention to a country's ability to generate foreign exchange. They fail to capture the potential for vicious cycles arising from interactions among fiscal tightening, higher interest rates, slower growth, and lower tax receipts. Further, current interest rate spreads may be poor predictors of the spread that markets will require in the future to meet a country's financing needs as domestic and external conditions evolve. Thus Goldstein concluded that more conservative approaches are warranted for estimating whether a country's debt is sustainable. He also strongly supported measures to make debt restructuring more timely and orderly. In this context, he ended his commentary with a discussion of the main initiatives that have been proposed recently.

Jose Luis Machinea, former minister of finance of Argentina, analyzes the period leading to Argentina's crisis from the perspective of a key decision-maker and in the context of existing literature on currency crises. The thrust of his argument is that Argentina's unique experience with convertibility poses new problems that challenge and improve upon conventional wisdom about the nature of these crises.

Machinea begins by reviewing the literature on currency crises, arguing that many of the lessons learned from the crises of the 1980s, such as the central importance of consistent monetary and fiscal policy decisions, are still relevant today. More recently, the magnitude of the crises in Mexico, Asia, and Russia has increased the focus on the link between currency crises and financial crises. Weak financial systems, short-term indebtedness of both the private and public sectors, and herding behavior among investors are seen as key causes of the meltdown in these countries. Machinea shows that according to these criteria the causes of Turkey's recent crisis were not ambiguous. Argentina's crisis, however, is somewhat exceptional, because the country was admired throughout the 1990s for high growth, low inflation, and a remarkably solid financial system.

Machinea focuses on the inflexible nature of the convertibility regime as central to Argentina's problems. He carefully weighs the criticisms of convertibility—that it was not sufficiently credible in the long run for investors, that it did not allow necessary procyclical fiscal policy and exaggerated external shocks, and that it was harmful to Argentina's competitiveness—against what he perceives to be the alternatives, and argues that it is unclear that a move to official dollarization or a more flexible regime would have been more effective. An alternative regime would not necessarily preserve low inflation and interest rate premiums or change the fundamental problems of high government deficits or labor market rigidity. In fact, by the time he took office in December 1999, Machinea argues, it would have been economically devastating and politically impossible to abandon convertibility. He defends the government's decision for fiscal adjustment and an IMF loan, and blames political disagreement and the worsening global economic climate for its failure.

Machinea draws several lessons from this crisis that should better inform policymakers in the future. Foremost, while convertibility was an effective short-run monetary stabilization tool, he believes it should have been abandoned in the good times. For political reasons, this did not happen in Argentina. Thus the Argentine crisis highlights the centrality of political consensus to economic policymaking. Ultimately, the economy must be able to make adjustments in the event of an external shock, and this puts particular stress on hard peg regimes. Argentina shows that inflexibility does not necessarily lead to discipline.

Machinea also concludes that this crisis has implications for financial market policy. Unlike other countries that suffered currency crises, he characterizes Argentina's financial system as extremely solid, fettered only by the potential cost of devaluation due to high liability dollarization. Therefore, Machinea concludes that liability dollarization should be discouraged. He also believes that market instruments, such as the Argentine mega swap, cannot be used to solve liquidity problems in the middle of a crisis.

Yung Chul Park explores the strengths and weaknesses of the development model in East Asia. He asks whether the region should overhaul its entire development model in favor of the American style of free capitalism, or should instead concentrate on reforming the current model. He notes that the IMF reform programs in East Asia, which are based on free market capitalism, have not led to precrisis success levels. But the precrisis model may have had serious flaws that precluded its success in the new global economy.

When the East Asian economies were opened to capitalism and free trade they boomed, but then crisis set in. Park identifies four structural weaknesses of the precrisis model. These weaknesses are all related to the inability to adjust the corporate banking sector quickly enough to market liberalization: an inadequate governance mechanism over the private sector; the absence of mature financial infrastructure and a legal and regulatory system; a closed, nontransparent corporate sector; and the market distortions and monopolies arising from dependence on an export-led development strategy. However, Park concludes that these weaknesses are not enough to completely abandon the old development model. The model's basic premise is still applicable, but its institutions must be reformed.

Updating the old model essentially amounts to building a new, mixed economy model combining the state and market to adjust to democratization, economic liberalization, and globalization. Different countries in East Asia will reform at different speeds and to different degrees, based on their individual situations and expectations. All of them would be smart to maintain the same growth policies: incentive schemes for saving and investment, encouraging investment in education along with research and development, upholding macroeconomic stability and market openness, and preserving the growth with an equitable social welfare strategy. The necessary reforms to the model include instituting a new democratic governance system, halting corruption in government, developing social welfare programs, providing for political participation for labor, regulating both market-based and bank-based financial systems, strengthening legal and judiciary oversight of industrial organization, implementing a managed floating exchange rate system, and improving regional integration and cooperation.

Thus Park suggests that reforming the precrisis East Asian development model so that it complies with the new requirements of open market capitalism and globalization will lead to more success than will simply imposing the American capitalist model on East Asia. He concludes that a gradual reform—sensitive to the realities of the region and flexible enough to adjust to societal, political, and economic changes—is the safest way to avoid further crises.

ANDREW POWELL

Universidad Torcuato Di Tella, Buenos Aires

Argentina's Avoidable Crisis: Bad Luck, Bad Economics, Bad Politics, Bad Advice

W as the Argentine crisis inevitable? One would think so, given the number of papers suggesting that Argentina's economic collapse was unavoidable. This paper counters that trend. While Argentina's currency may have been overvalued by conventional measures, especially after the devaluation of the Brazilian real, the current account had more or less adjusted by the end of 2000. This paper suggests that until the end of 2000—and arguably even until the second quarter of 2001—the fiscal adjustment that Argentina most certainly required to resolve its crisis was feasible. Instead, Argentina did virtually nothing. The real roots of the crisis had more to do with Argentina and the difficulties in effecting a fiscal adjustment than with the particular exchange rate regime.

Argentina's crisis was avoidable. If some combinations of key events and decisions at particular moments had turned out differently, the crisis could have been averted; if, for example:

—Argentina had managed to renegotiate the tax-sharing agreement between the provinces as the constitution demanded;

—Argentine public sector savings had been higher in 1996–98;

—the Peronist Party had not been split down the middle in 1998–99;

The author thanks Leandro Arozamena, Miguel Angel Broda, Joyce Chang, Susan Collins, Hugh Elliott, Javier Finkman, Miguel Kiguel, Michael Gavin, Beatriz Nofal, Martín Gonzalez Rozada, Pablo Guidotti, Jose Luis Machinea, Pedro Pou, and Féderico Sturzenegger as well as the participants in the Brookings Trade Forum for their help in writing this paper. The author wishes to thank Brookings for sponsoring this paper, Augusto Stabalito for excellent research assistance, and Centro de Informacíon Financiera (CIF), Universidad Torcuato Di Tella, for additional support.

1

—the Radical Party had held an outright majority in the new government in 1999;

—the new Alianza government had reduced (the right) expenditures immediately;

—the Radical Party had actively ditched Frepaso preemptively and sought an alliance with moderate Peronists and others;

—the Lopez-Murphy plan had been endorsed.

Had any one of these occurred, then the risk of default would have decreased.

The root of the crisis was the interaction between bad luck, a moderate but certainly required fiscal adjustment, a slow deflationary and recessionary current account adjustment process, and, very importantly, extremely messy politics—and hence the inability to reduce national spending without creating enormous political uncertainty. These interaction effects can also be thought of as vicious self-enforcing cycles, suggesting potential multiple equilibria, both within the economic variables and also between the economy and politics.

Authors have criticized both the role of the International Monetary Fund (IMF) in Argentina and particular decisions by the IMF. The characterization offered in this paper is that the IMF was in an impossible position—and will be in the same impossible position when faced with the next country in a similar trap. It is suggested below that, on the one hand, the IMF became increasingly uncomfortable with the policies that Argentina adopted—especially in 2001, as the limits to orthodox fiscal adjustment became clearer and other directions were tried. But at the same time the IMF knew that if it withdrew support it would create the conditions for a private sector run that would have ended (as it eventually did) in default and probable devaluation. The IMF was then caught between a growing concern regarding moral hazard and the possibility of a massive run that would create a crisis much deeper than actually warranted given the underlying problems in the economy. This more structural explanation for the difficult role of the IMF suggests that the international financial architecture is still incomplete and further creative thought is required to contain the incentives for countries in such an unfortunate position to pursue more risky policies as default becomes more likely.

The current economic crisis in Argentina can be traced back to at least mid-1998. This was the period when private investment began to decline and the economy began to slow more rapidly.[1] At that time Argentina suffered a set

---

1. Some might argue that the roots of the crisis can be traced back to 1991 and the convertibility regime itself. But the origins of that regime also would have to be contemplated.

of external negative shocks that might have rocked any economy. The events addressed in this section are roughly chronological: luck runs out; politics get messy; politics drive economics, or vice versa; and the IMF's role.

Luck Runs Out

The Asian crisis largely left Argentina unscathed, with a sharp but temporary hike in risk spreads with the attack on Hong Kong in October 1997. The impact of the Russian default was a different story altogether. The strong rise in the overall Emerging Markets Bond Index (EMBI) spread led to a significant impact on Argentina, affecting capital inflows and investment. Figure 1 shows the overall EMBI and the Argentine EMBI.[2] Argentina's persistent current account deficit reflected a dependency on international capital flows to foster growth. After many years of an open investment regime, the majority of the top 100 companies in Argentina were under foreign ownership. Thus a significant percentage of domestic fixed investment was accounted for by foreign-owned companies. The currency board, open capital account, and structure of investment made the passthrough from measures of country risk to real investment more direct than in many other emerging countries.

In 1998 Argentina also suffered a sharp decline in the terms of trade, mainly as a result of significant falls in agricultural prices. In addition there was a deepening recession in Brazil, Argentina's main trading partner and the destination for about 30 percent of Argentine exports. Another significant shock hit Argentina in January 1999, namely the devaluation of the Brazilian real. Argentine exports to Brazil were again strongly impacted, although the feared cheap imports from Brazil to Argentina never really materialized. Moreover, Argentine exports appeared to recover reasonably well toward the end of 1999 as the Brazilian economy recovered, although export levels were still below 1998 levels. Finally, given the exchange rate regime, the strength of the U.S. dollar clearly did not help Argentina either in exporting to Europe (the second-largest export market after Brazil) or in competing with other countries in exporting to the U.S. market (the third-largest export destination). While

Indeed, some might consider that the origins were the same as the problems that dogged Argentina throughout the second half of the twentieth century. This paper considers the origins since 1998. It is then a maintained assumption that the crisis was not inevitable given the initial conditions at that time.

2. The high correlation is not explained by Argentina's relatively high participation in the index.

Figure 1. Overall and Argentine EMBI Spread, 1994–2001

Spread over U.S. Treasuries (basis points)

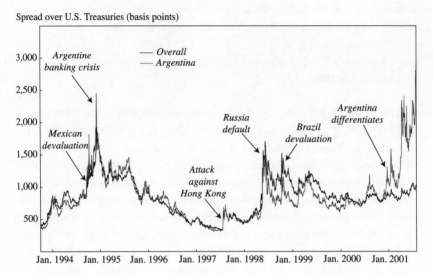

Source: JP Morgan Chase.

Figure 2. External Trade through Convertibility, 1993–2001

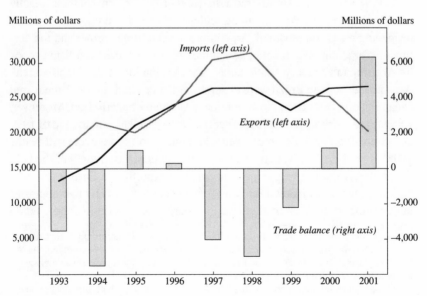

Source: Ministry of the Economy.

exports grew virtually every year over the currency board period, these factors ensured that export growth was limited. Figure 2 plots Argentine exports and imports and the trade balance.

Pou suggests that 1999 is a critical year to analyze, as in that year third quarter growth was flat and in the fourth quarter Argentina grew at an annualized rate of 5.6 percent. Pou claims that it is incorrect to consider the entire period of 1988 to the present as continuous recession. The growth in 1999 is surprising, given the Brazilian devaluation in January 1999, the supposed overvaluation of the Argentine peso, and the deflationary adjustment that Argentina was undergoing during that time. A possible explanation is a fiscal stimulus, in part due to the electoral campaign, but Perry and Servén find little fiscal stimulus at the federal level—about 1 percent of gross domestic product (GDP)—although the province of Buenos Aires also increased expenditure by some $2 billion over the year.[3]

Messy Politics

Late-1998 through 1999 coincided with a period of particularly messy politics. First, the end of then president Menem's second term heralded a waning concentration of power and more fractious politics. A common view was that many of Menem's actions during his second term were aimed ultimately at attempting to change the constitution to allow for a third term. This created a sharp divide within the Peronist Party between those who appeared to go along with this bid and those who did not, with subsidiary fights within the latter camp regarding a successor. This political turmoil made further major economic reforms more difficult.

In October 1999 de la Rua was elected president, beating Duhalde, the chosen Peronist candidate and former governor of the province of Buenos Aires. De la Rua was the leader of the Alianza, an alliance between the Radical Party and Frepaso, a smaller party. The political campaign was quite extraordinary. Duhalde held a marked lead in the polls early in the year, but he was ultimately defeated, in part due to his decision to focus on the debt position and his open call for a renegotiation of the foreign debt.[4]

3. Pou (2002); Perry and Servén (2002).
4. While Duhalde started to talk about debt renegotiations earlier, and *La Nación* ran the story that he visited the Pope, in part to discuss debt relief, this became a major issue after the Argentine Banking Association (ABA) conference in July 2001, which provided a major platform for Duhalde's position.

This stance did not help relations with then president Menem. Duhalde criticized Menem for undermining his campaign. The debt position had certainly worsened, arguably as a result of the political campaigns themselves. But the reaction of most Argentines to Duhalde's call for debt renegotiation was that such a move would threaten Argentina's hard-won economic stability. The voters rejected it.

Another interesting feature of the campaign was the rumor that Domingo Cavallo might forge an alliance with Duhalde. Cavallo headed his own political party, Acción por la República. To some extent this may have been meant to calm the nerves of those that were concerned about Duhalde's more populist political rhetoric. In a July 1999 interview with the *Financial Times*, Cavallo suggested that eventually the peso might float.[5] While the interview clearly stated that Cavallo would float the peso only from a position of strength, the article was published with a leading title that suggested otherwise. In a precedent of things to come, the markets reacted strongly, pushing country risk up significantly.[6]

President de la Rua took office in January 2000. The reaction of the private sector to the new Alianza government was one of suspicion, and might best be described as "wait and see." The suspicion stemmed from a number of factors, including:

—rumors regarding the personality and competence of the president himself;

—the Radical Party's history—the party's last experience in power led to the early resignation of President Alfonsín in 1989 amid economic crisis;

—the nature of the alliance—the Frepaso Party did not appear to share many of the views or policies of the de la Rua wing of the radicals; and

—the Alianza did not hold a majority in Congress and had to negotiate with the opposition Peronists to pass virtually all legislation, raising issues of governability.

Politics Drives Economics or Vice Versa?

As the economy stagnated and tax revenues began to fall, President de la Rua's first economy minister, Jose Luis Machinea, decided on a significant

5. "Cavallo Says Argentina Could Float Its Currency," *Financial Times,* May 17, 1999.
6. In an "event study" of how currency risk affects country risk, covering many years and countries, Powell and Sturzenegger (2000) find that this event was significant.

tax increase. This became known in Argentina as the first *impuestazo*, a play on the Spanish word for tax, *impuesto*. The idea was that with a significant increase in taxes (politically easier than reducing expenditure), the fiscal deficit would be narrowed and the private sector would feel more comfortable about the sustainability of the debt as well as the responsibility of the Radicals in power. More orthodox economists argued that this would then reduce country risk, cut interest rates, and aid recovery. Unfortunately, the *impuestazo* had a significant negative effect on activity that appeared to outweigh these potentially positive aspects. Indeed, the negative effect on activity could be seen after the announcement of the package in early 2000, even before taxes had actually risen.

During 2000 there was a new piece of bad luck, namely the fall in the Nasdaq. Moreover, further internal political squabbles ensued as the proposed austerity program angered the left wing of the Radicals, which was led by former president Alfonsín and members of Frepaso, such that the governing coalition appeared to be continuously at breaking point. Problems with the ability to govern appeared paramount, the real economy did not recover, and the private sector saw its wait-and-see attitude vindicated; indeed the private sector became more pessimistic. The IMF program, based on reasonably optimistic scenarios for growth, implied that many observers thought that the fiscal deficit targets were difficult to meet. Eventually, certain expenditure reducing policies were also effected, including a reduction in public sector salaries. This reduction was an attempt to maintain reasonable deficit figures despite falling revenues and stay within the IMF program. Also, a labor reform bill was passed, although at significant political cost. Toward the end of 2000, the continued political squabbling resulted in the resignation of the vice president, who was also the leader of the Frepaso party, putting the future of the alliance in further doubt.[7]

Through 2000 a double vicious cycle developed. On the one hand, a purely economic cycle included depressed economic activity that negatively impacted tax revenues, along with worsening the fiscal deficit. This was coupled with increasing concerns about debt sustainability, pushing country risk spreads and interest rates higher and reducing investment, feeding back to depressed economic activity. A second vicious cycle developed from the economics to politics and back to economics. The worsened fiscal position led to calls for adjustment and heightened political squabbling. The suggested adjustments,

7. The vice president's resignation was also a consequence, at least ostensibly, of a bribery scandal in the Senate, where it was alleged that senators accepted payments to support the passage of a labor reform bill.

Figure 3. GDP Growth, Fiscal Revenue, and EMBI+

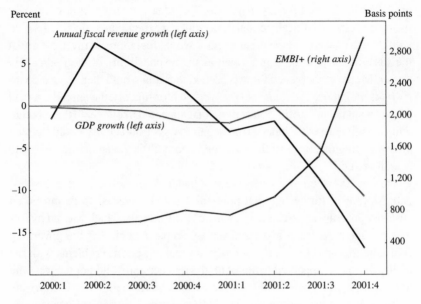

Source: Ministry of the Economy.

in terms of tax hikes and expenditure reductions, hurt interested parties. In turn the political squabbling also increased country risk. Market perception was that Argentine politics would prevent any forthcoming adjustments to make the fiscal position sustainable. Figure 3 plots growth, fiscal revenue, and the EMBI+ index for Argentina for 2000 and 2001.

At the end of 2000, and as stronger doubts began to emerge on the sustainability of the debt, Minister Machinea negotiated a support package from the IMF, other multilaterals, private banks, and the Spanish government to ensure funding for the following twelve to twenty-four months. This was known as the *blindaje* and included a substantial IMF contribution.[8]

The *blindaje* appeared to calm the nerves of international investors—at least temporarily. However, there was concern about the real commitment of the private sector market makers to roll over the debt. Also, there were doubts regarding the promised IMF support—again conditional on fiscal targets based on reasonably optimistic growth forecasts. Indeed, one interpretation is that

8. *Blindaje*, which is Spanish for armor, conveys well the idea that the package was to protect Argentina from speculative attacks (or runs) due to a lack of confidence about the liquidity position of the public sector. The total package was advertised as $30 billion, with the IMF contribution amounting to $15 billion. See Mussa (2002) for details.

the Argentine private sector simply did not believe in the promised recovery or the adjustment. These doubts were not helped by the resignation of Jose Luis Machinea in March 2001 after a period of sustained political pressure. One (generous) interpretation was that having spent his political force in forging an agreement to obtain the *blindaje,* Machinea thought it would be better for the country if he resigned and someone else took the economic reins to implement it. A less kind interpretation was that Machinea himself did not really believe that the recovery or adjustment was possible and wanted out while the going was good. Machinea was replaced with Ricardo Lopez-Murphy. Lopez-Murphy had a reputation as a strong fiscalist and had been a strong original candidate for economy minister, but had become unpopular among sections of the Radical Party by calling openly for cuts in public sector wages—cuts that Machinea had eventually implemented.[9]

Lopez-Murphy's plan included an immediate cut in public sector expenditure, with cuts in areas that directly hurt key and powerful lobbies within the Radical Party that supported de la Rua, including education. One might speculate that this was a deliberate strategy on the part of Lopez-Murphy to signal to the markets that he meant business, and to the de la Rua government that he should be allowed to do anything he wanted or he would leave. The result was that he left. Lopez-Murphy failed to convince his own party that these measures were really necessary. Following a political storm heralded by the resignation of the minister of the interior, Lopez-Murphy was forced to resign.

Domingo Cavallo replaced Lopez-Murphy. Cavallo left his own political party to become the minister of the economy for the second time. His strategy appeared to be quite different from those of Machinea or Lopez-Murphy, and his focus, at least initially, was not on orthodox fiscal measures, but was on more heterodox policies to try to get recovery. Perhaps he calculated that his reputation for sound economic management during his first period as economy minister (1991–96) was sufficient to allay the fears that Argentina might move back to more market unfriendly measures. These heterodox measures included pressuring the central bank to relax banking regulations (relaxing monetary policy, as he referred to it), introducing subsidies for particular sectors (through a scheme named the competitive plan, or *plan competitividad*), and trying to get more flexibility within the exchange rate regime (discussed below). A financial transaction tax was also introduced, which, being reasonably easy to monitor, helped to reduce substantially the fiscal deficit and arguably made the total package roughly revenue neutral.

9. Lopez-Murphy was originally appointed minister of defense.

However, two issues toward the start of Cavallo's new term resulted in sharply increased country risk. The first was a fight with the central bank and the eventual removal of the central bank president. The second was the change in the convertibility law to include the euro (once it achieved parity with the U.S. dollar) in the basket to fix the Argentine peso within the currency board regime. On the first issue, the central bank moved slightly in the direction of relaxing bank regulations, but it was clear that it would attempt to resist further changes. The analysis from the central bank was that measures to loosen monetary policy would not work, as the problem was a lack of demand for credit, not a problem of supply. Indeed, effectively reducing central bank reserves would simply weaken confidence, and hence demand, further. Pedro Pou, then central bank president, also made clear his objection to the introduction of the euro into the currency basket and publicly favored dollarization rather than increased flexibility.

At the same time, Pedro Pou faced a political inquiry into his conduct that focused mostly on the handling of several bank closures and other miscellaneous charges.[10] As no court had pronounced against him with respect to any of these cases, the inquiry had to be a political one. The investigating congressional committee could allege no statements regarding legal wrongdoing. The charter of the central bank states that the central bank is independent, but allows the country's president to remove a central bank president after the formation of a congressional committee and upon its recommendation. While a central bank president can be removed after some judicial process has proven guilt, it was also argued by the committee and their lawyers that the clause allowed for dismissal if the relevant committee discovered misconduct, with the final decision resting with the president. In the end the congressional committee recommended removal and President de la Rua signed the relevant decree, making a mockery of the independence of the institution. This process clearly eroded the already shaky reputation of institutions in Argentina.

It is perhaps ironic that the plan to introduce the euro into the basket met with such a hostile reaction from the markets. After all, the markets appeared to have been calling for increased flexibility, and this could have been interpreted as one way to get it—and without sacrificing the discipline of the

10. These charges included assisting banks too much before they were eventually closed, but also suggested that banks were not assisted enough. The charges also included references to money laundering (or that the central bank had not done enough to stop it) and suggested that the central bank president, by talking favorably about dollarization, was not defending the local currency. The charter of the central bank states that defending the value of the local currency is the central bank's first objective.

currency board. However, the market's interpretation was that if this change to the convertibility law (previously thought sacrosanct) could be made so easily, then other changes might also be introduced with ease. While Cavallo consistently stated that there would be no devaluation, his comments did not appear to calm the markets.[11]

The country risk over this period reached 1,000 basis points over U.S. Treasury bills and was clearly unsustainable. A huge debt swap was then launched, known locally as the *mega-canje* (*canje* is Spanish for swap). Indeed, this still stands as the largest debt swap in history. It covered bonds issued internationally, although the majority of those that participated were local residents. Still, there was a significant international tranche. The *mega-canje* represented a clear trade-off. It pushed out the debt profile, extending the maturities and reducing the debt service in the coming thirty-six months. However, the effective interest rate on the swapped debt rose. While the swap improved the government's liquidity position, the general conclusion was that it worsened its solvency.[12] On the anticipation of the *mega-canje*, the EMBI+ did drift higher (lower spreads), but it fell on its announcement, with, perhaps, some (small) net gain. This suggests that the operation did reduce default risk, at least up to the duration of the EMBI+, but that the market was disappointed by the terms.

Through June and July the increasingly uneasy relationship between Cavallo and the largely Peronist provincial governors generated much noise. However, the cause may well have been economic factors. On the one hand, arrears had built up in tax revenues that the federal government was supposed to share with the provinces. On the other hand, there were reports that banks were refusing to roll over loans to the provincial governments, putting further pressure on provincial finances. Also, and perhaps more important, there was still no good news on economic activity, fiscal revenues remained depressed (impacting the government's willingness to share the tax revenues), and it seemed that the magic of Cavallo was not working, this time around, to get the economy moving.

On June 15, perhaps as part of these pressures, a de facto dual exchange rate regime was announced, which operated through a system of variable export, subsidies, and import tariffs. The scheme cleverly brought forward the

11. There is also a view that Cavallo pushed for the change in the convertibility law at that time for political motives, to demonstrate that convertibility was not the same as dollarization. After all, it is difficult to explain the timing of the proposed change in terms of pure economics.

12. Mussa (2002) characterizes the *mega-canje* as an "act of desperation" (p. 41).

policy of bringing the euro into the basket for trade-related operations while keeping the exchange rate fixed for financial transactions.[13]

IMF's Role

At the time of the government's announcement regarding the de facto dual exchange rate, there was very serious concern that this measure might cause the IMF to withdraw support and effectively stop the program. However, the Argentine authorities (successfully) argued that the system was not a dual exchange rate but a system of export subsidies and import tariffs, where the rates of those subsidies and tariffs happened to operate through the movement in exchange rates.

The markets reacted very unfavorably to the measure, in large part due to the uncertainty that this policy created with respect to the IMF program. This interaction is crucial to an understanding of events in Argentina. The IMF had previously signaled its displeasure to the change in the convertibility law. It appeared to suggest that the *mega-canje* had been positive, but the weak-worded support, for many, indicated that the IMF was just going through the motions.[14] A common view was that the de facto dual exchange rate might be the final straw to break relations with the IMF. If the International Monetary Fund withdrew, many investors calculated that there most likely would be a run on the banks, and hence the possibility for further government financing would be dissipated. Maintaining engagement with the IMF was, then, crucial to Argentina finding some orderly solution to its problems.[15] The perceived displeasure of the IMF then increased nervousness among private investors. As country risk rose, the financial system also started to lose deposits again.

A zero deficit policy was announced, perhaps as part of the negotiating strategy with the IMF to increase the chances of an early disbursement, and in part due to the worsened fiscal position. The announcement came on July 15.[16] The reaction by the market was an extraordinary increase in risk spreads by some 400 basis points, to over 1,600 basis points.

---

13. The export subsidies and import tariffs were calculated on the basis of the dollar-euro exchange rate.

14. See the discussion in Mussa (2002).

15. This interaction between the IMF and private sector is incorporated into the simple game presented in appendix B.

16. Approved by Congress on July 30, 2001.

It is at first sight difficult to explain this very negative market reaction. It might be argued that the plan was not credible, but that would explain only the lack of a positive reaction, not such a pronounced negative one.[17] Joyce Chang, commenting on this paper, suggested that the market had actually expected a greater adjustment, or perhaps a more detailed plan, and was disappointed by the announcement. Pablo Guidotti suggested at the time that not only was the plan not credible, but also the announcement revealed that the situation was much worse than many market observers believed.[18]

Related to this view is an explanation based on how the plan was announced. The announcement stressed that a zero deficit was not really what Argentina wanted, but had been forced on the country as there was no further access to credit. At a time when the IMF had given no real indications that further funds would be forthcoming, there was now an admission that there was no prospect of any private sector funding either. In the terminology of game theory, this might be thought of as an event that changed the degree of common knowledge among investors. While each individual investor may have been reticent to lend to Argentina, each individual investor was not absolutely sure what the view of another investor was. And the second investor did not know for sure what the first investor knew about the second, and so on. The announcement by the Argentine authorities themselves confirmed what many might have thought but did not know for sure—no private investor was prepared to fund Argentina. This then became common knowledge.[19]

This announcement switched a bad situation into a terrible one and served as the trigger for the run from the financial system. Of course, it is likely that the private sector was already on the point of selecting this bad equilibrium, given the series of bad news and especially given the doubts regarding the continuance of the IMF program. The run can be seen clearly in figure 4, which graphs private sector bank deposits. Still, this run from the banks was mostly, but not entirely, by institutional investors and the more sophisticated (and larger) private depositors.

There then followed a couple of tense weeks and negotiations with the IMF as banking sector deposits fell and country risk hovered between 1,400 and 1,700 basis points. Despite repeated government announcements, there was significant uncertainty in Argentina as to whether a package would be agreed

17. The author of this paper is indebted to Féderico Strurzenegger for this observation.

18. See Guidotti (2001).

19. See Binmore (1992) on "Bob's your uncle" regarding who has a dirty face in a Victorian railway carriage—and the remainder of chapter 10—for an excellent account of common knowledge.

Figure 4. Private Sector Bank Deposits, Dollars and Pesos, January 2000–December 2001

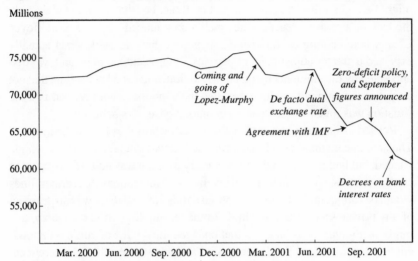

Source: Central Bank of Argentina.

to and what any package would look like. Many suggested that the IMF (or the U.S. Treasury) would call for private sector involvement as part of any agreed package. This, of course, only added to investor concern. Finally, an agreement with the IMF was reached on August 21. As can be seen from figure 4, this agreement clearly arrested the deposit run and also brought down country risk, but only to 1,400 basis points.

The agreement with the IMF was a strange animal indeed.[20] It included about $5 billion of new money to shore up central bank reserves and $3 billion to assist Argentina in some future (unspecified) debt restructuring.[21] At the same time the Contingent Repo Facility of the central bank was called, allowing a further $1.2 billion increase in reserves at that time from private sector international banks, plus a further $1 billion of World Bank and Inter-American Development Bank disbursements ($500 million from each institution) as enhancements to that facility.[22]

Over the subsequent month or so banking system deposits stabilized, but the run of some $8 billion (more than 10 percent of deposits) and the very high, continuing risk spreads implied a credit crunch that hit the real econ-

20. See Mussa (2002) for more details.
21. The $3 billion was not disbursed.
22. The facility has since been repaid fully to the private sector. Repayments to the multilaterals have followed their particular amortization schedules.

omy hard. This credit crunch was concentrated on the private sector—a private sector that had lost access to the international capital market. As the very poor fiscal revenue figures for September became known, risk spreads rose again. It looked increasingly clear that Argentina would now miss the fourth quarter fiscal target with the IMF—and would be far away from the zero deficit promised. This once again put in jeopardy the agreement with the International Monetary Fund. After the August package, the debate was now whether Argentina would get any more money from the IMF at all.

There was also a realization that the Argentine government was going to have no choice but to restructure its debt again—both domestic and foreign—and there was a growing perception that the IMF was going to require this before any new money arrived. Initially, the announcement was to seek a voluntary restructuring. However, it was not clear how this was going to be done. While domestic investors, including regulated banks and regulated pension funds, might be coerced into a restructuring that could be presented as at least quasi-voluntary, it was not clear how this was going to be achieved with non-regulated and international investors. Tellingly, official terminology changed from seeking a voluntary debt restructuring to seeking an orderly one. Country risk rose accordingly to over 3,000 basis points by November 20.

As it became a more widespread view that the IMF would seek this restructuring (now read default) before a new agreement was reached, there was also a growing realization of what such a restructuring implied for domestic banks' balance sheets. Domestic investors became more nervous. Not surprisingly, the decision of increasing numbers was safety first. Investors began shifting money abroad or placing dollars in safety deposit boxes—or simply under the mattress. A full-scale run developed in the financial system once again.[23]

In fact the causality between the run on the banks and the run on country risk was not entirely clear, as there was also a growing realization by international bondholders that if domestic banks lost funding, then the government also lost funding, and hence any haircut applied to international investors would have to be greater. And as bond prices fell, the solvency position of banks—heavily exposed to the sovereign—looked more and more shaky, alarming depositors. While deposit holders watched country risk, international bond-

---

23. The final trigger for the severest run on the banks was a measure that effectively limited the interest rates that banks could pay on new deposits. *Comunicación A 3365* from the central bank, dated November 26, 2001, established 100 percent reserve requirements on deposits paying an interest rate higher than specific reference rates.

holders monitored deposits in the local financial system. The causality most likely ran both ways.[24]

The authorities at that time then had little room to maneuver. Controls on deposit withdrawals were swiftly imposed, as were capital controls to limit the outflow of capital from the country. This set of controls became known as the *corralito*.[25] The *corralito* was deeply unpopular with those who got trapped, and to a large extent helped to provoke the *cacerolazo* of the middle classes.[26] Together with the more serious demonstrations, as well as riots and attacks on supermarkets and other stores, the more peaceful *cacerolazo* first led to the downfall of Minister Cavallo, and subsequently to the downfall of the de la Rua government. Since that date, Argentina has formally defaulted (under former president Rodriguez Sáa) and devalued (under current president Duhalde). Duhalde's devaluation was accompanied by a forced and asymmetric pesification of dollar contracts within the financial system such that dollar deposits were converted to pesos at the exchange rate of 1.4 to 1, loans were converted at 1 to 1. As of July 2002, at the time of writing, Argentina was still attempting to resolve the problems in the financial system and lift the banking controls, and had not commenced to renegotiate the external debt.

24. This account reflects this paper's view that the banking system was essentially a victim of the macroeconomic situation and not a major cause of the instability in itself. Perry and Servén (2002), however, suggest that the strict Argentine banking regulations were a strong façade, and de la Torre, Levy Yeyati, and Schmukler (2002) suggest that understanding certain risks in the banking system is vital to understanding the crisis. In my view, these authors are right to criticize the relaxation of certain regulations, but other criticisms are largely misplaced. Banking regulations are like automobile seatbelts: they are extremely useful to protect against 30 mile per hour crashes, but provide little protection if a car is driven off a cliff. To be assured of absolute safety the car should not leave the garage. Similarly, to be perfectly safe a banking sector should only invest in AAA (foreign) paper. The overall lessons from Argentina with respect to financial systems are, unfortunately, very well known. First, financial stability is vulnerable—even with very high initial liquidity and solvency ratios—when the macroeconomic policy framework does not add up and there is fear of expropriation of one sort or another. Second, there is a fine but important distinction between countercycle policy that might allow a government to rollover debt when there is a temporary lack of access to international markets and gambling for resurrection, which deserves a deeper analysis.

25. This name is reputed to have multiple origins. My favorite interpretation is that it comes from a corral into which cattle are herded. After queuing, the cattle are, with luck, allowed out one at a time, having been washed or injected or having suffered some other indignity. If they are less lucky, they leave the corral one at a time onto a truck to be taken to slaughter.

26. *Cacerolazo* refers to the beating of casserole dishes and other kitchenware in a noisy but largely peaceful demonstration.

Four Hypotheses

This paper's description of events in Argentina raises a set of potential hypotheses that might explain the proximate roots of the country's crisis.[27] In this section four potential hypotheses—fiscal unsustainability, current account unsustainability, political risk, and multiple equilibria—are described analytically and tested empirically.[28]

Fiscal Unsustainability

Argentina defaulted in January 2002. Hence by definition, at some point there was a problem of fiscal unsustainability. It is difficult to pinpoint exactly when the debt position became clearly unsustainable, and individuals may have their preferred dates.[29] While the date at which things became unsustainable is an interesting question, a more important question to ask is whether fiscal unsustainability was the underlying cause of the crisis or it was something else that resulted in fiscal unsustainability. As this paper discusses below, competing causes include a lack of growth for some other reason (due to an external constraint or high political risks) that then made the fiscal position unsustainable.

Argentina has been plagued by fiscal problems throughout much of its recent past. Indeed, it would strange if fiscal sustainability was not an issue in this crisis. Throughout the 1980s the fiscal and quasi-fiscal deficit played a significant role in driving price expectations toward eventual hyperinflation. Prior to the adoption of the currency board, an attempt was made at a significant fiscal reform. But this still did not lead to exchange rate (and money demand) stability. The establishment of the currency board itself could be traced back to Argentina's fiscal problems and the monetary instability that they helped to create.

One view was that the currency board—by imposing hard budget constraints and eliminating the possibility of the inflation tax—might serve to enhance fiscal discipline. The fiscal reforms, and in particular the privatization of large loss-making public enterprises, certainly went in that direction. However, an

27. This paper assumes that the crisis was not inevitable, but that events post-1997 made the crisis a reality.

28. These hypotheses are not mutually exclusive, but indeed may be complementary and mutually reinforcing.

29. It is this paper's view that the market, which predicted around January 2001 a significant default probability but clearly much less than unity, was about right (750 basis point spread), but that default and devaluation became virtual certainties after the bank run in August 2001.

opposing view is that the currency board made access to international debt markets easier and hence relaxed the financing constraint, allowing for larger fiscal deficits.[30]

Most notably, in the fourth quarter of 1994 Argentina missed a fiscal target with the IMF. An announcement was made that the IMF program would lapse just days before the devaluation of the Mexican peso that heralded the start of the tequila crisis.[31] An additional statement in February 1995, which said that Argentina would not return to negotiate a new program with the IMF, sparked the systemic bank run in the first two weeks of March 1995. In turn, that led to a new IMF agreement and, finally, a set of promised fiscal and other reforms.[32]

Argentina grew strongly after the tequila period. Yet fiscal deficits remained and debt levels grew faster than the fiscal deficit. Figure 5 demonstrates that total public sector consolidated debt levels grew much faster than deficits due to a set of nonbudgetary items. These items included the recognition of old debts (or nonbudgeted payments with bonds); the costs implied by (nonprovisioned) court cases against the state, including pensions and compensation payments to families of those disappeared in the so-called dirty war; and significantly, by the growing deficits of the provinces. Over the 1995–2001 period, the accumulated difference between the change in debt and the accumulated fiscal deficit was a very substantial $30 billion, with an increasing amount of this difference stemming from provincial deficits in the later years.

Teijeiro makes perhaps the strongest case for fiscal irresponsibility as the underlying cause of the current crisis.[33] He estimates that in the ten-year period 1991–2000, the actual overall accumulated fiscal deficit, corresponding to the increase in debt, was $108 billion—not the officially budgeted $33 billion— with $31 billion of the difference being made up in terms of "payments with bonds" and $16 billion in provincial debts. Teijeiro calculates this as 4.1 per-

---

30. This view presupposes some creditor irrationality; or, for example, the view that in good times market discipline is very weak, perhaps due to competing lenders, harking back to models of the 1980s debt crisis (see Kletzer [1984]). See Aizenmann and Powell (1998) for a model where a divided government with a weak center may borrow as much as it can from external markets due to an internal type of prisoner's dilemma.

31. While the economy slowed notably in the second half of 1994, the fiscal target for the year was missed despite a growth rate of almost 5.8 percent (Ministry of the Economy).

32. See D'Amato, Grubisic, and Powell (1997) for a description of the tequila shock and its effects on the banking system. Ganapolsky and Schmukler (1998) conduct an event study to attempt to identify the causes of the bank run.

33. Teijeiro (2001).

Figure 5. Fiscal Deficit and Change in Public Debt, 1995–2001

Millions of dollars   Millions of dollars

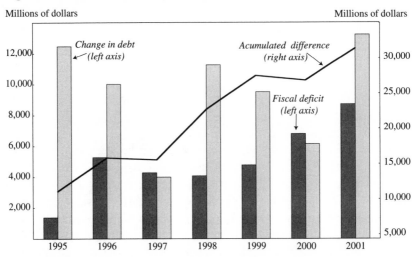

Source: Ministry of the Economy.

cent of GDP on average, but reaching 6.6 percent in 1999 and 5.4 percent in 2000. However Teijeiro, similar to Mussa, essentially calculates all transient receipts as temporary (for example, revenue from privatizations) and all transient costs as permanent (for example, pension system reform).[34] According to Teijeiro, spending increased from 23 percent of GDP in 1992 to a record 29 percent in 1999. The analysis of the increase in spending suggests that up until 1994 the major increase was in current primary spending, whereas after 1994 primary spending only increased marginally, but interest payments increased substantially—up from almost $6 billion in 1995 to $11.5 billion in 2000.

By the end of 2000, Argentine public sector debt had reached 46.5 percent of GDP. While that level may not be high by continental European standards, some suggested that it was too high for a country of Argentina's characteristics. Mussa cites five reasons why a debt level of over 40 percent of GDP might be sustainable for an industrialized economy but not for a country of Argentina's characteristics.[35] These include:

34. See Hausmann and Velasco, this volume, for an interesting discussion of the pension fund reform. However, they appear to mix up the change to a "pay as you go" to a capitalization system with changes in the amount paid into the obligatory system due to changes in rates.

35. Mussa (2002).

—poor performance in collecting taxes (total tax and Social Security revenue have been only about 20 percent of GDP);

—Argentine debt is mostly issued in foreign currency and is foreign held (discussed later in this paper with respect to current account sustainability);

—the dynamics of the debt ratio, which had risen from 19 percent in 1993 to over 40 percent in 1998;

—vulnerability to external real shocks (for example, the Brazilian devaluation); and

—vulnerability to financial market sentiment.

These last two reasons suggest an interaction between the competing hypotheses considered in this section. In other words, given the external environment in terms of the stability of neighbors and other issuers in external debt markets, along with the threat of contagion, a safe debt level for an emerging country may be much lower than that for, say, a European country with a more stable set of trading partners and more liquid and stable debt markets.

Around the end of 2000, the opinion from the markets was clearly divided. Notably, JP Morgan suggested that Argentina's "debt problem" was "much ado about not very much."[36] The JP Morgan study consisted of modeling the Argentine debt profile and then thinking through different scenarios for interest rates, growth, and the primary fiscal surplus. The analysis suggested that if growth remained constant (real growth of 1.8 percent and nominal growth at 0.68 percent), then Argentina would have to increase the primary fiscal surplus to 1.8 percent of GDP (from 1.2 percent of GDP) to keep the ratio of debt to GDP constant. This was calculated as the equivalent of $4.5 billion of spending cuts, or 4.8 percent of total consolidated public sector spending. It was suggested that this did not, then, imply a too high level of adjustment to be necessary to obtain a stable ratio of debt to GDP.[37]

The JP Morgan analysis is based on an analysis of debt dynamics. This paper employs a similar analysis to further shed light on this hypothesis. It is easy to show that the next period's ratio of debt to GDP is related to this period's ratio of debt to GDP via the following formula:[38]

---

36. On the other hand, Lehman Brothers (2001) saw the situation as unsustainable, suggesting that Argentina should default, devalue, or both.

37. For example, at the time Brazil had a primary fiscal surplus of about 3.3 percent of GDP, Ecuador 6.6 percent, and Russia 5.9 percent; JP Morgan (2000).

38. This assumes that there is no other source of financing for the government, for example, through money creation.

$$d_{t+1} = \frac{1}{1+g_t}\left(f_t + d_t\left(1+r_t\right)\right), \tag{1}$$

where

d: ratio of debt to GDP,

f: primary fiscal deficit (if f is negative, it would be a surplus),

r: interest rate on debt,

g: growth rate.

The subscripts refer to the time period. Hence the ratio of debt to GDP becomes larger the

—higher the current debt level,

—higher the primary fiscal deficit,

—higher the interest rate,

—lower the growth rate.

Using this formula, one can calculate the fiscal surplus that yields a stable ratio of debt to GDP, $(d(t + 1) = d(t))$. This turns out to be:

$$s_t = d_t(r_t - g_t), \tag{2}$$

where s is now the fiscal surplus ($s = -f$). One can use this simple formula to calculate the level of primary fiscal surplus required to yield a stable ratio of debt to GDP for each quarter through 2000 and 2001. Figure 6 plots the results. The debt ratio is the level of debt divided by deseasonalized GDP corresponding to that quarter, and the growth rate is that quarter's deseasonalized growth rate. This paper uses two different assumptions regarding the interest rate. The first (Interest Rate 1) is that quarter's actual interest payments divided by the previous quarter's debt level. The second (Interest Rate 2) starts at the same level (roughly 8.5 percent annualized), but then assumes that the annualized rate of interest rises 2 percent each quarter. The actual primary surplus attained in each quarter is also plotted in figure 6.

Figure 6 shows that through 2000 and, arguably, the first half of 2001 the required adjustment in terms of increasing the primary fiscal surplus did not appear very large. Indeed, in the second quarter of 2000, it is about 0.5 percent of GDP over the quarter (or less than 2 percent on an annualized basis and very close to JP Morgan's calculation). Taking 2000 as a whole, it is about 3 percent of GDP on an annualized basis. Moreover, even under the stiff assumption that interest rates were rising by 2 percent (annualized) each quarter, the required primary fiscal surplus was still under about 4 percent of GDP on an annualized basis in the third quarter of 2000.

Figure 6. Required and Actual Primary Fiscal Surplus (as a Percentage of GDP), Quarterly, 2000–01

Percent of GDP

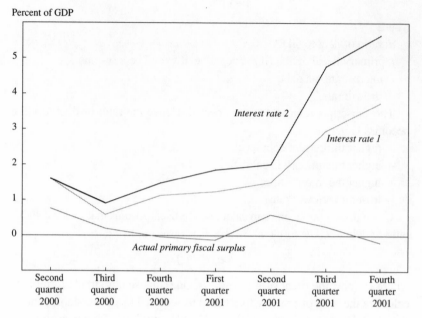

Source: Author's calculations.

Figure 6 also illustrates that, *ex post*, Argentina only achieved an extremely modest primary fiscal surplus in the third quarter of 2000, and in the fourth quarter of 2000 or first quarter of 2001 achieved no primary fiscal surplus at all. While the gap between the actual primary fiscal surplus and the required primary fiscal surplus then increased in the first quarter of 2001, it narrowed again in the second quarter as the actual primary fiscal surplus rose (in part due to the financial transaction taxes). However, in the third quarter of 2001—perhaps as a result of sharp increases in country risk as a response to the more heterodox economic program and its effects on the real economy—the more negative GDP growth started to imply implausible levels of primary surpluses required for stable debt levels.

While this analysis can be criticized for some of the underlying assumptions, the message is very clear. The required fiscal adjustment to achieve a stable ratio of debt to GDP was relatively modest. Surprisingly, these modest levels of required adjustment continued, arguably until the second quarter of 2001. The Argentine story does not appear to be one of sharp fiscal adjustment that was not enough, but rather of the lack of a (relatively modest) fiscal adjustment at the right time. Given the undoubted inefficiencies in Argentine public spending and tax collection, it is quite extraordinary that virtually no adjustment was achieved.

There are at least two competing explanations.[39] The first is that it was simply not feasible politically. The evidence in favor of this hypothesis was the lack of support for the Lopez-Murphy plan to cut expenditures and his forced resignation. The second is that Argentina could not in a technical sense, in that if it did attempt to adjust by reducing expenditures or increasing taxes, then the effect on the real economy would be such that fiscal revenues would fall and hence the increased primary balance would never actually materialize. There is some evidence in favor of this hypothesis, given Machinea's *impuestazo* and its effects on the real economy.[40]

Both of these hypotheses suggest that the problem, fundamentally, was not the level of debt but rather a problem of politics or vicious cycles/multiple equilibria. It would be correct to conclude, however, that given that the existence of these vicious cycles/multiple equilibria, or political constraints to adjustment, the safe level of debt to GDP for a country with Argentina's characteristics was, very clearly *ex post*, less than 45 percent of GDP.

Current Account Sustainability

A second hypothesis is that the Argentine crisis was really a result of an external constraint; in other words, an unsustainable current account. There are different aspects to this explanation. One view, as reviewed earlier in this paper, is that Argentina was hit by a set of fierce external shocks, and that due to the fixed exchange rate and inflexible domestic labor markets, Argentina

39. Commenting on this paper, Pedro Pou suggested a third explanation, namely the inability to roll over the debt. The spirit of the analysis here is one of solvency, and hence if the result is that the government was solvent then there should be no problem with respect to rolling over. However, it is certainly the case that the required primary fiscal surplus increases with more pessimistic assumptions about the percentage of the stock of debt that can be rolled over. While the debt maturity structure in Argentina was relatively long, such that the rollover problem was less than it might have been, the analysis presented is conducted under the maintained hypothesis that rolling over debt coming due was feasible.

40. However, increasing taxes is not the same as reducing (inefficient) expenditures. Indeed, one view might be that the political constraint acted on reducing expenditures and the technical one acted more on increasing taxes. However, Teijerio (2001) argues strongly in favor of the hypothesis that during 1991–98 higher spending financed by higher external debt was highly expansionary, and that post-1998 tax rises and higher domestic debt helped to provoke the recession that led to an unsustainable debt position.

found it difficult to adjust. Indeed, the only adjustment possible was through a slow and painful process of recession and deflation. Only through recession could imports be reduced, and only through deflation would domestic prices adjust to start to make exports more competitive. According to this view Argentina would only grow once this adjustment process had been completed. At the same time, recession and deflation made the fiscal position much worse. Recession reduced tax revenues and deflation increased public sector wages and other fixed nominal expenditures in real terms.

However, exports grew each year (with the exception of 1999) through convertibility (see figure 2). It is also quite extraordinary to note that Argentine agricultural exports, particularly grains, increased substantially over the years. This occurred despite high taxes in Argentina and lower world prices, in part sparked by large subsidies to European and U.S. producers. Still, these are only partial replies as it may still be the case that, given the terms of trade and other shocks, exports perhaps had to increase by much greater rates in order to avoid recession and deflationary adjustment and maintain programmed foreign debt payments. Indeed, as can be seen in figure 2, in each period of strong growth the trade deficit widened substantially, as imports grew much stronger that exports. While during the 1995 recession the trade balance turned around quite rapidly, helped by a booming (and not very competitive) Brazil, this did not happen with anywhere near the same speed through 1999–2001, with Argentina in recession and Brazil with low growth and a very competitive exchange rate.

Another complementary view is that for whatever reason, the high levels of capital inflows that Argentina enjoyed through the first half of the 1990s stopped. Given a sudden stop in capital flows, Argentina had to adjust to achieve current account balance. This adjustment necessitated increased exports and reduced imports. Again, due to the fixed exchange rate and internal inflexibility, Argentina was able to achieve only a modest increase in exports, and hence had to reduce imports via recession, provoking an unsustainable fiscal position.

However, at best this is only a partial explanation, as it does not explain why there was such a sudden stop in private capital. If the stop in private capital was due to the perceived risk of the Argentine public sector defaulting, then we are back to the unsustainable debt story. If, however, the explanation of the sudden stop is due to a change in risk aversion of foreign investors— perhaps due to experiences in Russia—then that is more a story of an external shock.

Table 1. Argentina Consolidated Public Sector Debt by Different Criteria, End of 2000

Billions of dollars

Criterion	External	Internal	Total
Residence	85	60	145
Currency	118	27	145
Legislation	97	48	145

Source: Ministry of the Economy.

To analyze the sustainability of the current account a little further, it is also necessary to discuss the structure of Argentine debt. Elsewhere, I propose three different definitions of external debt, appropriate for three different purposes.[41] A currency definition is appropriate for analyzing what would happen in the case of devaluation, assuming no pesification. A definition depending on where the debt is issued would be appropriate for analyzing what would happen in the case of default and hence how much debt is written under different contracts and different legal jurisdictions. However, to analyze the sustainability of the current account, the correct definition, consistent with all current account definitions, would appear to be residence. Table 1 presents an estimation of the structure of Argentine public sector debt at the end of 2000 according to these different definitions. While some $118 billion of Argentine consolidated public debt was in foreign currency, some $97 billion of total debt was issued outside of the country, and an estimated $85 billion held by nonresidents.[42]

While $85 billion is not as high as $97 billion or $118 billion, it is still a very significant figure and almost four times the level of exports. Moreover, this is only external public sector debt. To complete the picture, one must also add to this private sector external debt, which at the end of 2000 amounted to some $62 billion, according to the same residency basis (see table 2).

The substantial and persistent current account deficit in Argentina reflected, in part, the interest payments on these high external debt figures. Figure 7 shows the trade balance and current account balance. The persistent and growing difference between the two, in part, reflects the sale of domestic companies to foreign ones, and hence the growing retained earnings of those companies (an outflow in the current account and an inflow in the capital account). It also reflects the growth in interest payments on foreign debt. However, while both

41. Powell (2002).
42. Ministry of the Economy.

Table 2. Argentine External Assets and Liabilities: Public and Private Sector^a

Billions of dollars

Sector	1994		2000		Change	
	Debt	Assets	Debt	Assets	Debt	Assets
Public	61	18	85	27	24	9
Private	25	47	62	91	37	44
Total	86	65	147	118	61	53

Source: Argentine balance of payments, Ministry of the Economy; public sector assets, Central Bank of Argentina.

a. Balance of payments definition includes government deposits held at the central bank, excludes government bonds in U.S. dollars. Private sector is sum of financial and nonfinancial private sector. Figures are net of external assets with no return.

private and public sector debt grew through convertibility, it is noticeable that the Argentine private sector built up substantial reserves of external assets. In some years it is very clear that the substantial capital inflows, through debt and foreign direct investment (FDI), also led to high outflows by residents and subsequent high levels of external private assets.

Table 2 provides figures on Argentine private and public sector external debts and external assets as of the end of 1994 and 2000. The bottom line is that while private sector external debts grew over this period by $37 billion, private sector external assets grew by $44 billion. At the same time, external public sector debt grew by $24 billion, but external public sector assets (essentially central bank reserves) grew by only $9 billion.

Thus while the growth in interest payments that Argentine private sector companies paid on their foreign debt had a counterpart in the earnings on increased foreign assets, there was no similar counterpart (or at least a much smaller one) to the growth in interest payments on increased public sector external debt.

However, these somewhat alarming ratios and trends constitute only partial analyses of current account sustainability. Indeed, a more complete analysis can be conducted regarding the sustainability of the current account in very similar vein to the analysis above on fiscal sustainability. In particular, to maintain a constant external ratio of debt to GDP requires a trade surplus (as a percentage of GDP) given by

$$ts_t = d_t(r_t - g_t) - o_t, \tag{3}$$

where (the assumption is that reserves remain constant)

d: ratio of external debt to GDP,

Figure 7. Trade Balance and Current Account, 1992–2001

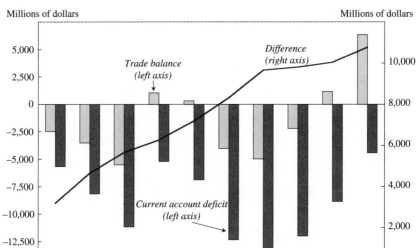

Source: Ministry of the Economy.

r: interest rate on external debt,

g: GDP growth rate,

o: ratio of other (net) inflows as a percentage of GDP,

t: time period.

Other net capital inflows might include stable or persistent net flows, such as FDI and earnings on overseas assets.

Figure 8 plots the estimated required trade surplus for each quarter in 1999–2001 (required to keep the external debt level and reserves constant) versus the actual trade surplus for different assumptions regarding other flows (represented by o in equation (3)). Other net inflows include:

—net service balance,

—net flow of dividends,

—interest earned on foreign assets by Argentine residents,

—and inflows in the capital account net of the change in the external debt of Argentine residents, including, for example, FDI.

The first assumption is that o is the actual figure for other flows for each quarter. Figure 8 includes the actual change in reserves as information. The second assumption is that o is fixed as the average for the period 1998–2001,

Figure 8. Trade Balance Required for Current Account Sustainability, Quarterly, 1999–2001[a]

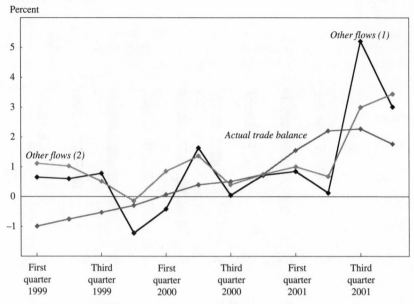

Percent

Source: Author's own calculations.
a. Changes in reserves: 1999 = +$1.2 billion; 2000 = –$0.4 billion; 2001 = –$12 billion.

which is a net inflow of 0.5 percent a quarter (about 2 percent a year). Figure 8 also provides the actual trade balance for comparison.

Assuming that actual other net inflows remained roughly at these historic levels, the main message from figure 8 is that the actual trade balance was a little below the required level through 1999, but that by 2000 it was roughly at the required level for external debt sustainability. The situation then blows up later in 2001. The striking aspect of figure 8 is that it appears to suggest that the required adjustment in the trade balance was more or less complete through 2000. Certainly, what happened in 2001 does not seem as if it could have been a consequence of a deterioration of this measure through 2000.

A potential criticism of this analysis, however, is that other net inflows may not remain at these levels. For example, Argentina received a substantial amount of FDI in the period 1998–2000, and it might be posited that this would not continue. However, this argument forgets that Argentine residents placed much of the proceeds of these inflows abroad, as evidenced in table 2. Moreover, the average other net inflows (line 2 in figure 8) is averaged including 2001, a very negative year for the private capital account. It might, however, be suggested that the Argentine resources abroad might not be repatriated if things got tough. This is certainly true, but it is not an explanation of why things got tough. Moreover, if the theory is that capital inflows were going to stop, and thus the current account would become unsustainable, then an explanation is needed as to why capital inflows were going to stop. This is not an explanation regarding the sustainability of the current account, but rather about the nature of capital flows or a story of multiple equilibria. The conclusion is that a simple story of a lack of current account sustainability does not fit the facts of the case.

Political Risk

The descriptive account of the Argentine crisis in the previous section also suggests that Argentine politics became particularly messy from 1998 onward. On the one hand, politics became more factious, and through 2000 and 2001 there were very severe concerns regarding governability. An alternative view is that there was a substantial shift in Argentine political risk that affected the perceived risk of investment and hence growth. In this view, while the debt position may have been perfectly sustainable with more stable politics, the increased fractious nature of the political environment meant that the inherited debt level became unsustainable.

One approach would be to subjectively select a set of political events during the period.[43] However, in an attempt to obtain an independent and impartial view of the deteriorating nature of Argentine politics, figure 9 plots an index of political risk developed by the International Country Risk Guide.[44] This indicator of political risk is designed to be consistent across time with a set of standard questions. The types of factors included are government stability; public satisfaction with the government program; the government's attitude to inward investment, internal conflict (for example, political violence), and external conflict (trade restrictions and embargoes); corruption; the role of the military in government; religious tension; law and order; ethnic tension; democratic accountability; and bureaucratic quality. Figure 9 shows that Argentine political risk was not considered particularly high through much of 1997–99.

43. Candidate events might include Duhalde's address to the Argentine Banking Association in July 1999; the October 1999 election result; the vice president's resignation in October 2000; Jose Luis Machinea's resignation and the coming and going of Ricardo Lopez-Murphy as economy minister in March 2001; Cavallo's resignation as economy minister in December 2001.

44. See International Country Risk Guide (1999), www.prsgroup.com.

Figure 9. Political Risk Index for Argentina, 1997–2001

Index

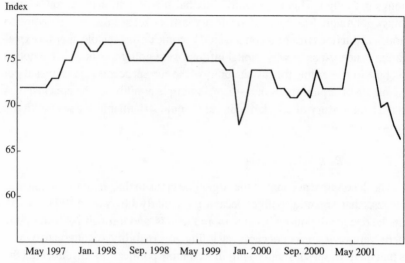

Source: International Country Risk Guide (1999).

There is a sharp dip in October 1999, coinciding with the election result and presumably concerns about governability. However, the index recovers. Through 2000 there is a downward, if volatile, trend, but once again the index recovers in the early part of 2001. A very sharp decline, however, begins in July 2001.

While particular events or perceptions of political risk may have impacted country risk, economic activity, or other variables, it is interesting to consider whether these events were simply random occurrences or there is a deeper and more fundamental reason why Argentine politics became so messy. Political scientists, for example, have noted that the interaction of the decentralized structure of the national parties, the federal nature of the parties, and the over-representation of underpopulated areas of the country have led to divisions both within the parties and between the federal government and the govern-ments of the provinces.[45] There has also been substantial criticism of Argentina's particular form of proportional representation and party electoral lists.[46] In turn, one hypothesis is that these factors have led to problems of excessive divisions within parties and across regions, a high political cost of

45. See Calvo and Abal Medina (2001).
46. See Jones and others (2001).

government, a low level of accountability, and low levels of efficiency of public spending.[47]

Multiple Equilibria

The three hypotheses discussed above are not mutually exclusive, but rather complementary or reinforcing. This paper's fourth and final hypothesis is that Argentina's crisis resulted from a particular dynamic between the three hypotheses discussed above and some relatively minor mistake. Simply put, bad luck in conjunction with existing economic and political weaknesses put Argentina in a very bad equilibrium from which it could not escape without default and devaluation.

As noted above, a double vicious cycle developed. A purely economic cycle ran from poor economic performance to lower fiscal revenues, to a higher fiscal deficit, to higher risk spreads, higher interest rates, and back to lower economic performance. This implies that Argentina fell into a kind of economic trap from which it could not escape. In particular, it implies that higher risk spreads were both a cause of the problem, in terms of reduced growth, and also an effect, in that higher fiscal deficits increased risk spreads.

A second vicious cycle included politics. In particular, poor economic performance and higher fiscal deficits led to the increased need for adjustment, greater political squabbling, a high risk spread, and thus poorer economic performance. Under this view, political risk was not just a cause of the economic crisis, but poor economic performance also led back to create heightened political risk.

These types of vicious cycles imply that there may have been multiple equilibria. In other words, while a particularly poor outcome was observed, in fact other outcomes were also feasible but not found. Unfortunately, the science of economics has not developed a good theory for why, under conditions of multiple equilibria, one equilibrium was chosen and not another.

The issue as to whether there are multiple equilibria or not is an important one in relation to the role of the IMF. If there are no multiple equilibria then the IMF's role might be thought a great deal simpler, as everything would flow reasonably easily from a simple analysis of countries' fundamentals. However, if there are multiple equilibria it is quite possible that a major IMF support package could shift a country from a bad equilibrium to a better one. If that

---

47. This paper does not discount this more fundamental view of the political risk, but it notes that it is difficult to identify whether or not it is correct with the data and methodology adopted in this paper.

is the case, then what might be considered a hopeless situation in terms of low growth, high interest rates, and capital flight might potentially be turned around to a virtuous one of capital repatriation, lower interest rates, and higher growth.[48]

Empirical Evaluation

This section conducts an empirical analysis of the period leading up to the Argentine crisis (1997–2001) to attempt to discern which, if any, of the above hypotheses may have empirical support. It is clear from the descriptive analysis that in attempting such a study there is an almost pathological problem of endogeneity. Indeed, this endogeneity is the key to one of the hypotheses, namely the existence of multiple equilibria. It would be beyond this paper's scope to develop a full structural model of the Argentine economy. For these reasons, this paper's approach is to select a small number of key variables and investigate the temporal relations between those variables using a vector autoregression (VAR) analysis. This technique uses the bare minimum of structural assumptions (discussed below) and allows for consideration of the full set of causal relations among these variables.[49]

The variables chosen for this analysis are (i) the indicator of political risk, (ii) fiscal revenue (deseasonalized), (iii) private sector bank deposits, (iv) imports (deseasonalized), and (v) the EMBI+ spread (this paper uses monthly averages). Integration tests reveal that all variables were nonstationary, $I(1)$, and so this paper works with first differences to avoid problems of nonstationarity.[50] Positive changes to imports may be considered in two different ways. They might represent good news on economic activity or bad news on the trade balance, and hence the sustainability of the current account. Positive shocks to deposits may be thought of as good news regarding the capital account and also on the potential to finance government debt. This paper inter-

48. This suggests a tension between an "it's-mostly-fundamentals" IMF, or an IMF that must "impetrate market feelings." With apologies, especially to Catholic theologians, the verb *impetrate* is to ask something from God.

49. The concept of causality within a VAR is similar to that of Granger causality. In other words, causality is determined if the past of one variable is significant in explaining the future of another, or vice versa.

50. For the series of log deposits, $I(0)$ was rejected at the 5 percent level. For other series, it was rejected at the 10 percent level. There was weak evidence of one co-integrating vector between these variables. This paper leaves the possibility of a vector error correction model for future research.

prets positive shocks to fiscal revenues as good news regarding the sustainability of the debt position and uses the political risk indicator as an objective proxy for political developments in Argentina. This selection of variables allows for light to be shed on the hypotheses regarding the roots of the crisis. For example:

1. If there is evidence that lower fiscal revenues drive the EMBI spread higher, then this would be evidence in favor of the debt-sustainability hypothesis.

2. If higher imports drive the EMBI spread higher, then this would be evidence for the current account sustainability hypothesis. If, on the other hand, higher imports drive EMBI lower, then this would mean the good news on economic activity outweighed the bad news on the current account sustainability.[51]

3. If political risk drives the EMBI spread higher, then this would be evidence for the hypothesis that political risk was also important in the story.

4. If lower bank deposits are found to be significant for EMBI, then this might be interpreted as evidence in favor of both the current account sustainability hypothesis and fiscal sustainability. It would also be evidence of the importance of the sudden stop in capital flows.

The VAR approach and this paper's choice of variables also allows one to test slightly more complex hypotheses:

5. If hypotheses 1 through 4 are supported by the data and it is found that the EMBI spread feeds back to fiscal revenues, imports, or political risk, then there would be evidence of a feedback relation within the economic variables that would support the idea of multiple equilibria.

6. If the other variables were significant in explaining political risk and deteriorating political risk led to lower fiscal revenues, lower imports, or higher EMBI, then there would be evidence of a feedback and potential multiple equilibria through the politics.

This paper's approach is to specify an unrestricted VAR with a large number of lags and then cut down the lag length according to the Akaike information criteria, which allow for a system with just one lag. The results of the VAR analysis are presented in appendix A.

The VAR regression results indicate a number of significant interactions including, for example, that changes in:

---

51. This paper notes that as fiscal revenues are included in all equations, higher imports would only carry news regarding economic activity that was not already reflected in higher fiscal revenues.

—bank deposits and imports help to explain changes in the EMBI index;

—imports and political risk help explain changes in deposits;

—deposits, imports, and political risk help explain changes in fiscal revenues;

—bank deposits and fiscal revenues help explain changes in imports;

—and fiscal revenues and imports help to explain changes in political risk.

However, the coefficients in the empirical model of a VAR are less interesting than the analysis of the so-called structural model, which takes into account the relevant interactions between variables when considering the effect of a shock to one variable on another. This latter information is summarized in the impulse response functions. Nonetheless, to move from the empirical model to the structural model requires some assumptions regarding the relations between these variables. This paper employs the so-called Choleski decomposition, which implies a particular ordering of the variables in terms of their contemporaneous relations.

The model has five endogenous variables and the following ordering is adopted: EMBI, deposits, fiscal revenues, imports, and political risk. The paper posits this ordering as the EMBI index for a particular month is available immediately, whereas the other variables only become available with a lag. This lag is at a minimum for bank deposits (four days), followed by tax revenues, then imports, and then political risk. This ordering implies that the contemporaneous relations are restricted such that EMBI can affect all four other variables, deposits can affect three other variables (not EMBI), fiscal revenues can affect two other variables (neither EMBI or deposits), imports can affect one other variable (political risk), and political risk cannot affect any other variable contemporaneously. It is important to note, however, that after one period and for all other periods thereafter, there are no constraints, that is, all variables can affect all others. These restrictions are only on contemporaneous effects.[52]

In this preferred ordering, the impulse responses (see appendix A) show a number of interesting interactions. In particular, there is evidence that:

—higher EMBI leads to lower deposits and lower fiscal revenues;

—higher deposits lead to lower EMBI, higher fiscal revenues, and higher imports;

—higher fiscal revenues lead to higher imports initially, although after one period the effect turns negative;

—higher imports lead to lower EMBI, higher deposits, higher fiscal revenues, and a higher political risk index (lower political risk); and

52. Moreover, this ordering is changed to test the robustness of the results.

Figure 10. Virtuous and Vicious Circles

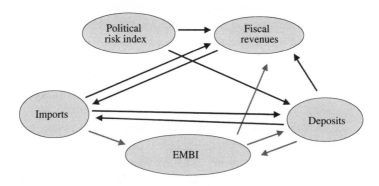

—a higher political risk index (lower political risk), leads to higher deposits, and higher fiscal revenue.

One interesting result is that EMBI spreads rise if imports fall. This appears to go against the current account sustainability hypothesis and in favor of the debt sustainability hypothesis, suggesting that rising imports as a sign of more growth outweigh any negative effects on current account sustainability. EMBI also rises if deposits fall. As noted, this can be interpreted in favor of the debt sustainability (less financing) or current account sustainability (sudden stop) hypotheses. Political risk does not feed directly into EMBI (perhaps EMBI already incorporates the information in this index), although it does feed through to economic fundamentals.

There is strong evidence of vicious/virtuous cycles operating through the economic variables. In particular: (1) lower deposits lead to higher EMBI and higher EMBI feeds back to lower deposits; (2) lower deposits lead to lower imports, which lead to higher EMBI, which leads to lower deposits; (3) lower deposits lead to lower fiscal revenues, which lead to (initially) lower imports, which lead to lower deposits. There is also evidence of a feedback through the political risk index. In particular, a higher political risk (lower index) drives lower deposits that drive lower imports, which feed back to higher political risk. Figure 10 summarizes the many different interactions between the variables.

Appendix A also contains the variance decompositions from the VAR. These are also of significant interest. In particular, this paper notes that while there is evidence of feedback through the politics, only 13 percent or so of the variation in the political risk index is explained through the other variables, with some 87 percent exogenous to the system.[53] This implies that exogenous (new) shocks to political risk were extremely important in explaining the variation of this variable over time. On the other hand, 46 percent of the variation in imports is explained by the other variables—in particular EMBI (3 percent), deposits (20 percent), and fiscal revenues (23 percent)—and 33 percent of the variation in fiscal revenues is explained by the other variables—especially EMBI (9 percent), deposits (10 percent), imports (8 percent), and political risk (6 percent).

This suggests that while exogenous events were also important, a significant amount of the variation in these variables is explained within the system. On the other hand, only 25 percent of the movement in deposits is explained by the other variables (especially political risk) and 75 percent of the variation in this variable is explained by exogenous events. We also note that only some 13 percent of the variation in EMBI is explained by the variables within the VAR.[54]

As is often the case, changing the order of the variables produces some differences in the impulse response functions. Reversing the variable sequence results in the following ordering: political risk, imports, fiscal revenues, deposits, and EMBI. EMBI is now the most endogenous variable rather than the most exogenous, and we find that the effect of EMBI on some of the other variables remains but becomes less significant (for example, EMBI on deposits). Therefore, the significance of some of the feedback relations within the economic variables is lost. Higher EMBI spreads are still, however, driven by lower deposits (sudden stop), lower fiscal revenues (debt sustainability), and lower imports (less growth and hence less debt sustainability), although this latter effect, once again, is not significant under this ordering. Under a third ordering (fiscal revenues, imports, EMBI, political risk, and deposits), the economic feedback effects once again become positive, especially between EMBI and deposits. The broad message is that the direction of the effects is reasonably constant across these different orderings, while the significance levels do change.

The general conclusion from this analysis is:

—there is some evidence to support the debt sustainability hypothesis;

—there is little evidence to support the current account sustainability hypothesis (that is, higher imports resulted in lower country risk);

53. The ordering adopted implies that this variable is the most endogenous.
54. This figure rises substantially, however, on changing the variable ordering within the VAR.

—the bank deposits (sudden stop) variable was critical and might be interpreted as in favor of either the current account or the debt sustainability hypotheses, but coupled with the other evidence the interpretation offered here is that this variable was important with respect to fiscal sustainability and potential government financing;

—there is evidence to suggest that political risk affected economic variables that then certainly made the debt position worse; and

—there is strong evidence in favor of vicious cycles at work and hence multiple equilibria through solely economic variables, as well as from the economic variables to the politics and back to the economics.

Role of the IMF

Argentina is a major emerging economy. At the end of 2000 it had GDP of some \$290 billion, the third largest in Latin America. The country had a disproportionate share of international debt markets and is an important member of the IMF. Moreover, in many respects Argentina went from being a role model to financial pariah in the matter of only some three years.[55] When a previously successful major bank collapses, the regulator is always asked what was to blame and why the collapse was not prevented. Similarly, it is natural to consider what the role of the IMF—as the main international agency concerned with countries' macroeconomic prospects and international financial market stability—was with respect to the Argentine crisis.[56]

To Support or Not to Support?

There has been much general criticism of IMF-type programs that focused on public sector austerity and exchange rate devaluations. In the case of Argentina, the IMF actually supported the exchange rate policy consistently through the tequila crisis and, at least tacitly, through the late 1990s and into the first quarter of 2001, objecting to the Cavallo idea of introducing the euro.

55. Indeed, President Menem was given the rare honor of addressing the IMF assembly in 1997.

56. Bank regulators normally state that their role is not to prevent a bank from failing, and indeed that the possibility of bank failure is healthy in terms of promoting bank competition. It is not clear that this analogy can be pushed to the case of countries. While the possibility of failure may reduce moral hazard, countries do not compete in the same way as banks, and citizens do not have the automatic right to change countries as bank depositors may switch to better banks.

The austerity programs, to the extent that they were implemented, were designed by Argentina. There is no doubt that the Argentine crisis was very largely a result of policies produced in Buenos Aires. And, for reasons explained below, that the solution will most likely have to be one produced from Buenos Aires as well.

Mussa argues persuasively that the IMF was right to (eventually) support the currency board in Argentina post-1991 and to maintain that support through the tequila crisis of 1995.[57] He goes on to criticize the IMF for not being tough enough on Argentina during the so-called good times of 1996–98, but suggests that the major support package extended to Argentina at the end of 2000 was appropriate. However, he returns to criticism with respect to the August 2001 package, characterizing it as one of the worst decisions that the IMF has ever made.

In this paper's second section, the broad conclusions were that (1) the fiscal adjustment that Argentina needed to make was not feasible, even by the end of the first quarter 2001, and (2) the trade balance had adjusted through 2000 such that current account sustainability was not the critical issue. However, the conclusion of the previous section was that political risk was a significant factor and that the Argentine economy had fallen into a vicious cycle or bad equilibrium path. These conclusions broadly support the view that, depending on one's reading of political risk, the IMF was right to maintain engagement and a program, at least through the first quarter of 2001.

However, the lack of political support for the Lopez-Murphy plan suggests that at that point the political boundaries for potential adjustment had been drawn. And, given that the only politically feasible alternative to close the fiscal deficit was new increases in taxes, it was becoming clearer that Argentina would not make it out of the bad equilibrium. As the more heterodox economic policies were introduced, the reaction of the markets simply pushed Argentina further into the trough of that bad equilibrium, with EMBI spreads of over 1,000 basis points.

As spreads reached these levels, one view might be that the IMF had a decision to make. The IMF either had to say that the markets were wrong and to support Argentina very strongly indeed to attempt to break the vicious cycle, or it had to say that the situation was no longer viable and that Argentina should seek a renegotiation of the debt and cut its losses. As it turned out, the IMF did neither. The IMF appeared to vacillate. On the one hand, the IMF signaled some displeasure at elements of the more heterodox strategy, such as the

57. Mussa (2002).

entrance of the euro into the currency basket and the introduction of the de facto dual exchange rate; on the other hand, the program appeared to continue.[58] The perception was that the IMF was unsure whether to continue the program or pull the plug.

The rumors—especially after the introduction of the de facto dual exchange rate—were that the IMF was about to withdraw. This created the environment for the bank run in late July. Finally, the IMF came through with a package for $8 billion in August. Although there was much talk that private sector involvement of some sort would be sought, in fact the package included roughly $5 billion of new money to shore up central bank reserves, plus $3 billion for some unspecified debt restructuring enhancement.[59] However, it was never very clear whether this was to be voluntary (in which case $3 billion looked dramatically insufficient or forced), and if so, how exactly that would happen.

The August package clearly arrested the bank run, but the sharp liquidity crunch had a very negative impact on the economy. As the fiscal figures for September became known and it became obvious that Argentina would not make the annual fiscal target for the IMF, the preconditions for another run were in place. The announcement of the zero deficit plan, subsequent increase in country risk (see this paper's first section), and decrees limiting interest rates on bank deposits were the final trigger. This bank run was not met with an IMF package. Indeed, the IMF declined to send any more funds, provoking the *corralito* and subsequent downfall of the de la Rua government.

Understanding the Strategic Interactions

While one approach is to argue in favor of or against particular decisions made by the IMF at particular times, a more useful strategy would be to attempt to understand the nature of the strategic relationship between the IMF and the country. Perhaps if one understands why this vacillation outcome occurred, one may then attempt to design a set of institutions that would help to prevent such outcomes from occurring in the future. Appendix B presents a very simple game along these lines, where the IMF decides to "assist" or "not assist," and the country decides whether to play "safe" or "risky." The four potential outcomes are labeled: First Best (IMF assists and country plays

58. Mussa (2002) cites a set of more institutional reasons as to why the program was most likely continued.
59. The IMF package did also go alongside the central bank triggering a Contingent Repo Facility with private sector banks.

safe); Moral Hazard (IMF assists and country plays risky); On Your Own (IMF does not assist and country plays safe); and Worst Case (IMF does not assist and country plays risky).

An interesting feature of this game is that in its noncooperative, one-shot (static) form, there is no (Nash) equilibrium in so-called pure strategies. There is, however, a unique (Nash) equilibrium in mixed strategies, where the players randomize between their possible actions. What this means in practice is that in equilibrium, the IMF can never unequivocally assist and the country can never unequivocally claim that it will play safe. In its most literal interpretation, the players randomize. One way to think about this is a rationalization of the case-by-case (or constructive ambiguity) doctrine.

However, assuming the game is repeated, there is a possibility of cooperation developing such that the First Best is attainable. This is feasible because the incentive for the country to deviate to the risky strategy (to get the Moral Hazard outcome) is contained by the threat that then the IMF will respond with the mixed strategy equilibrium forever, which in the long run may be worse for the country. It turns out that if the country has a high enough discount factor—or in other words, if the country derives sufficient benefit from future payoffs relative to the payoff today—this cooperative First Best outcome may be supported. However, it also follows that if something changes (for example, the payoffs) then the country may well deviate and the IMF will respond with the mixed strategy.

Relating the Game to Argentina

The interpretation offered here is that Argentina and the IMF had achieved the cooperative First Best outcome at some point during the latter half of the 1990s, with Argentina following a reform policy and the IMF assisting with a program. Admittedly, this position is debatable, although it seems consistent with the decision of the IMF to continue to support Argentina through the 1990s and the major *blindaje* program at the end of 2000. The position is also consistent with the analysis above that the debt position and current account actually were not too far away from sustainability. However, for whatever reason, during 2001 Argentina deviated to the risky strategy. One view is that having obtained the *blindaje,* the Moral Hazard outcome (and hence deviation) became more attractive. The evidence in favor of deviation is, first and foremost, the rejection of the Lopez-Murphy plan, and then secondly, the swathe of heterodox measures that attempted to get the economy moving while risking higher country risk spreads.[60] As it turned out, this so-called gambling for resurrection failed to turn the economy around. As predicted, the IMF returned with a mixed strategy, vacillating between assistance and nonassistance.

Implications for Institutions

It is interesting to consider what this story implies for the role of the IMF as a country gets closer and closer to default. It can be shown in a slightly more complex version of the model (see Powell, forthcoming) that the incentives to deviate rise as the probability of default rises in the case of risky play. It is then likely that a country will have the incentive to deviate to the risky strategy and gamble for resurrection before actually defaulting. There is, then, a structural problem in the role of the IMF, which given current institutions appears without solution. One may argue over the minutiae of IMF decisions and whether the IMF should have withdrawn support earlier or later, but the fact is that for a country that enters default, the country will most likely have previously gambled and the IMF will have vacillated.

One solution to this problem is to provide the country with an alternative. One candidate solution is a bankruptcy procedure, as advocated recently by Anne Krueger.[61] The above approach appears to set some limits as to how attractive or painful such a process should be. If the country is to decide for that alternative, then at the point where the country has the incentive to deviate to the risky strategy, that alternative would need to be superior to the discounted payoff from deviation. Obviously, it should otherwise be less attractive than the First Best. If such a procedure had been available to Argentina through 2001, perhaps it would have provided for a better set of strategic interactions between the country and IMF.[62]

Moreover, this paper has not discussed explicitly the role of the private sector, although this is incorporated into the game explained in appendix B in a very simple manner. Given the severe coordination problem within the pri-

60. Some might argue that Argentina had deviated before, perhaps even during Menem's second term. Others might suggest later, for example, with the introduction of the *de facto* dual exchange rate, or even later, with the decrees limiting interest rates on banks. Adopting one these alternatives would change the details of the story but not the underlying message regarding institutions that follows.

61. Krueger (2002).

62. A bankruptcy procedure may not be the only solution to this problem. However, it seems the one that would be most likely to genuinely provide an alternative for an incumbent government, rather than the risky strategy. This does not mean, however, that the current proposals necessarily comply with the restrictions advanced here. We leave that as a further interesting topic for research.

vate sector and the lack of a solution to the problem as suggested above, in the case of Argentina the private sector ran, placing substantial capital offshore through 2001. Reserves fell by $12.2 billion and the private sector capital account registered a fall of some $12 billion, with errors and omissions most likely reflecting further capital flight of another $3.5 billion.[63] The risky strategy adopted by Argentina through 2001—this massive loss of liquidity (plus the subsequent default and asymmetric pesification)—has now bankrupted what was a highly solvent and liquid banking sector and made the potential recovery process very difficult indeed. This process does not appear to be an efficient one to rectify a problem of public sector insolvency, current account unsustainability, increased political risk, or multiple equilibria, depending on one's preferred hypothesis. If the analysis above is correct and Argentina's fiscal problems were not so dramatic, the current account was not so far away from sustainability—at least before Argentina "deviated"—and the problem was more one of heightened political risk and multiple equilibria, then indeed what followed in Argentina was an extremely inefficient crisis resolution procedure, to say the least.

Conclusions

This paper has been one of history, attempting to understand what happened. After a brief description of the events, four hypotheses were posed as potential roots of the current crisis. While Argentine public sector debt had increased sharply, the adjustment required to make the debt ratio stable did not appear so large, even as late as the first quarter of 2001. While the external debt had also risen sharply, an adjustment process in the trade balance appeared to have been more or less completed again by the end of 2000, and the collapse of 2001 certainly did not seem to be a result of a wildly unsustainable current account. The preliminary conclusion from this analysis is that political risk, playing together with the mild level of required adjustment in the fiscal accounts, put Argentina into a bad equilibrium from which it did not escape without eventual devaluation and default. There is also support for this explanation using a vector autoregression analysis that showed a set of inter-

63. Note that consistent with the predictions of the model in appendix B, the recent uncertainty over further official assistance for Uruguay has also helped to spark a very significant run from that country's banking system and provoked a set of banking suspensions complicating the situation quite dramatically.

relations between key economic variables. Political risk fed through to worsened economic fundamentals, and these fed back to increased political risk. Low fiscal revenues and lower imports fed through to higher EMBI spreads, which in turn fed back to lower imports and lower fiscal revenues.

The fact that fiscal sustainability and current account sustainability were not far from Argentina's grasp justified the IMF's continued involvement through 2000 and into the first quarter of 2001. Perhaps if political events had been different and Argentina had had some good luck, the *blindaje* may even have turned things around. As it was, more messy politics made things even worse. The lack of support for the Lopez-Murphy plan appears to have been a watershed and marked the boundaries of the politically feasible adjustment in government spending under the de la Rua government. It is suggested above that with the *blindaje* in place, Argentina adopted a more risky strategy, attempting to get the economy moving with more heterodox measures and risking negative market sentiment and IMF disapproval.

At that point, it might be argued, the IMF had to make a decision—assist Argentina strongly or withdraw. However, it did neither. A more formal, game theoretic analysis suggests that this deviation to risky play might have been a rational strategy for the country. Cooperation between the IMF and Argentina then broke down, and in the formal analysis it was shown that the noncooperative game between the IMF and the country had no pure-strategy equilibrium. The only equilibrium is with the IMF vacillating between assist or not assist. This was exactly the perception in Buenos Aires, where the perceived probability of the IMF program continuing varied each day, according to the new announcements.

Indeed, the August package came as something of a surprise for many, and clearly arrested the bank run in progress at the time. But the run had already done its damage to the real economy. Eventually, the IMF did withdraw support and a second, major bank run ensued. This provoked the *corralito* and *cazerolazo,* which together with a set of more violent protests eventually brought down the government.

At the time of writing, Argentina has entered into a very deep crisis, and there is still no clear solution in sight. Argentina has defaulted and still has not entered into negotiations with external creditors. It has devalued with no clear vision with respect to future monetary policy. And through asymmetric pesification and default, it has broken its banks. The IMF and world leaders called for a sustainable policy and President Duhalde's repost was that there was little chance of a sustainable solution without an IMF agreement.

This interchange suggests that the game with no pure-strategy equilibrium continues. The IMF will not assist for fear of moral hazard, but if it does not assist then the private sector will not have confidence to invest, even if the country plays safe. The repeated game suggests that a cooperative first best strategy will only become available when the threat of the removal of IMF assistance is meaningful. This implies sustained IMF assistance will be available only once the crisis has been resolved. The conclusion is, then, that a sustainable policy must be found in Buenos Aires. Curiously, this argument suggests that the IMF, at least under its current modus operandi, may be largely irrelevant to a country in a crisis as deep as Argentina's. The only thing the IMF can do is point to the benefits that there would be in the future, once the sustainable policy had been found and IMF assistance subsequently granted.

In terms of the current policy debate, the government is caught between the banking sector controls (being eroded by the courts) and the monetary overhang caused by the lack of confidence in domestic institutions, and its effect on the exchange rate, if released. This paper is not the place for a detailed analysis of potential solutions—that would deserve another fifty pages. However, it is clear that a resolution to the crisis in the financial system is a necessary condition for Argentina to grow.

The analysis also suggests a structural problem with respect to institutions. The game analyzed suggests that a country with an IMF program in place but heading toward default, will at some point deviate to a risky strategy and gamble for resurrection. In turn, the IMF will most likely find itself adopting a mixed strategy (that is, vacillating) in order to attempt to control the moral hazard. As the IMF finally withdraws support, the country will face a liquidity crisis (as well and on top of whatever problem there is in fundamentals) that will make the recovery process much more complex. This is not an efficient crisis resolution process. There appears to be much work still to be done to construct a more efficient crisis resolution process. A bankruptcy procedure for sovereigns might be one candidate solution, although further analysis is required to see if current proposals would satisfy the right restrictions. The analysis suggests that this procedure should (normally) result in a payoff to the country worse than that of the first best (where the IMF assists strategy), but slightly better than the risky strategy at the point where the country otherwise has the incentive to deviate. This may, then, help to put some bounds on how attractive or painful such a procedure should be.

Comments on this article follow on page 105.

Appendix A

Table A-1. Vector Autoregression Results

	DLEMBIPRO	*DLDEPOSITS*	*DLRECAUD*	*DLIMPORTS*	*DLPOL_RISK*
DLEMBIPRO(–1)	0.226797	–0.017166	0.051301	0.098501	–0.011706
	(0.14111)	(0.01630)	(0.04877)	(0.07678)	(0.02032)
	(1.60719)	(–1.05311)	(1.05188)	(1.28286)	(–0.57617)
DLDEPOSITS(–1)	–2.273865	0.326157	1.103569	2.037212	0.178669
	(1.10698)	(0.12787)	(0.38259)	(0.60233)	(0.15937)
	(–2.05412)	(2.55070)	(2.88451)	(3.38225)	(1.12107)
DLRECAUD(–1)	0.276356	–0.056002	–0.603383	–0.389032	–0.079693
	(0.40360)	(0.04662)	(0.13949)	(0.21960)	(0.05811)
	(0.68473)	(–1.20123)	(–4.32570)	(–1.77152)	(–1.37150)
DLIMPORTS(–1)	–0.493969	0.085768	0.291216	–0.127296	0.082465
	(0.27207)	(0.03143)	(0.09403)	(0.14804)	(0.03917)
	(–1.81557)	(2.72903)	(3.09698)	(–0.85987)	(2.10525)
DLPOL_RISK(–1)	–0.058391	0.292837	0.726221	0.004169	0.052793
	(0.94742)	(0.10944)	(0.32744)	(0.51551)	(0.13640)
	(–0.06163)	(2.67579)	(2.21787)	(0.00809)	(0.38704)
C	0.040720	0.004002	–0.008959	–0.027389	–0.001133
	(0.02175)	(0.00251)	(0.00752)	(0.01183)	(0.00313)
	(1.87255)	(1.59342)	(–1.19206)	(–2.31477)	(–0.36184)
R-squared	0.192240	0.296988	0.361280	0.273711	0.100256
Adj. R-squared	0.114571	0.229391	0.299865	0.203876	0.013742
Sum sq. resids	1.237727	0.016515	0.147844	0.366446	0.025655
S.E. equation	0.154280	0.017821	0.053321	0.083947	0.022212
Log likelihood	29.26940	154.4552	90.89072	64.56766	141.6814
Akaike AIC	29.47630	154.6621	91.09762	64.77456	141.8883
Schwarz SC	29.68944	154.8753	91.31077	64.98771	142.1014
Mean dependent	0.041862	0.003924	–0.004516	–0.012942	–0.001370
S.D. dependent	0.163958	0.020301	0.063725	0.094083	0.022366
Determinant Residual Covariance	2.50E–14				
Log Likelihood	496.7361				
Akaike Information Criteria	497.7706				
Schwarz Criteria	498.8363				

Sample (adjusted): 1997:03 2001:12
Included observations: Fifty-eight after adjusting endpoints.
Standard errors and *t*-statistics in parentheses.

Figure A-1. Impulse Response Functions

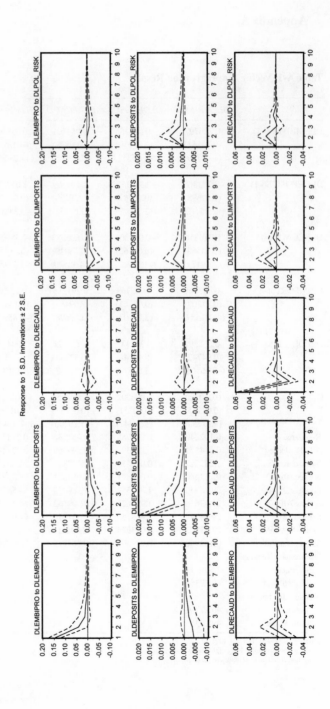

Response to 1 S.D. innovations ± 2 S.E.

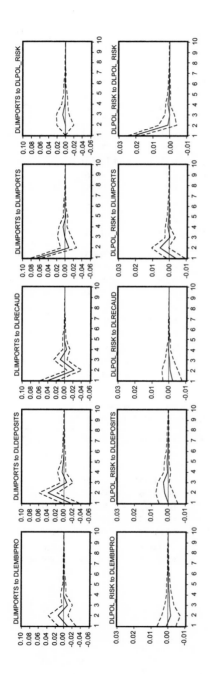

Table A-2. Variance Decompositions

DLEMBIPRO:

Period	S.E.	DLEMBIPRO	DLDEPOSITS	DLRECAUD	DLIMPORTS	DLPOL_RISK
1	0.146083	100.0000	0.000000	0.000000	0.000000	0.000000
2	0.158831	91.68486	3.835118	0.112104	4.362202	0.005713
3	0.163096	87.69037	7.244177	0.207663	4.480810	0.376978
4	0.164484	86.60354	7.835709	0.204200	4.674678	0.681873
5	0.165081	86.07690	8.192186	0.215003	4.751962	0.763952
6	0.165282	85.91640	8.306047	0.214934	4.768082	0.794536
7	0.165363	85.84839	8.348129	0.215433	4.779515	0.808529
8	0.165393	85.82352	8.365770	0.215581	4.782350	0.812783
9	0.165404	85.81423	8.371780	0.215613	4.783694	0.814683
10	0.165409	85.81060	8.374235	0.215639	4.784182	0.815345

DLDEPOSITS:

Period	S.E.	DLEMBIPRO	DLDEPOSITS	DLRECAUD	DLIMPORTS	DLPOL_RISK
1	0.016874	5.892666	94.10733	0.000000	0.000000	0.000000
2	0.019337	7.738253	76.68230	0.001617	5.883758	9.694074
3	0.020204	7.939735	76.00374	0.290661	6.354741	9.411126
4	0.020449	8.337228	75.34968	0.284838	6.452618	9.575635
5	0.020558	8.395966	75.09127	0.297331	6.584735	9.630698
6	0.020595	8.433268	75.03388	0.297724	6.597985	9.637147
7	0.020610	8.446401	74.99783	0.297928	6.611695	9.646143
8	0.020615	8.450763	74.98812	0.298212	6.615272	9.647636
9	0.020617	8.452746	74.98374	0.298229	6.616707	9.648576
10	0.020618	8.453396	74.98213	0.298260	6.617321	9.648894

DLRECAUD:

Period	S.E.	DLEMBIPRO	DLDEPOSITS	DLRECAUD	DLIMPORTS	DLPOL_RISK
1	0.050488	9.368210	1.697509	88.93428	0.000000	0.000000
2	0.061986	9.016540	8.966953	68.74649	7.468317	5.801701
3	0.062827	9.534781	9.441760	67.31379	7.996151	5.713517
4	0.063154	9.475836	9.371637	66.63155	8.483720	6.037257
5	0.063235	9.467766	9.578466	66.46976	8.461851	6.022154
6	0.063254	9.479967	9.580870	66.43333	8.467729	6.038106
7	0.063263	9.479149	9.595994	66.41595	8.470297	6.038607
8	0.063265	9.480415	9.599278	66.41118	8.470086	6.039043
9	0.063266	9.480568	9.600441	66.40898	8.470565	6.039445
10	0.063266	9.480658	9.601073	66.40821	8.470573	6.039486

Table A-2. Variance Decompositions (continued)

Variance DLIMPORTS:

Period	S.E.	DLEMBIPRO	DLDEPOSITS	DLRECAUD	DLIMPORTS	DLPOL_RISK
1	0.079486	1.127737	4.085083	22.45058	72.33660	0.000000
2	0.092463	2.851045	19.86687	22.95546	54.32653	8.59E-05
3	0.093782	3.622430	19.69655	23.40880	52.81627	0.455941
4	0.094210	3.596917	19.86150	23.42333	52.62816	0.490100
5	0.094262	3.629372	19.88450	23.40842	52.58810	0.489599
6	0.094286	3.630964	19.87844	23.39704	52.58691	0.506647
7	0.094293	3.631714	19.88812	23.39413	52.57942	0.506615
8	0.094295	3.632636	19.88825	23.39331	52.57813	0.507669
9	0.094295	3.632731	19.88899	23.39296	52.57749	0.507828
10	0.094296	3.632836	19.88917	23.39284	52.57726	0.507890

DLPOL_RISK:

Period	S.E.	DLEMBIPRO	DLDEPOSITS	DLRECAUD	DLIMPORTS	DLPOL_RISK
1	0.021032	0.122929	9.87E-07	1.085061	3.235715	95.55629
2	0.021933	0.838037	0.938036	1.132190	8.981417	88.11032
3	0.022168	1.008100	2.745425	1.137043	8.854056	86.25538
4	0.022233	1.140059	2.776974	1.140218	8.977865	85.96488
5	0.022261	1.152602	2.953003	1.153993	8.982757	85.75765
6	0.022268	1.170063	2.978392	1.153797	8.981737	85.71601
7	0.022271	1.173278	2.991717	1.154074	8.985804	85.69513
8	0.022272	1.175007	2.997536	1.153997	8.985706	85.68775
9	0.022272	1.175647	2.999159	1.153966	8.986036	85.68519
10	0.022273	1.175861	2.999976	1.153965	8.986094	85.68410

Ordering: DLEMBIPRO, DLDEPOSITS, DLRECAUD, DLIMPORTS, DLPOL_RISK.

Appendix B: Simple, Game-Theoretic Approach to Strategic Interactions between a Country and the IMF

This appendix describes a very simple model to fix ideas, drawing on previously unpublished work.[64] The model can be thought of as a three-player game, where the actors are a country, the International Monetary Fund, and private sector lenders. Suppose, for simplicity, that one restricts the potential actions of each to a bivariate decision. In particular, that the country must decide a "safe" strategy or "risky" strategy, the IMF must decide whether to "assist" or "not "assist," and the private sector must decide whether to "lend" or "run."

64. Gavin and Powell (1998).

Figure B-1. The Game in Extensive Form

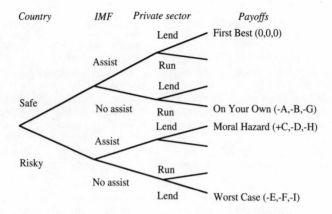

Simultaneous Game between the Country and IMF

This game with three players, each with two possible actions, has eight potential outcomes. The game is presented in extensive form in figure B-1. However, in what follows the outcome is restricted in a way that depends on some other features of the problem. In a first case, assume that there is a simultaneous game between the IMF and country. Then the private sector conditions its decisions on the outcome of that game, in particular on what the IMF does. This intertemporal structure can be justified in at least two different ways. First, the private sector is making decisions every second in real time, whereas the IMF and country policy discussions have a more defined structure and timetable. Second, the private sector, as it is composed of many different actors, may be thought of as incapable (or less capable) of making any commitment. Hence its actions must be conditioned on the actions of others. However, as discussed below, one interpretation of the current debate is precisely to attempt to change the intertemporal structure of this game. Therefore, this appendix explores different sequential structures below. It should come as no great surprise that the results are highly sensitive to the particular assumed intertemporal structure.

Furthermore, assume that the private sector's actions crucially depend on those of the IMF. In particular, assume that the private sector runs unless the IMF assists. This may seem a harsh assumption, but it makes little difference if one says instead that there is a greater probability of the private sector running without IMF assistance so long as that greater probability results in expected payoffs that satisfy certain conditions outlined below. Hence, while this particular assumption is harsh, weaker assumptions along the same lines would have similar results.

At least two more theoretical interpretations for this assumption are available. First, as discussed above, the private sector has a severe coordination problem, and hence may run unless the IMF coordinates in some fashion. Or, by assisting, the IMF directly rules out a run equilibrium through its promise of liquidity. A second interpretation is that there is some (unmodeled) information problem, and the private sector only trusts the country (and IMF) if the IMF puts down its own money rather than any cheap talk without committing resources. The assumption—that the private sector runs without IMF assistance—is how the liquidity school argument is introduced into this version of the model. With this assumption, there are then only four relevant outcomes (as in the standard prisoner's dilemma), as the private sector's action is really determined by the IMF's actions.

As there are only four outcomes that depend on the actions of the country and the IMF, one can also represent the model in a two-by-two matrix, as in figure B-2. The four potential outcomes are labeled: First Best, On Your Own, Moral Hazard, and Worst Case. These labels refer to some general notion of world welfare and not the payoffs of particular players. First Best is a case where the country plays safe, the IMF assists, and the private sector lends. Worst Case is when the country plays risky, the IMF does not assist, and the private sector runs. A third outcome is where the country plays Safe, IMF does not assist and private sector runs, which is labeled On Your Own. It also might be referred to as the case where the discipline of the IMF and the private sector is operating most fully. The final outcome is where the country plays risky, the IMF assists, and the private sector lends. This is referred to as the Moral Hazard case.

Discussion of the Payoffs

The equilibrium of this game naturally depends on the assumed payoffs. As the actions of the private sector are assumed to follow those of the IMF, it is only the payoffs of the IMF and country that matter. Assume that the base case is First Best, and the payoffs—both for the country and the IMF—are zero. The payoffs are written as a vector with the first element the payoff to the country, and the second, the payoff to the IMF.

Figure B-2. Reduced Form of Game[a]

IMF

		Assist	No assist
	Safe	First Best (0,0)	On Your Own (–A,–B)
Country			
	Risky	Moral Hazard (C,–D)	Worst Case (–E,–F)

a. Assuming the IMF "coordinates" the private sector if the IMF assists, and the private sector runs if not.

In order for there to be a moral hazard problem, it must be the case that, given that the IMF is assisting, the country will prefer not to play safe but would rather play risky. This appendix assumes then, following the moral hazard school, that in the Moral Hazard outcome the payoffs are {C, –D} with C, D > 0 where one assumes that the country is better off and the IMF is worse off relative to the base case.

In Worst Case, the country plays risky, the IMF does not assist, and the private sector runs. Here, the payoffs are –E, –F, where E, F > 0. This appendix assumes that –D < –F. Or, in other words, for the IMF Moral Hazard is worse than Worst Case. An interpretation of recent lobbying of the moral hazard school economists is precisely to ensure that this is the case. This particular issue is discussed further in the next section, noting that recent authors have suggested otherwise.[65] For the country, however, the Worst Case outcome is the worst of all, that is, –E is the lowest payoff the country may receive.

Finally, in the On Your Own outcome, the payoffs are –A, –B, where A, B > 0. This appendix assumes that –E < –A. In other words, while this is clearly worse for the country than the base case (if the IMF does not assist, On Your Own is preferred to Worst Case. Or, if the IMF does not assist, it is then better for the country to play safe rather than risky. This appendix also assumes that the payoff to the IMF here is –B, where B > 0. This implies that if the country is playing safe, then the IMF would prefer to assist than not assist.

65. See Eichengreen and Ruhl (2000).

Discussion of Potential Equilibria

If the country and the IMF are acting simultaneously, with the payoffs as defined above, it is simple to see that this game has no Nash equilibrium in pure strategies. In particular, start from First Best. If the IMF is assisting, the country then prefers to play risky—thus the country prefers the Moral Hazard solution to First Best. But if the country is playing risky, then the IMF prefers to not assist; hence the IMF prefers Worst Case to Moral Hazard. However, if the IMF does not assist and the private sector runs, then the country prefers to play safe (that is, the country prefers On Your Own to Worst Case). But then, if the country is playing safe, the IMF should sssist, and one is back to First Best. Hence there is no Nash equilibrium in pure strategies.

However, it is well known that in such a situation there is at least one equilibrium in mixed strategies, where the IMF plays randomly between assist and not assist and the country plays randomly between safe and risky. In particular, suppose that the probability that the IMF plays assist is p and the probability that the country plays safe is q. It follows, given the payoffs, that there is a particular pair of probabilities, p and q, that make the country indifferent between playing safe and risky, and the IMF indifferent between assist and not assist. This probability pair then defines the mixed-strategy equilibrium.

To find the probability that the IMF will assist in this equilibrium, p, consider the position of the country. To ensure that the country is indifferent between playing safe and risky, it must be the case that the expected payoff to the country from playing safe—calculated using the probabilities of the IMF playing assist or not assist—is equal to the expected payoff to the country of playing safe, again weighted by the probabilities of the IMF deciding to assist or not assist. In mathematical terms:

$$p0 + (1 - p)(-A) = pC + (1 - p)(-E) . \tag{B-1}$$

It then follows that by rearranging this equation that

$$p = \frac{E - A}{E - A + C} . \tag{B-2}$$

The existence of moral hazard is critical in the explanation of why there is no equilibrium in pure strategies, only in mixed strategies. If there were no moral hazard, then C would not be positive but would be zero or negative (C is the payoff to the country if it plays risky, given that the IMF assists). If there were no moral hazard present, then the probability p would be unity (or would not be well defined, as it would be greater than one). And, if the other payoffs remained unchanged, then Best Case would be a pure-strategy equilibrium.

In a similar vein, the probability that the country plays safe, q, can also be found by considering the position of the IMF. The IMF will be indifferent to assist or not assist if its expected payoff from playing assist is equal to the expected payoff of not assist, that is, if

$$q0 + (1-q)(-D) = q(-B) + (1-q)(-F) . \qquad (B-3)$$

Rearranging this equation we find that

$$q = \frac{D-F}{D-F+B} . \qquad (B-4)$$

It is easy to check from the assumptions regarding payoffs above that $0 < p < 1$ and $0 < q < 1$.

One interpretation of the mixed-strategy equilibrium is the case-by-case approach to countries with difficulties regarding international payments that has indeed been the norm. There is a close analogy here between the case-by-case approach applied to countries and the apparent affinity for constructive ambiguity of central banks when it comes to helping banks in distress. There are at least two interpretations of the reasons why case-by-case or constructive ambiguity may be useful. One is that the world is just too complex to write down the right set of rules, and hence flexibility is required to deal with particular cases as they arise. This might be referred to as the incomplete contracts view. However, the other interpretation is that case-by-case or constructive ambiguity really implies unpredictability. As is shown in the game above, if there is moral hazard and other conditions are met, then unpredictability may be necessary for there to be an equilibrium. Under this interpretation, to ensure an equilibrium the IMF must never assist with certainty, and the country will respond by never being absolutely clear that it will play safe.[66]

Note that the probability that the country plays safe depends on the relationship between $(D - F)$ and B, the payoffs to the IMF. If $(D - F)$ is large,

66. Gavin and Powell (1999) develops a slightly more complex model with imperfect information, where the IMF prefers a mixed-strategy equilibrium to a Nash equilibrium in pure strategies, and the IMF always assists in the case of a systemic problem and opts to not assist in the case of an individual problem—giving a slightly different interpretation of the constructive ambiguity doctrine. See Fischer (1999) for a further discussion of the analogy between case-by-case and the constructive ambiguity doctrine of central banks and the interpretation that such approaches are in part designed to control moral hazard.

relative to B, then the probability increases that the country will play safe in this mixed-strategy equilibrium. This means that if the Moral Hazard outcome is very bad for the IMF compared to the Worst Case outcome (summarized by the difference, D – F), then the probability that the country plays safe rises in equilibrium. On the other hand, if (D – F) is reduced, the probability that the country plays safe diminishes.

The welfare of the country in the mixed-strategy equilibrium is equal to $(1 - p)(-A)$, or $-AC/(E - A + C)$.[67] This is increasing in E but decreasing in A and C. This implies, for example, that increasing E (that is, making –E more negative, and making the risky strategy combined with the IMF's not assist more painful for the country), would actually increase country welfare in the equilibrium, as the IMF would have to assist more frequently for an equilibrium to be found. This is somewhat analogous to the result that increasing the pain of a country in default might actually make a country better off, *ex ante*, as it would support greater private lending, although the mechanism for this result is quite different.

Repeating the Game: Opportunities for Cooperation

Returning to the original game, with simultaneous play between the country and the IMF, it is possible to ask what might happen if the game is repeated. In the one-shot game, the only equilibrium was one in mixed strategies. And given the assumption of simultaneous play, the country could not commit to a safe strategy, nor could the IMF commit to only assist if the country played safe.

However, in a repeated game there may be an opportunity for cooperation between the IMF and the country. Note that the best outcome for the IMF is First Best. Suppose that the IMF offers First Best, but with the threat that if the country deviates (and plays risky to obtain the Moral Hazard outcome), then the IMF will respond with the Nash (mixed-strategy) equilibrium forever. As one had before, the payoff to the country in the Nash equilibrium is equal to $(1 - p)(-A)$, and the country is then clearly worse off than in First Best, which is equal to zero. It is then possible that First Best can be attained through this approach.[68]

67. Note that in the Nash mixed-strategy equilibrium, the country is indifferent to playing safe or risky, by definition, and so the payoff to the country can be calculated as simply the payoff to playing safe.

68. Naturally, this is only one potential cooperative outcome. The IMF, for example, might be able to impose On Your Own on the country forever, where the IMF does not assist and country prefers to play safe. On Your Own in this game is the country's security level (or max-

In this example, the country must weigh up the welfare of staying in First Best forever, which is equal to zero, versus the alternative of deviating and obtaining the payoff C from the Moral Hazard outcome for one period, and then welfare of the mixed-strategy equilibrium for the rest of time. First Best can then be supported if

$$C + \frac{\delta}{1-\delta}(1-p)(-A) < 0 , \tag{B-5}$$

where δ is the discount factor of the country, and hence the second term on the left-hand side gives the payoff to playing the Nash equilibrium forever, discounted by one period.[69] Substituting for p in terms of the payoffs and re-arranging, this yields the following condition for First Best to be supported:

$$\delta > 1 - \frac{A}{C+E} . \tag{B-6}$$

Remembering this original assumptions, A, C, E > 0, equation B-6 gives a threshold discount factor of less than one.[70] The larger is C (the payoff from deviating and obtaining the Moral Hazard outcome for one period), then the higher is the threshold discount factor. In other words, if C is large, then the country must weigh future payoffs more highly for First Best to be supported. This is because increasing C increases the reward from deviation. The threshold discount factor also rises if E is increased. If the country's pain from playing risky and the IMF's opting for not assist is greater, then as the welfare in the Nash equilibrium rises, the discount factor now has to be greater to support First Best. Perhaps, somewhat surprisingly, if one presumes default is most likely in the scenario where the country plays risky and the IMF does not assist, and then default is made less costly, then the First Best has more chance of being supported. This result appears to go against the standard view of a trade-off between *ex ante* provision of credit and *ex post* efficiency of default

---

min), in the sense that it gives the best payoff for the country, assuming that the IMF will always choose the worst action for the country given the country's choice. However, whether this is a credible threat is a complex issue and is not discussed further here. See Fudenberg and Maskin (1986).

69. The discount factor δ ($0 < \delta < 1$) can be thought of as $(1/(1 + r))$, where r is the positive discount rate.

70. Note that if $C + E > A$, then the threshold discount factor is greater than zero too, although there is no obvious reason why that is the case. If, then, C or E are sufficiently small, or A sufficiently large (subject to the restrictions to obtain the unique Nash mixed-strategy equilibrium), any positive discount factor would support First Best.

resolution, and may provide some theoretical support for collective action clauses in bond contracts.

References

Aizenman, Joshua, and Andrew Powell. 1998. "The Political Economy of Public Savings and the Role of Capital Mobility." *Journal of Development Economics* 57: 67–95.

Binmore, Ken. 1992. *Fun and Games: A Text on Game Theory.* Lexington, Mass.: DC Heath.

Calvo, Ernesto, and Juan Manuel Abal Medina. 2001. *El Federalismo electoral Argentino: sobrerepresentación, reforma política y gobierno dividido en la Argentina.* Buenos Aires: UDEBA.

D'Amato, Laura, Elena Grubisic, and Andrew Powell. 1997. "Contagion, Bank Fundamentals or Macroeconomic Shock? An Empirical Analysis of the Argentine 1995 Banking Problems." Working Paper 2. Central Bank of Argentina (July).

De la Torre, A., E. Levy Yeyati, and S. Schmukler. 2002. "Argentina's Financial Crisis: Floating Money, Sinking Banking." Mimeo. World Bank and Universidad Torcuato di Tella.

Eichengreen, Barry, and Cristof Ruhl. 2000. "The Bail-in Problem: Systematic Goals, ad Hoc Means." Working Paper 7653. Cambridge, Mass.: National Bureau of Economic Research (April).

Fischer, S. 1999. "On the Need for an International Lender of Last Resort." *Journal of Economic Perspectives* 13 (4): 85–104.

Fudenberg, Drew, and Eric Maskin. 1986. "The Folk Theorem in Repeated Games with Imperfect Public Information Discounting or with Incomplete Information." *Econometrica* 54: 533–54.

Ganapolsky, Eduardo J. J., and Sergio L. Schmukler. 1998. "The Impact of Policy Announcements and News on Capital Markets." Working Paper 5. Central Bank of Argentina (June).

Gavin, Michael, and Andrew Powell. 1998. "Domestic and International Lender of Last Resort: Constructive Ambiguity and Cheap Talk." Mimeo. Central Bank of Argentina.

———. 1999. "Should the International Lender of Resort Be Privatized?" Mimeo. Central Bank of Argentina.

Guidotti, Pablo. 2001. "Adónde Apunta el Déficit Cero y el Programa con el FMI." Mimeo. Universidad Torcuato Di Tella.

International Country Risk Guide. 1999. "Brief Guide to the Ratings System" (www.prsgroup.com).

Jones, Mark P., and others. 2001. "Keeping a Seat in Congress: Provincial Party Bosses and the Survival of Argentine Legislators, or Why Argentina Legislators Are So Ugly." Mimeo. Universidad de San Andrés.

JP Morgan. 2000. "Argentina's Debt Dynamic: Much Ado about Not Very Much." Market Brief. New York (September 6).

Kletzer, Kenneth M. 1984. "Asymmetries of Information and LDC Borrowing with Sovereign Risk." *Economic Journal* 94 (374): 287–307.

Krueger, Anne. 2002. "New Approaches to Sovereign Debt Restructuring: An Update on Our Thinking." Presented at Conference on Sovereign Debt Workouts: Hopes and Hazards. Institute for International Economics, Washington, April 1.

Lehmann Brothers. 2001. "Argentina: Speaking the Unspeakable." *Global Weekly Economic Monitor*. New York (March 2).

Mussa, Michael. 2002. "Argentina and the Fund: From Triumph to Tragedy." Mimeo. Washington: Institute for International Economics.

Perry, Guillermo, and Luis Servén. 2002. "The Anatomy of a Multiple Crisis: Why Was Argentina Special and What Can We Learn from It?" Mimeo. Washington: World Bank.

Pou, Pedro. 2002. "The Argentine Crisis." Presentation prepared for the National Bureau of Economic Research Conference on Argentina. Cambridge, Mass., July 17.

Powell, Andrew. 2002. "Safety First: Monetary and Financial Policies for Emerging Economies." In *Financial Risks, System Stability, and Economic Globalization,* edited by O. Johnson, 267–311. Washington: International Monetary Fund.

———. Forthcoming. "Countries in Payments Difficulties: What Can the IMF Do?" In *The IMF and the International Financial Architecture*, edited by C. L. Gilbert and D. Vines. Cambridge University Press.

Powell, Andrew, and Federico Sturzenegger. 2000. "Dollarization: The Link between Devaluation and Default Risk." Mimeo. Central Bank of Argentina and Universidad Torcuato di Tella.

Teijeiro, M. 2001. "Una Vez Mas, La Política Fiscal." Mimeo. Buenos Aires: Centro de Estudios Públicos (June).

RICARDO HAUSMANN *and* ANDRÉS VELASCO

Kennedy School of Government, Harvard University

Hard Money's Soft Underbelly: Understanding the Argentine Crisis

A rgentina has imploded, and among policy gurus and op-ed writers there is no shortage of simple reasons why. Some blame the International Monetary Fund (IMF), others the neo-liberal model (whatever that may be), yet others a singularly corrupt and incompetent batch of politicians. The implication is often clear: had Argentina just done this or that differently, the tragedy surely could have been averted.

If only life were that simple. Argentina's was not a crisis that caught people by surprise. Instead, it was a protracted affair that, as it marched inexorably toward a catastrophic demise, attracted the attention of some of the best minds in Washington, Wall Street, and Buenos Aires for months on end. During this long agony, many well-trained economists proposed various diagnostics and innovative policy initiatives. The country's much-maligned politicians and parties supported austerity policies (such as cutting nominal public sector wages) that would be very hard to swallow in most democratic societies; and, until late in the game, the international community provided ample financial support. Yet the catastrophe proved impossible to avoid.

It may seem like ancient history now, but not long ago Argentina was thought to be a development model. Through much of the 1990s, Washington and Wall Street toasted Argentina's success in axing inflation, privatizing, deregulating, and linking its currency to the dollar through the so-called convertibility system. This was not pure ideology. In the 1991–97 period the Argentine economy grew 6.7 percent a year (on average), a performance sec-

The authors are grateful to Joyce Chang, Susan Collins, Michael Gavin, and Dani Rodrik for comments. The Center for International Development at Harvard provided generous support.

ond only to Chile's within Latin America. Most important, Argentines themselves relished this new combination of low inflation and strong, if erratic,
growth. In 1995 they reelected Carlos Menem—the president who had first
applied the reform policies—in spite of double-digit unemployment and
Menem's penchant for fast cars and tainted associates. In 1999 they elected
Fernando de la Rua, who promised to be like Menem minus the antics: a solid
if boring politician committed to responsible, market-friendly policies. It was
not until very late (the crucial date is October 2001, when congressional elec-
tions were held) that Argentine voters reacted with dismay to the deteriorating
economic situation.

True, Argentina's convertibility had been in trouble before. During the
tequila crisis of 1995, the system had been tested by a massive collapse in capital inflows and deposit demand. But the economy came out roaring in 1996–97
without any changes in its currency regime. Moreover, Argentine authorities
used the experience to lengthen the maturity of public debt, improve the liquidity of the Treasury, upgrade banking regulation, and create a novel liquidity
policy that helped reassure investors and kept deposits growing through the
recession that started in 1999 and until as late as February 2001.[1]

The theories put forward as the crisis deepened spanned the whole scope
of the academic literature. For some, the problem had a fiscal origin and
required a fiscal response.[2] Proponents argued that a fiscal contraction could
even be expansionary, since it would eliminate fears of insolvency and make
capital markets more forthcoming. These ideas led to a series of fiscal adjustment efforts that in fact increased the non–Social Security national primary
fiscal surplus by over 2 percentage points of gross domestic product (GDP)
in spite of the recession.[3] They involved raising taxes, and by the summer of
2001 even cutting nominal public sector wages, pensions, and mandated intergovernmental federal transfers.

For others, it was a multiple equilibria story, in which self-fulfilling pessimism kept interest rates too high and growth too low for the numbers to add
up. Analysts pointed to liquidity needs and rollover risks. In order to reassure
the markets and reestablish access, the government negotiated a $40 billion

---

1. For a description of Argentina's banking reforms, see Calomiris and Powell (2000).
2. Tejeiro (2001) and Mussa (2002).
3. Ministerio de Economia, Republica de Argentina, www.mecon.gov.ar. The de la Rua
administration started in January 2000 with a major fiscal adjustment—the *impuestazo*— that
did not generate an expansionary contraction, but instead was later blamed for having killed
an incipient recovery in its bud. Three additional attempts at this strategy were made in 2001,
without any expansionary consequences.

lending package led by the IMF in December 2000, and negotiated a $30 billion debt exchange in May 2001.[4] Neither had the expected effects.

In this same vein, some analysts blamed investor pessimism on the lack of conviction of policymakers and demanded a more forceful leader. This concern led to the return of Domingo Cavallo, the architect of the convertibility plan of 1991 and allegedly a legend in the minds of Argentines and Wall Streeters alike. He demanded and was granted special powers to fix the economy by decree. The market reacted with a sharp rise in country risk.

Other students of the Argentine situation blamed the exchange rate, which had moved in the wrong direction because of the dollar's strength and the real's weakness. Fearful of the balance sheet and credibility consequences of an exchange rate move, the government in 2001 engineered a fiscal devaluation (that is, a tariff for imports accompanied by a subsidy for exports, leaving financial transactions and hence balance sheets untouched) of about 8 percent.[5] It accompanied this measure with a planned gradual transition away from a pure U.S. dollar basket and into an evenly divided dollar-euro peg. The markets reacted very negatively.

For others—including Domingo Cavallo, in one of his incarnations—the problem was growth and required a supply response. Here again, a massive attempt was made at fostering competitiveness through assorted sectoral plans. Markets again remained unimpressed.

Finally, there have been many who blamed the Argentine crisis on political gridlock, but this is a hard case to make. In spite of an unrelenting recession and with little to show for their efforts, the government consistently got from Congress an unprecedented level of delegation of power. All major policy requests were granted: labor market reforms (albeit in watered-down form), several tax increases, a special powers act in April 2001, and a zero-deficit rule in the summer of 2001 that involved cutting wages and pensions and making their recipients junior to bondholders. And yet, as in a Greek tragedy, destiny proved unavoidable.

Which of these stories makes more sense? Even though there were elements of self-fulfilling pessimism in the Argentine debacle, it is hard to make the case that multiple equilibria alone were to blame. The reestablishment of

4. The program never added up to $40 billion. This number included unidentified operations with markets for $20 billion. The main component was an approximately $14 billion loan from the IMF, and $5 billion from the Inter-American Development Bank (IADB) and the World Bank. The latter amount was mainly previously planned lending and not much in additional finance.

5. The consequences of such policy are analyzed by Fernández-Arias and Talvi (2000).

enough confidence to assure moderate growth, given hard-to-change relative prices, would have required maintaining a current account deficit in excess of 5 percent of GDP and the accumulation of an additional $20 billion in external debt between 1998 and 2001. Perhaps in an idealized world of perfect capital markets such a path would be feasible. In a more realistic setting of sovereign risk and imperfect commitment to repay, it seems like a pretty unlikely bet indeed.

In spite of the strong temptation to blame everything on the politicians and their irresponsibility, the simple fiscal explanation is also inadequate. There is no evidence of a spending boom: as a share of GDP, primary government expenditures remained roughly constant in 1993–2001. True, public debt grew rapidly. But this paper shows the accumulation of debt was driven mainly by the transition costs of the Social Security system, recession, and recognition of preexisting debts, not by a lack of adjustment effort.

This paper sketches a framework for understanding the nature of the Argentine crisis. To make sense of what went wrong one has to focus on the interaction between two factors: the real exchange rate, which became grossly misaligned in the run-up to the crisis, and the country's capacity to borrow abroad, which went from ample in the early 1990s to nil by 2001. In this framework, export prospects determine the access of financially constrained countries to external resources. Starting in 1999, expectations of future export growth arguably declined sharply: expected returns to capital in this sector fell, alongside low export prices and an appreciating real multilateral exchange rate. The drastic tightening of the financing constraint explains the onset of Argentina's investment decline and recession. Thereafter negative factors fed on each other: higher risk premiums and smaller capital flows meant less demand for domestic investment, which in turn depressed aggregate demand and output, further curtailing creditworthiness and the ability to borrow.

True, other countries in the region suffered similar capital account shocks and were forced to undertake rapid current account reversals. But those countries, especially Chile and Brazil, could rely on sharp changes in relative prices to help speed up the adjustment. And those countries were much less dollarized than Argentina, a fortunate factor that reduced the significance of negative balance sheet effects. Since relative prices could not adjust quickly (deflation did its painful job, but very slowly), quantities had to. The economy began contracting sharply in 1999 and has remained on that course ever since. In this sense, Argentina's financial crisis is a growth crisis: if incomes keep dropping, at some point debts become impossible to pay.

Something similar can be said of Argentina's public finances, which have deteriorated sharply since 1999. True, there was a spending blip late in Menem's term, as the president attempted to gain political backing to run again. But the bulk of the fiscal problems were a consequence, not a cause, of the overall mess. As the economy went on a tailspin, balance could only be maintained by ever-rising tax rates and spending cuts, which would only further the collapse. In this context, spreads charged on loans to Argentina went from huge to obscene. This drove up the deficit, which then spooked investors, who demanded even higher spreads, and scared consumers, who spent even less (causing revenues to decline yet again), all of which enlarged the deficit further.

The situation presented policymakers with an unusually nasty menu of options. Standard fiscal contraction ran the risk of further contracting an already depressed economy, while having a highly uncertain impact on expectations, investment, and future growth. Using the exchange rate as textbooks recommend was no easier. Argentina clearly suffered from exchange rate over-valuation. But given the large stock of dollar-denominated debt, both private and public, devaluation by itself would have most likely made matters worse. Arguably a devaluation accompanied by the pesification of financial claims might have resolved the overvaluation while minimizing the negative balance sheet effect.

This paper outlines what happened in Argentina—and what did not happen—and analyzes the limitations of the three major paradigms with which actors and analysts tried to understand events as they unfolded. A framework for making sense of the crisis is presented, along with an examination of what might have happened had authorities pursued other policy options. The paper also asks how reasonable a picture this is of the Argentine crisis and ponders some troublesome issues—an understanding of which might help forecast (and perhaps even prevent?) the next emerging market financial crisis.

What Happened

Argentina collapsed into hyperinflation in the late 1980s, but was able to right itself by adopting a radical market-oriented reform anchored by a currency board. The reforms delivered rapid growth in the early 1990s, with a very rapid recovery of investment (see table 1 and figure 1). Then came the tequila crisis in 1995. Financial flows from abroad and investment collapsed, causing a deep recession. Notice, however, that during the crisis exports sky-

Table 1. GDP and Its Components, 1994–2001[a]

	1994	1995	1996	1997	1998	1999	2000	2001
GDP	5.8	−2.8	5.5	8.1	3.9	−3.4	−0.8	−4.5
Private consumption	6.1	−4.4	5.5	9.0	3.5	−2.0	−0.7	−5.8
Public consumption	0.4	0.8	2.2	3.2	3.4	2.6	0.6	−2.1
Investment	13.7	−13.1	8.9	17.7	6.5	−12.6	−6.8	−15.9
Exports	15.3	22.5	7.6	12.2	10.6	−1.3	2.7	2.9
Imports	21.1	−9.8	17.5	26.9	8.4	−11.3	−0.2	−14.0
Export prices[b]	2.9	5.7	6.5	−3.5	−10.4	−11.2	10.2	−3.5

Source: Ministerio de Economia, Republica de Argentina.
a. Annual rates of growth, constant 1993 prices.
b. Annual rate of growth in U.S. dollars.

rocketed, growing at real rates in excess of 30 percent in 1995. The subsequent period of 1996 and 1997 brought what seemed like very healthy export- and investment-led growth. Concerns over the competitiveness of the country were (temporarily) laid to rest as the economy was able to extricate itself from the tequila crisis and rebound to high growth through exports, without the disruptive devaluation that the Mexicans had undergone. Also in contrast to Mexico, Argentina's banks were able to weather the storm, in spite of a drastic but short-lived decline in deposits.

Figure 1. GDP Component Growth, March 1993–September 2001

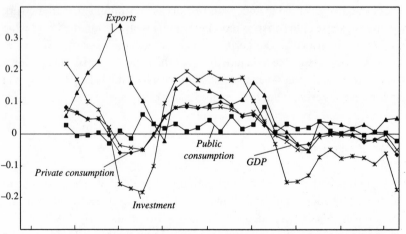

Source: Ministerio de Economia, Republica de Argentina.

Figure 2. Export Price and Volume Growth, 1990–2001

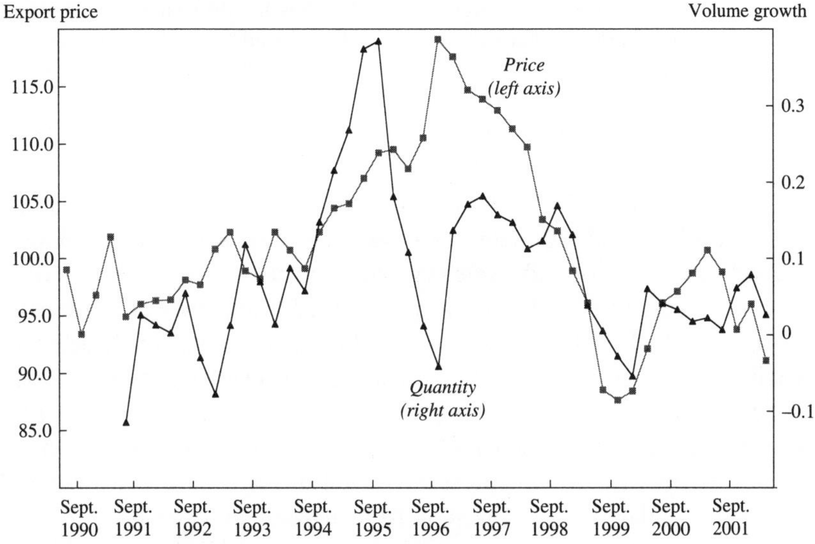

Export price   Volume growth

Source: Ministerio de Economia, Republica de Argentina.

That was the happy part of the story. It was not to last. The East Asian crisis caused a fall in the terms of trade in the second half of 1997 (see figure 2). Then came the Russian crisis in August 1998, and later, the Brazilian devaluation of January 1999. Just as under the tequila crisis, output declined, led by a collapse in investment. Optimists hoped that the economy would soon turn around, just like the last time. But this time export volumes stagnated and investment continued to decline. The recovery never came. The earlier magic was not repeated.

For much of the period after the Russian crisis of 1998, in which the Argentine economy was deteriorating, financial markets seemed convinced that the situation was under control. It is striking that until the Brazilian devaluation in January 1999, markets perceived Argentina as just another Mexico. Spreads for the two countries were close. After that the dangers were seen as somewhat larger, yet Argentina's country risk was well below that of Brazil, Venezuela, or the Emerging Markets Bond Index Plus (EMBI+) average. It was only in the summer of 2001 that asset prices began to reflect an ominous future.

The IMF was equally sanguine, arguing it was just a matter of keeping heads cool and policies focused until the economy turned around. This was the view expressed by the IMF board in May 1999:

Argentina is to be commended for its continued prudent policies. As with a number of other countries in the region, Argentina has had to bear the adverse consequences of external shocks, which have taken a significant toll on economic performance. Nevertheless, the sound macroeconomic management, the strengthening of the banking system and the other structural reforms carried out in recent years in the context of the currency board arrangement, have had beneficial effects on confidence, and have allowed the country to deal with these challenges.[6]

Why the difference between Argentina's performance in 1995–96 (during the tequila effect) and in the late 1990s? Part of the explanation has to do with bad luck. The terms of trade were negatively impacted after the Asian crisis in the second half of 1997. Financial markets dried up after the Russian default in August 1998. Brazil abandoned its crawling band and massively depreciated its currency in January 1999. The euro sank by over 20 percent in 2000, further weakening Argentina's competitiveness vis-à-vis the important European market. The world entered into recession in 2001, not only weakening commodity prices and export prospects, but also creating additional turmoil in financial markets after the burst of the high technology bubble. Throw in underwhelming new authorities at the U.S. Treasury and IMF, along with the implications of September 11, and there are the makings of a perfect storm.

But any complete explanation must also recognize that, while large, these adverse shocks were not much worse than those suffered by other Latin American countries—at least until the Argentine endgame of 2001 played itself out. Country risk rose for all after Russia, yet Argentina's risk remained below the EMBI+ average until mid-2000. And, as was seen in 1998–2000, Argentina was perceived as a much safer bet than either Brazil or Venezuela, at least until the first quarter of 2001.

The evolution of the terms of trade implies a similar story. After a rise in 1996–97, Argentina's terms of trade fell by over 10 percent in the following two years and recovered thereafter. Other countries in the region fared much worse. Oil exporters like Ecuador, Mexico, and Venezuela suffered more during the oil price slump of 1997 and 1998. And over the last five years, the terms of trade deterioration has been larger and more persistent for Chile and Peru.[7]

In all of these countries investment and growth slowed. But none except Ecuador crashed. It is not hard to understand why adverse capital and current account conditions can trigger a recession. But they ordinarily do not cause a fiscal and financial crisis, default on foreign and domestic debt, collapse of

6. International Monetary Fund, news brief 99/24, May 26, 1999.
7. See the detailed discussion in Perry and Servén (2002).

the exchange rate system, meltdown of the domestic banking system, and downfall of a succession of governments, as has happened in Argentina. What else was at work in Argentina to render it so vulnerable to adverse external conditions? What had changed between 1995 and 2000, so that the old medicine of holding tight, sticking to the fixed exchange rate, and hoping for the best could no longer work? This paper now turns to such questions.

What Did Not Happen

As the drama unfolded, three major views developed as to the nature of the problem and the appropriate policy response. The dominant view put the accent firmly on self-fulfilling bad expectations. A second view—not completely unrelated—emphasized problems of fiscal sustainability. Yet another view stressed lack of competitiveness and the rigidity of the exchange rate regime. Each of these views was influential in policy circles and led to important changes in actual policies.

Self-Fulfilling Pessimism

The self-fulfilling pessimism paradigm probably became dominant as it was seen as the most convincing explanation of the 1995 tequila crisis, which was associated with a sudden and systemic collapse in capital inflows and the demand for deposits in the banking system. Without a lender of last resort, the country was vulnerable to liquidity crises. To avoid future similar crises, the authorities developed after the 1995 crisis a highly praised liquidity policy, which involved imposing high liquidity requirements on banks, negotiating contingent credit lines with foreign banks, lengthening the maturity of the public debt, and keeping a liquid fiscal position. These policies were handsomely rewarded by the markets through improved confidence and market access. In fact these policies, together with the currency board, were seen as providing robust institutions to cope with financial turmoil.[8] They proved their mettle during much of the subsequent crisis: deposits in the banking system kept growing until February 2001.

---

8. "Argentina's convertibility regime and the liquidity defenses of the banking system are important pillars of the country's economic strategy and have been vital in helping withstand turbulent financial conditions. The Fund, therefore, welcomes the authorities' reaffirmation of their commitment to these policies." IMF, press release 01/37, September 7, 2001.

With the banking system under control, self-fulfilling negative expectations were seen as potentially originating from rollover problems in the public debt. To avoid such bad equilibria, the authorities negotiated a major expansion of international official support in November 2000—the so-called *blindaje*. They repeated this strategy in the spring of 2001 with a $30 billion debt exchange designed to lengthen the maturity of debt coming due in the subsequent three years and achieve a temporary reduction in interest payments.

Negative expectations were also seen as becoming self-fulfilling, not just through liquidity channels but also through fiscal conduits. Pessimism would lead to high interest rates, which would depress growth and weaken the fiscal position, complicating debt service and thus justifying the initial pessimism. The IMF itself seemed to take this view in its press release 01/3, dated January 12, 2001:

> Despite substantial efforts by the Argentine government to implement the economic program it had announced in December 1999, and which the IMF has supported with a stand-by credit since March 2000, economic performance in 2000 was worse than expected. A major disappointment was the failure to recover from the recession affecting economic activity since mid-1998. After a short-lived pickup in the last quarter of 1999, the economy again stagnated. This reflected in part the impact of the fiscal tightening on domestic demand, but was mainly the result of a drop in business and consumer confidence, and the progressive hardening of financing conditions in international markets, that resulted in rising borrowing costs and reduced market access for Argentine private and official borrowers.

In designing a strategy to deal with the crisis the IMF program—revised in May 2001 and issued in IMF news brief 01/44, dated May 21—argued as follows (italics added):

> Argentina's program aims at *strengthening confidence* through fiscal consolidation to achieve the program's targets for 2001 and fiscal balance by 2005, while promoting the recovery of investment and output through fiscal incentives and regulatory changes. Firm implementation of the program is needed *to initiate a virtuous circle of stronger public finances, lower interest rates, and a recovery of economic activity.*

To check some implications of this story, a simple simulation was run for this paper. The assumption was that enough confidence was reestablished to secure a 3 percent growth rate, starting in the fourth quarter of 1998. This simulation intends to illustrate a possible counterfactual path, had the Russian crisis not affected the availability of finance and prompted a move toward a bad equilibrium. The simulation intends to use very crude relationships, just to gauge the potential implications of alternative paths. This simulation does not take account of other real shocks that the economy experienced throughout this period.

To keep things simple, a minimum number of behavioral equations are included, but the identities required by the national accounts are kept. First, this simulation incorporates the impact of the higher output on a higher demand for imports. It calculates the marginal propensity to import, by running a regression between imports and output. The econometrically estimated coefficient was 0.261, but the simulations used a more modest 0.2. It also includes the higher external debt needed to run the wider current account deficit and the debt service caused by the additional debt. The simulation also takes account of the impact of the higher output on the primary fiscal balance. It calculates from the data the marginal propensity to save the additional fiscal revenues, by running a simple regression. The estimated effect is 0.088. This simulation leaves all other fiscal variables as they are, except that it counts the impact of the lower path for public debt on the interest burden. It does not include the potential negative impact of the higher domestic demand on the level of exports, as this would only make the story even more compelling.

The simulations are presented in figures 3a, 3b, and 3c. As can be seen clearly, the increased activity would have been enough to maintain the ratio of public debt to GDP relatively stable, below 40 percent of GDP, instead of rising as it did up to almost 50 percent of GDP by the first quarter of 2001. However, in order to achieve this path, the current account deficit would have had to average in excess of 5 percent of GDP instead of declining to a four-quarter moving average of 3.1 percent of GDP by the first quarter of 2001.[9] This larger deficit implies that external obligations would have had to rise by an additional 12 percent of GDP, even after correcting for the larger denominator, given the higher growth. This implies an increase in the ratio of debt to exports of over 100 percentage points.

Hence, leaving all other shocks aside, the good equilibrium—that is, the reestablishment of enough confidence to maintain growth at 3 percent—

9. Some would argue that if the fiscal adjustment had translated into a lower country risk, interest rates on new debt would have declined, making the debt dynamics less unfavorable. However, much of the old debt in Argentina was long term and had been contracted at rates well below those faced by even countries like Mexico post-Russian crisis. In the simulations, this paper assumes that the additional debt pays an 8 percent interest, which is about 300 basis points over the U.S. Treasury, a spread significantly below that of the average EMBI+, let alone the more than 700 point spread that Argentina faced during this period. Moreover, the bulk of the additional debt is explained by the trade deficit accumulated between 1998:4 and 2001:2 ($19.9 billion) and not to the additional interest payment ($1.8 billion).

Figure 3a. Ratios of Public Debt to GDP, Third Quarter 1998–Second Quarter 2001[a]

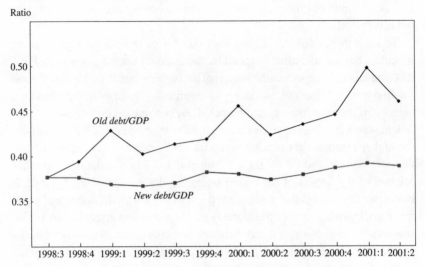

Source:
a. Simulations from model. Assumption is GDP growth of 3 percent after the second quarter of 1998.

Figure 3b. Current Account, Third Quarter 1998–Second Quarter 2001[a]

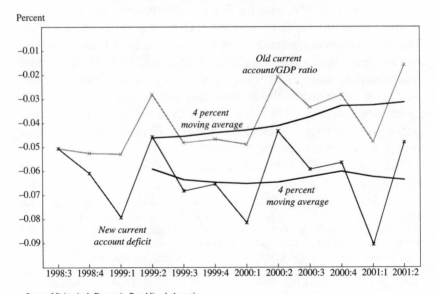

Source: Ministerio de Economia, Republica de Argentina.
a. Simulations from model.

Figure 3c. Additional External Debt, Third Quarter 1998–Second Quarter 2001[a]

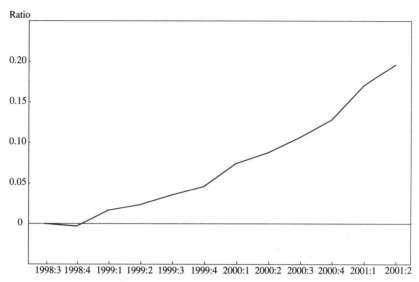

Source: Ministerio de Economia, Republica de Argentina.
a. Corrected increase in debt-to-GDP ratio. Simulations from model.

would have done away with the fiscal imbalance, but would have required the funding of sustained 5 percent current account deficits and the accumulation of an additional 12 percent of GDP in external obligations. Of course, this assumes that external financial constraints do not bind. If for some reason this amount of financing were not available, then the good equilibrium would not be feasible.

Fiscal Unsustainability

A second view of the crisis put the accent not so much on self-fulfilling pessimism and multiple equilibria, but on the more banal problem of fiscal solvency. After all, the public debt went from $80.3 billion at the end of 1994 to $144 billion in 2001. Is this not proof that the fiscal accounts were on an unsustainable path? True, the fiscal problem had been aggravated by the recession, but the debt had increased by $15 billion in the three boom years of 1996–98. Was this not proof that the country could not enforce a budget constraint?[10]

The need for fiscal balance was paramount in the minds of the authorities and the IMF throughout the evolving crisis. In fact that was the diagnosis with

10. Mussa (2002).

which Minister Jose Luis Machinea defined the economic situation in early 2000 in order to justify his so-called *impuestazo*. It was also the interpretation of Minister Ricardo Lopez-Murphy, who took office briefly in March 2001. When Minister Domingo Cavallo took over after Lopez-Murphy, he immediately implemented a financial transactions tax to improve the fiscal situation. He later adopted the zero-deficit policy in the summer of 2001.

The view that Argentina was somehow irresponsible in its fiscal management and that this may have been a major cause of the crisis—and not just one of its consequences—has become a dominant story *ex post*.[11] This paper does not share this view. The fiscal imbalance was not large and was backed up to a significant extent by increased savings in the privatized pensions system. Moreover, as the simulation above illustrates, the fiscal imbalance that emerged was related to the recession and hence is best understood as a consequence rather than a cause of the crisis. It is hard to make the case that a more forceful fiscal adjustment would have made a very significant difference. This paper presents facts that support a rather different interpretation.

Table 2 contains the basic fiscal accounts. The numbers quickly dispel any argument based on a spending feast. Government spending remained remarkably flat as a share of GDP from 1993 onward. If Social Security payments and transfers to the provinces are excluded, other national primary spending actually declined by 1.9 percent of GDP (from 8.0 to 6.1 percent) during the precrisis period of 1993–98.

It is important to understand the dynamics governing the fiscal accounts in Argentina. First, there was a rising interest burden of the debt. As shown in table 2, factor payments increased from 1.3 percent of GDP in 1994 to 4.1 percent of GDP in 2000. This was due mainly to three reasons:

—Some of the Brady Bonds issued during the early 1990s had rising interest rates.

—The increase in the official public debt exceeded the accumulated deficit flows between 1994 and 2000 by about $21 billion, half of which was the recognition of preexisting debts, and the rest represented the purchase of financial assets (see table 3).

—After the Russian crisis, the country faced an interest rate on new debt that was higher than the average rate paid on the existing stock.

A second force affecting the fiscal accounts was Social Security reform. This caused revenues to the Social Security system to be diverted toward the new private fund administrators. Social Security revenues declined from

11. Mussa (2002) and Tejeiro (2001).

Table 2. Fiscal Accounts, 1993–2001

Percent of GDP

	1993	1994	1995	1996	1997	1998	1999	2000	2001
Primary Spending	24.6	24.3	24.1	22.7	23.2	23.3	25.4	24.5	24.4
Provinces	11.3	11.3	11.3	10.8	10.8	11.3	12.3	11.9	12.0
Social Security	5.3	5.9	6.1	5.7	5.9	5.8	6.1	6.1	6.1
Rest of the national									
government	8.0	7.1	6.8	6.2	6.5	6.1	7.0	6.4	6.3
Ordinary Revenues	26.0	24.4	23.6	21.8	23.3	23.6	24.5	24.9	23.9
Provinces									
(excludes transfers)	4.9	4.8	4.6	4.6	4.7	4.8	4.9	5.1	5.1
Social Security	5.6	5.5	5.3	3.8	4.2	4.0	3.8	3.8	3.5
Rest of the national									
government	15.5	14.1	13.7	13.5	14.5	14.8	15.8	16.0	15.2
Primary Balance	1.5	0.1	−0.5	−0.8	0.3	0.4	−0.8	0.5	−0.5
Social Security	0.4	−0.4	−0.7	−1.9	−1.7	−1.8	−2.3	−2.4	−2.6
Provinces	−0.7	−0.7	−1.1	−0.3	−0.1	−0.4	−1.1	−0.5	−1.0
Rest of the									
national government	1.8	1.3	1.3	1.4	2.1	2.7	2.6	3.3	3.1
Debt service	0.8	1.3	1.4	2.7	2.3	2.6	3.4	4.1	4.6
Overall balance	0.7	−1.2	−1.9	−3.5	−2.0	−2.2	−4.2	−3.6	−5.1
Memo: transfers									
to provinces	5.8	5.7	5.6	5.8	6.0	6.1	6.3	6.3	5.8

Source: Ministerio de Economia, Republica de Argentina. UBS-Warburg for the consolidation of provincial data.

5.6 percent of GDP in 1993 to 3.8 percent by 2000 (table 2). This did not represent a reduction in the economy's contributions to the system, only a change in the mechanism of allocation and administration. By December 2000, the private pension fund administrators had assets totaling $20.3 billion. By contrast, Social Security payments rose from 5.3 percent to 6.1 percent of GDP by 2000. This caused the Social Security balance to swing from a surplus of

Table 3. Accounting for the Increase in National Public Debt

Billions of U.S. dollars

Debt as of December 1994	80.3
Debt as of december 2000	128.0
Total increase in gross debt	47.7
Increase in gross assets (collaterals and cash)	11.7
Increase in net debt (1995–2000)	36.0
Cumulative deficit (1995–2000)	21.8
Social Security deficit	30.9
Capitalized interest and valuation changes	−1.2
Recognized debt, provinces and other	16.4
Memo: assets of the private pension funds December 2000	20.3

Source: Ministerio de Economia, Republica de Argentina.

0.4 percent in 1993—before the reform—to a deficit of 2.4 percent of GDP by 2000. The cumulative deficit of the Social Security component of the budget between 1995 and 2000 was $30.9 billion (table 3).

Finally, the provinces maintained fairly flat spending and revenue levels, except for a spurt in spending in the 1998–99 period. However, this meant that the provinces were running consistent primary deficits between zero and 1 percent of GDP, making them unable to service their growing debt without recourse to more financing.

In order to confront these pressures on the budget, the national authorities pursued a policy of improving the primary surplus of the remaining parts of the budget (excluding the Social Security system and the provinces). This surplus increased from 1.3 percent of GDP in 1995 to 3.3 percent in 2000. In this sense, excluding the Social Security system, the primary surplus achieved by Argentina is comparable to that achieved by Brazil, a country that has not privatized its Social Security system.

Did the authorities really tighten fiscal policy when they found themselves in trouble in 2000—or was it all just talk? Table 4 explores this issue by running regressions of government revenues and primary spending as a function of GDP and including a dummy for the post-*impuestazo* period, that is, the period starting in the second quarter of 2000. Several features merit highlighting. First, tax revenues show much more buoyancy than does spending. The estimated elasticity of tax revenues to GDP is 1.47, while it is only 0.72 for primary spending excluding Social Security. This implies that during the booming years of 1996 and 1997 government spending was kept subdued relative to revenues.[12] Second, after the fiscal adjustment in the first quarter of 2000— the *impuestazo*—revenues are estimated to have been 11 percent ($1 billion per quarter) higher than would have been expected given GDP changes. By contrast, the dummy variable for spending is not statistically significant, meaning the government was essentially just able to cut spending by the expected amount. During the recession revenues would have fallen more than spending, but the significant policy reaction prevented this from happening and secured a continued improvement of the non–Social Security primary surplus.

Bringing it all together (see figure 4) it appears that one way to describe the situation emanates quite naturally from the data: The government was able to improve the primary surplus (excluding Social Security) to accommodate

12. This fact is also clear in figure 1, where government consumption appears as the least dynamic component of aggregate demand during the boom periods. It does tend to show less downward adjustment in recessions.

Table 4. Accounting for Changes in Primary Revenues and Spending, First Quarter 1994–Third Quarter 2001[a]

	Tax revenue		Primary spending	
	Levels	*Logs*	*Levels*	*Logs*
GDP	0.19	1.47	0.09	0.72
	(10.6)	(10.7)	(5.5)	(5.5)
Dummy post 2000:1	1,000	0.11	185	0.015
	(4.9)	(4.7)	(0.5)	(0.7)
R^2	0.84	0.84	0.54	0.53
N	31	31	31	31

Source: Authors' own calculations based on data published by Ministerio de Economia, Republica de Argentina.
a. *t* statistics in parentheses.

a large proportion of the increase in debt service, while the overall deficit was essentially explained by the deficit of the Social Security system, and to a smaller extent by that of the provinces. However, the savings of the privatized pension system backed two-thirds of the Social Security deficit.

These calculations account for the published deficits. What about the assertion that the growth of debt was out of control? While this paper acknowledges that the provincial debt was growing in an unsustainable fashion, the debt of

Figure 4. Fiscal Balance and Its Components, First Quarter 1994–Third Quarter 2001

Percent of GDP

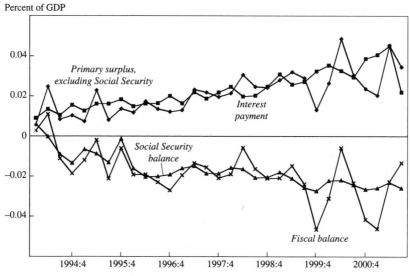

Source: Ministerio de Economia, Republica de Argentina.

the federal government supports a different interpretation. Table 3 shows the increase in federal debt during the 1994–2000 period. As can be seen, the total increase in debt of $47.7 billion exceeds the cumulative deficit by $25.9 billion. A bit over half of the difference is explained by the accumulation of assets ($11.7 billion), while some $16.4 billion can be explained by the recognition of preexisting debts. Note that the cumulative overall deficit is $9.1 billion larger than the cumulative Social Security deficit, and is equal to the accumulation of assets in the pension system.

In conclusion, excluding the Social Security system, the national government was able to generate a primary fiscal surplus in excess of 3 percent of GDP. This would have been sufficient to cover the increased cost of debt service of the national debt. In fact the primary surplus was of the same magnitude as that of Brazil, in spite of the deeper recession. The overall deficit was affected by the growing deficit of the Social Security system and by a moderate primary deficit in the provinces. In addition, there was a significant accumulation of assets and documentation of preexisting debt.

Obviously, the country could have tried to run a tighter fiscal ship. But the numbers here are not those of a profligate country, and are hard to square with the catastrophe that followed. Where is the dramatic shift in fiscal outcomes between the time when Argentina was perceived as one of the safest emerging markets (say, in 1999) and its eventual demise?

Exchange Rate Rigidity

The third influential theory was associated with the peculiar exchange rate system chosen by Argentina: a currency board with the dollar and a bimonetary financial system, one in which both the U.S. dollar and the Argentine peso were legal tender. The system achieved price stability, but left the country vulnerable to inconvenient movements in the multilateral exchange rate. This possibility of inconvenient movements became a reality after the Brazilian devaluation of January 1999 and the euro slide of 2000. The story is clearly evident in the data.

It is clear that the nominal appreciation of the multilateral nominal exchange rate of Argentina took place at a most inconvenient time. The Brazilian devaluation of 1999 had caused an appreciation in Argentina's multilateral nominal rate of 14 percent. Between January and July 2001, this rate appreciated a further 13 percent.[13] An increasing real exchange rate misalignment developed:

13. IMF (2002).

Figure 5. Real Exchange Rate Misalignment, 1990–2001

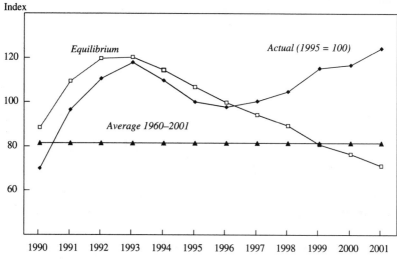

Source: Perry and Servén (2002), p. 21, figure 3.1.

the worsening external conditions called for a depreciated equilibrium
exchange rate, while the actual rate appreciated. Perry and Servén have estimated the underlying equilibrium real exchange rate, taking into account
changes in Argentine productivity, as well as the country's deteriorating net
foreign asset position.[14] Their index appears in figure 5, plotted along with
the actual multilateral real exchange rate. The result is striking: if Perry and
Servén are right, in 2001 the Argentine peso was overvalued by more than 40
percent.

The misalignment, coupled to the adverse external conditions and a rising
cost of capital, wreaked havoc on the profitability of the export sector and thus
on its ability to expand supply. Export volume growth, which had averaged
over 14 percent a year between 1993 and September 1998, stalled and never
again managed to recover its earlier dynamism, in spite of the declining levels of domestic absorption (see table 1 and figure 2).[15]

This standard logic can explain the protracted recession and increasing tension between the achievement of external balance and full employment. But
why would it lead to a financial crisis? As shown in the simulations described
in figures 3a, 3b, and 3c, at the prevailing real exchange rate even modest growth

14. Perry and Servén (2002).
15. Argentina still managed 3.8 percent growth from the third quarter of 1999 to the third
quarter of 2001, roughly in line with the export performance of other countries in the region.

Figure 6. Multilateral Exchange Rate and Spread between Argentina and Mexico, January 1998–December 2001

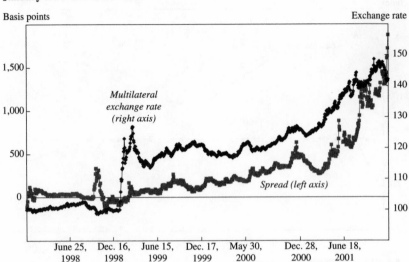

Source: Ministerio de Economia, Republica de Argentina; International Monetary Fund; and authors' own calculations.

of 3 percent could only be achieved at the expense of large current account deficits and rising debt ratios. Argentina thus found itself in a bind: if it tried to grow, it risked accumulating debt to the point of insolvency; if it chose to achieve external balance, it would have to achieve strongly negative growth rates, which would also imperil its solvency.

Markets increasingly began to fear this latter risk, as shown in figure 6. The multilateral exchange rate tracked remarkably well the evolution of the spread between the country risk of Argentina and that of Mexico, especially after the 1999 Brazilian devaluation. This paper takes Mexico as a benchmark, since both economies had very similar country risk spreads until the 1999. Both countries suffered a common shock when emerging markets floundered after the Russian default, but after the Brazilian devaluation, Argentina started to move in a different direction.[16]

16. Skeptics might wonder whether this correlation says anything about the perceived risk of exchange rate misalignment. An alternative interpretation of figure 6 is that both variables respond to a common driving force, namely Brazilian risk. Under this interpretation, Argentine risk moves with Brazil's because the countries are economically intertwined, while the multilateral exchange rate moves mainly because of fluctuations in the dollar price of the real, which also reflects Brazil's risk. This sounds sensible, but does not fit the facts. The correlation between the EMBI spreads of Brazil and Argentina, which had been very high from 1996 to 1998, was only 0.75 in 1999, 0.68 in 2000, and 0.39 in 2001.

There is an unmistakable sense, then, that Argentina did have an exchange rate problem. What is much less clear, however, is whether it had an exchange rate solution available to it. It was the combination of relative price misalignment with increasingly scarce financing that made the situation vulnerable. And, with a large accumulated dollar debt, both private and public, the competitiveness gains of a potential devaluation had to be weighed against the balance sheet damage it would inflict and the additional market access this would bring. The next section puts these different factors together and tries to assess the policy trade-offs involved.

How to Think about What Happened

If the conventional stories alone do not account for the Argentine crisis, what other factors do? How did the fiscal and current account deficits, exchange rate overvaluation, and borrowing limits interact to constrain policy alternatives? What policy options were available to Argentina? Might fiscal contraction, devaluation, or dollarization have worked, and under what circumstances? What follows is a model to help tackle such questions.

Imagine a world that has two periods, current and future; two goods, foreign and domestic; and two kinds of people, entrepreneurs and workers.[17] Workers only consume. Entrepreneurs' own capital, which they lend to firms, and also consume. They finance investment in excess of their own net worth by borrowing from foreigners. The government may also run a deficit and attempt to finance it abroad. A key point in the story is that such public and private borrowing may be constrained.[18]

Production of domestic goods is carried out using capital and labor with the Cobb-Douglas technology:

$$Y_t = K_t^\alpha L_t^{1-\alpha}, 0 < \alpha < 1. \tag{1}$$

---

17. These goods are both tradable, but are imperfect substitutes, so their relative price is endogenous. This paper will refer to it as the real exchange rate.

18. In its treatment of borrowing constraints, the model resembles the work by Krugman (1999) and Aghion, Baccheta, and Banerjee (2001), though the precise specification of collateral is forward looking rather than backward looking, as in those two papers. The model also borrows liberally from Céspedes, Chang, and Velasco (2000), a paper with a different financial imperfection, but whose modeling of labor and goods markets is very close to that found here.

Capital depreciates fully, so that in the final period capital stock equals investment, I. Firms are competitive: total payments to capital are αY_t, and total payments to labor are $(1 - \alpha)Y_t$.

Workers consume and supply labor. The consumption quantity, C_t, is an aggregate of home and imported goods, with shares γ and $1 - \gamma$, respectively. Let the foreign good have a price of E_t in terms of the domestic good—which can be thought of as the real exchange rate—so that the cost of one unit of consumption is $E_t^{1-\gamma}$. To make things simple, assume that workers cannot borrow or lend abroad. Then, their consumption is

$$E_t^{1-\gamma}C_t = W_t L_t - T_t,\tag{2}$$

where T_t is a lump-sum tax paid by workers.[19]

To describe the behavior of entrepreneurs it is necessary to distinguish explicitly between the initial and final periods. Let no subscript indicate an initial period variable, while a subscript 1 indicates a final period variable. Investment, like consumption, is an aggregate of domestic and foreign goods, with the same shares, γ and $1 - \gamma$. Hence the price of investment in terms of domestic goods is $E^{1-\gamma}$. At the beginning of the initial period, entrepreneurs collect the income from capital (equal to αY), pay taxes, invest, and repay foreign debt. As a consequence, their budget constraint is

$$ED_1 = IE^{1-\gamma} + (1+r)ED + T - \alpha Y,\tag{3}$$

where D is inherited foreign debt and r is the international real interest rate.[20] The size of the debt will play a crucial role.

If they are not financially constrained and can borrow as much as they want, entrepreneurs choose an amount of investment such that the percentage return to capital is equal to the domestic goods' expected cost of borrowing, so that[21]

$$\frac{\alpha Y_1}{E^{1-\gamma}I} = (1+r)\left(\frac{E_1}{E}\right).\tag{4}$$

---

19. What about the labor supply decision of workers? If their period utility function is $\log C_t - \xi v^{-1}L_t$, where $v > 0$ is the elasticity of labor supply and ξ is a constant, then labor supply is set to equate the marginal disutility of labor to its marginal return, and is therefore equal to $L_t = 1$ whenever real wages are flexible and the labor market clears.

20. For simplicity, entrepreneurs do not pay taxes. Little would change if they did.

21. This is optimal if entrepreneurs consume in the closing period only. To make things simple, this model assumes that, in true capitalist style, they consume only imports.

Next, introduce government. In the initial period government spends G on home goods only, receives tax revenue T, and repays its inherited foreign debt, B. Its budget constraint is[22]

$$EB_1 = G - T + (1+r)EB .\qquad(5)$$

Market clearing for home goods requires that domestic output be equal to demand. Domestic consumption of home goods is a fraction γ of the value of total consumption. The same is true of investment. In addition, the home good may be sold to foreigners: the value of home exports in dollars is exogenous and given by some fixed X.[23] This implies that in the first period the market for home goods will clear when

$$Y = G + \gamma(C + I)E^{1-\gamma} + EX .\qquad(6)$$

Using the workers' budget constraint, equation (5), to eliminate consumption, one obtains

$$\beta Y = \gamma I E^{1-\gamma} + G - \gamma T + EX ,\qquad(7)$$

where $\beta = 1 - \gamma(1 - \alpha)$. This is the IS schedule, which slopes up in Y, I space: higher investment leads to higher aggregate demand and output.

Since by assumption there is no investment and government spending in the last period, market clearing yields $\beta Y_1 = E_1 X_1$. Using this in equation (4), one has

$$I = \frac{E^\gamma X_1}{\beta(1+r)} .\qquad(8)$$

This is the quantity entrepreneurs would like to invest if unconstrained. By analogy with the Mundell-Fleming framework, call this the BP schedule: along it the balance of payments is in equilibrium. This schedule is vertical in Y, I space.

Turn finally to the national borrowing constraint. Consolidating the private and public sectors yields the evolution of total foreign debt:

$$EF_1 = G - T + IE^{1-\gamma} + (1+r)EF - \alpha Y ,\qquad(9)$$

---

22. This model is agnostic as to which taxes are raised, if necessary, to repay this debt. One possibility—the simplest in this case—is to levy a lump sum tax on entrepreneurs only, so that $T_1 = E_1(1 + r)B_1$.

23. This is similar to the assumption in Krugman (1999), and can be justified by positing that the foreign elasticity of substitution in consumption is 1, but that foreigners' expenditure share in domestic goods is negligible.

Figure 7. Before and After the Sudden Stop.

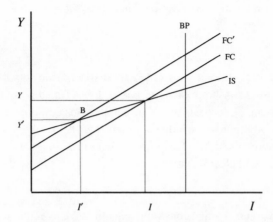

where $F = D + B$ is total foreign liabilities. Assume that, because of limitations of sovereignty, court jurisdiction, and the like, lenders can seize at most a portion $\mu < 1$ of national income in case of nonpayment. Hence they will not lend at the initial period an amount generating obligations larger than the resulting collateral: $(1+r)E_1 F_1 \leq \mu Y_1$.[24] Combining this with equation (9) and market clearing for the next period one arrives at

$$\alpha Y \geq IE^{1-\gamma} + G - T + E\left\{(1+r)F - \frac{\mu}{\beta}\frac{X_1}{1+r}\right\}. \qquad (10)$$

Term this the FC (financial constraint) schedule. It slopes up in Y, I space: investing more requires that national income be higher today if the constraint is to be satisfied. Notice that the tightness of the financial constraint depends on the size of old debts, because for a given level of output, higher payments on old debt mean less investment today.

It is easy to check that the FC is always steeper than the IS. They cross in the positive quadrant if the IS cuts the vertical axis above the FC, meaning that initial debt is not too large.[25] This is the case depicted in figure 7: a constrained but not-yet-bankrupt economy finds its equilibrium at a point such as A.

24. Notice this formulation implies that, after being used for production in the terminal period, total installed capital, $K_t = I$, cannot be used for anything else, and hence has no market or collateral value.

25. This requires

$$(1-\alpha)G - T < (1-\gamma)^{-1} E\left\{\alpha X + \mu\frac{X_1}{1+r} - \beta(1+r)F\right\}.$$

Hence inherited total debt cannot be too large. If this intersection is to the left of the BP curve, one has a constrained equilibrium. That is the case depicted in figure 8.

Notice that the real exchange rate, E, is treated as an exogenous variable. This is sensible over the short run if the nominal exchange rate is fixed and goods prices are sticky, as was the case in Argentina. This means that domestic output is demand determined, and therefore pinned down by the intersection of IS and FC.[26] Below, this paper asks what happens to this equilibrium if the government unexpectedly devalues, raising the real exchange rate E in the initial period.

What Might Have Happened

This paper is now ready to tell Argentina's story using this framework described above. Two things arguably happened after the Russian crisis of August 1998 and again after the Brazilian devaluation of February 1999. First, international investors lost some of their appetite for emerging country securities in general. In the setup above this can be thought of as a fall in μ: for every future level of output and exports, foreigners are willing to lend less. Second, external conditions facing Argentina worsened considerably, leaving the country less likely to export and grow: again, in terms of our toy model, this represents a fall in expected X_1.

Figure 7 also depicts the consequences of this shock. The FC shifts up, because with less financing, higher domestic output is now necessary to fund a given level of investment.[27] The new equilibrium is at point B. Investment and output fall. With less capacity to borrow, domestic entrepreneurs invest less, which in turn depresses demand for domestic output and the quantity produced in equilibrium.

This account fits Argentina's experience in several important respects. One is the startling decline in export dynamism observed starting in the fourth quarter of 1998, which stood in sharp contrast to the buoyant exports Argentina had displayed since 1993.[28] Some of the export decline was due to the shock

26. Technically, if output is demand determined, then workers must be supplying more labor than equation 6 requires. Over the longer haul—that is, in the final period—it seems sensible to assume that prices adjust, rendering the real exchange rate endogenous for any nominal exchange rate. In this case labor supply is given by equation 6 and domestic output is supply determined: $Y_1 = I^\alpha$.

27. The BP shifts left, because, even if unconstrained, domestic entrepreneurs would like to invest less. *Ceteris paribus,* lower future exports mean a more depreciated future real exchange rate, which makes repaying foreign loans more expensive. But as long as this shift is not too large, the economy remains financially constrained.

28. Documented above. See figures 1 and 2.

to the terms of trade and to other adverse international developments. Another portion was arguably caused by the sharp appreciation in the multilateral real exchange rate. Cautious observers, unsure of how much of this shock was transitory and how much was permanent, must have attributed at least some persistence to it. This meant that future Argentine exports would be lower than they had been previously forecasting, and so would be Argentina's capacity to repay debt. It made some sense, then, to curtail lending.

Why was Argentina hit so badly by this shock? One factor had to do with initial debt levels and the role of the exchange rate. This point is explored below. Another key factor is the degree to which Argentina was a closed economy. It is easy to show with a bit of algebra that the fall in output is given by

$$\Delta Y = \left(\frac{\gamma}{1-\gamma} \right) \left(\frac{\mu}{1-\lambda(1-\alpha)} \right) \left(\frac{1}{1+r} \right) E \Delta X_1, \tag{11}$$

so that the size of the contraction is increasing in γ, the share of domestic goods in domestic consumption, and investment spending. The more closed the economy, the larger is the fall in domestic investment and output necessary to equilibrate the external accounts after the tightening of the borrowing constraint. This magnifies the home effects of disturbances to the capital account.[29]

The other dimension along which this story seems to fit the Argentine facts has to do with the behavior of investment. As table 1 shows, investment growth became strongly negative in 1999. The correlation across time of investment and GDP is also exactly that suggested by figure 8, which shows how this pair of variables evolved over time. As borrowing capacity collapsed so did investment, pulling down demand and domestic output.

Fiscal Tightening: The Right Policy Response?

An often suggested option to deal with these nasty developments was to tighten fiscal policy: for the many observers who felt fiscal laxity was at the heart of the problem, the solution entailed curtailing current government spending and borrowing, thereby increasing the room the private sector had to borrow and invest. If this crowding in was sufficiently large, advocates of this policy claimed, one could even have a case of expansionary fiscal contraction: private spending would rise so much as to more than fully offset the fall in government spending, causing an increase in demand and output. This was

29. Calvo, Izquierdo, and Talvi (2002) make the same point in the context of a different model.

Figure 8. GDP and Investment, 1993–2001

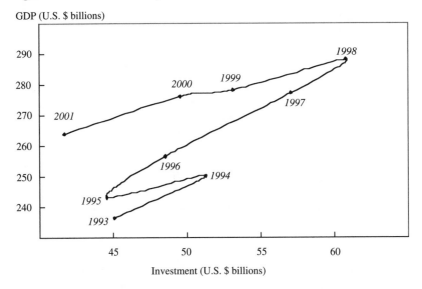

Source: Ministerio de Economia, Republica de Argentina.

an explicit justification of the *impuestazo* (tax increase) put into place by Economy Minister Machinea in the early days of the de la Rua administration, and of the zero-deficit policy pursued by Domingo Cavallo very late in the game.

But the expansionary fiscal contraction argument stands on shaky ground. The model here is predisposed to generate this result, since private borrowing capacity rises by the same amount as government spending falls—that is, there is full crowding in. In spite of this, total demand for domestic goods does not rise in response to a cut in government spending. That is because investment typically has a larger component of imports than does government spending. In the model, a portion $\gamma < 1$ of all investment spending goes to domestic goods, while all government spending falls on domestic goods. The net result of a contraction in fiscal policy is that demand for domestic goods falls, and so does output. The comparative statics are depicted in figure 9. The intercepts of both the FC and the IS shift downward, but the FC shifts farther. The new equilibrium has lower output and higher investment.

How large is the fall in domestic output, and what does this depend on? It is easy to show that $\Delta Y = \Delta G$, which might seem surprising at first. Is not the reduction in government borrowing allowing the private sector to borrow and

Figure 9. Fiscal Contraction

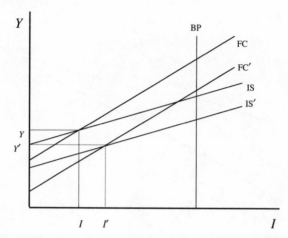

invest more, thereby offsetting (at the very least) the fall in government demand for output? Yes, indeed. Holding investment constant, it is easy to see from the IS schedule that $\Delta Y = \beta^{-1}\Delta G$, where $\beta^{-1} > 1$ is the standard Keynesian multiplier. The increase in investment offsets the extra bang of the multiplier, making current output fall one-to-one with government spending. Investment does rise, but less than proportionately, in response to the cut in government spending. It is easy to show that $\Delta(IE^{1-\gamma}) = -(1 - \alpha)\Delta G$, where $IE^{1-\gamma}$ is the domestic goods value of I units of investment.

Does this account leave out anything crucial? Perhaps. An advocate of fiscal tightening might claim that less spending today would mean more investment today, leading to higher output in dollars tomorrow, and hence to a looser borrowing constraint today. That in turn could increase investment sufficiently to avoid a short-run recession, perhaps yielding even an immediate output increase as a result of the fiscal cut. That mechanism is absent from the model so far, because output in dollars tomorrow is pinned down by future export demand, which is exogenous. Greater current investment and output simply yield a more depreciated real exchange rate tomorrow, so that repayment capacity in dollars does not rise.

This paper's appendix shows how the model can be expanded to include the kinds of effects fiscal contractionists arguably had in mind. Figure 10 depicts a situation with that flavor. The FC curve is now nonmonotonic, with positively and negatively sloped segments. If initial government spending is

Figure 10. Fiscal Contraction and Self-Fulfilling Pessimism

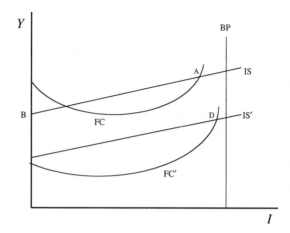

sufficiently high, then the FC cuts the vertical axis above the IS. This situation gives rise to two potential equilibria. There is a good (though constrained) equilibrium at a point such as A, and a bad one at B. Here the economy is bankrupt: investment is zero, the financing constraint is violated, and equilibrium output is at the point where the IS cuts the vertical axis. Pessimistic expectations can trigger a crisis. If investors believe domestic investment and output will collapse, leaving the economy unable to repay its debts, they will curtail lending. The result will be precisely the fall in *Y* and *I* they had anticipated. If government spending is sufficiently high that at the new level of income private and public debts cannot be serviced, then lenders will be glad they fled the country in question.

In this situation, contractionary fiscal policy can play a crisis-preemption role. A cut in spending shifts the intercepts of both the FC and the IS down, but the FC shifts farther. If the fall in *G* is sufficiently large, so that the FC now cuts the vertical axis below the IS, the bad equilibrium vanishes, and the only possible outcome is at a point such as D. But notice that one can show that D is always below A, so that if the starting point was indeed the constrained but nonbankrupt equilibrium, output has to fall as a result of the spending cut.

In this story, whether fiscal contraction is a good or a bad policy depends crucially on two factors, both of which are hard to quantify. The first is that initial spending and inherited debt have to be sufficiently high that if investment and output collapse, debts do become impossible to service. The second is that the probability of going to the bad equilibrium, if one exists, must be sufficiently high; only in that case is the actual contraction in output (between the two good equilibria) actually worth enduring. On both counts, Argentina seems to have been vulnerable. The public and private debts were too large to be serviced normally in a recession, as is abundantly clear by now. And the country's checkered financial history made it a prime candidate for self-fulfilling bouts of pessimism.

In this sense, then, there may have been a role for fiscal tightening among policies for dealing with the Argentine crisis. But it is very different from the role most of its advocates probably envisioned. It is preemptive: lower spending prevents even worse things from happening.

One must also wonder how realistic is the very strong rationality the story assumes. To begin with, this model assumes that all domestic output is exportable. In real life, an increase in investment is likely to be only partially reflected in increased export capacity, especially when relative prices do not make those activities particularly profitable. In addition, it is not obvious that investment would rise as much as the model assumes. Whether in a single equilibrium or a multiple equilibria context, tight fiscal policy works by releasing funds for private investment, thereby making higher investment and future output possible, even at the cost of lower output today. But can domestic investors and foreign lenders really be expected to risk funds if the economy is sinking today? There is surely an element of extrapolation in everyone's decisions. In a situation of limited information and great uncertainty, low output today may be signaling something about a host of adverse factors (declining productivity, weak export demand, and so on), most of which are likely to be persistent. Therefore any policy strategy that bets on an expansion tomorrow made possible by a megacontraction today is a risky strategy indeed.

This is not just an academic conjecture. There is some evidence that it was recession, not simple fiscal misbehavior, that prompted worsening expectations and rising country risk. Powell runs a vector autoregression analysis for 1997–2001 and reports that imports (a close proxy for activity) drive both the EMBI spread and fiscal revenues, and not the other way around.[30] And, of course, there is the striking fact that on the day (July 15, 2001) Domingo Cavallo announced the zero-deficit policy, implying an immediate cut in public sector wages and pensions of around 13 percent, Argentina's country risk spread rose from 1,200 to 1,600 basis points. No country can be run on that basis, investors plausibly conjectured. Events thereafter proved them right.

30. Powell, this volume.

Devaluation: Contractionary or Expansionary?

What about the exchange rate? An abandonment of the currency board and a drastic realignment of relative prices was advocated by many observers, and their numbers grew as time passed and the situation deteriorated. From some perspectives this made perfect sense. In the story so far, there is one sense in which there is indeed an exchange rate problem: output is low because aggregate demand is insufficient; if both exports and investment can be stimulated by changing relative prices, then the economy can be pushed toward recovery.

But can it? Is devaluation expansionary in a financially constrained economy, just as it is in the textbook model? Maybe yes and maybe no, depending on the size of old debt vis-à-vis current and future exports. It is easy to show that

$$\Delta Y = \left[X + \frac{\gamma\mu}{\beta} \frac{X_1}{1+r} - \gamma(1+r)F \right](1-\gamma)^{-1} \Delta E, \qquad (12)$$

where the term in square brackets could be positive or negative. It is negative if total initial debt is large relative to current and future exports.[31] In that case a devaluation is contractionary: the increase in the current debt service costs causes investment demand to fall by more than current export revenues increase, curtailing total aggregate demand. Investment also falls, as one can readily check.

Comparative statics appear in figure 11. With an unexpected devaluation the IS shifts up and becomes steeper. The slope of the FC rises by more than that of the IS, and its intercept shifts up if initial debt is sufficiently high. It is clear that depending on parameter values the devaluation could increase output and investment or decrease them. As drawn (and as will happen in the case of a high ratio of debt to exports), the FC moves farther up than does the IS, so a contraction takes place.

The intuition should be clear: the change in relative prices is expansionary insofar as it increases the domestic output value of current and future exports. But it also increases the domestic output value of debt service, making the FC constraint tighter. With enough debt relative to exports, the latter effect outweighs the former, causing the devaluation to reduce investment and output.

Was this the relevant case for Argentina? Opponents of abandoning the currency board certainly thought so, arguing that a drastic change in relative prices

31. Notice that if the equilibrium is interior and investment is positive, then the equation in footnote 25 still has to be satisfied. For this to be true and for the devaluation to be contractionary, it must be the case that $(1 - \alpha)G < T$.

Figure 11. Contractionary Devaluation

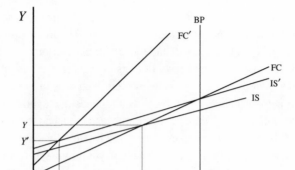

would render debt impossible to pay, bankrupting the government as well as many corporations. But what do the data suggest? Table 5 computes debt service–to–exports ratios for a number of so-called emerging markets. One column shows total debt service (gross) and the other shows interest payments, both as a share of total exports of goods and services. The table reveals that, along with Brazil, Argentina is an outlier in this regard.

The nasty side effects of devaluation in a context of large dollar debt prompted one of us to call for the pesification of all debts, domestic and foreign, coupled with the floating of the currency.[32] The mechanical logic behind this proposal is apparent from equation (12): once debts are denominated in pesos, the term involving $(1 + r)F$ drops out of that expression, making devaluation unambiguously expansionary. But this is far too simple, charged many critics. Pesification plus devaluation clearly meant a fall in the rate of return to holders of old debt. Why should these same lenders (or others much like them) be willing to provide new debt? And why should domestic investors be willing to acquire additional real assets if they too could be expropriated in the future?

Those are all sensible objections. But whether a *suitably engineered* pesification-plus-float is unbearably painful depends on the alternatives.[33] Start from the situation in figure 12, where the economy is already bankrupt, in the

32. Ricardo Hausmann, "A Way Out for Argentina: The Currency Board Cannot Survive Much Longer," *Financial Times*, October 30, 2001.

33. *Suitably engineered* is emphasized because since the demise of the de la Rua administration, both pesification and floating have been tried, but in a manner so confusing and chaotic that not much good can be expected to come of it.

Table 5. Ratios of Debt Service to Exports, Selected Countries, 2000[a]

Percent

Country	Total debt service/exports	Interest payments/exports
Argentina	71.3	30.3
Bolivia	39.1	11.1
Brazil	90.7	21.8
Chile	26.0	9.4
China	7.4	2.6
Czech Republic	12.7	3.7
Ecuador	17.6	8.4
Estonia	8.7	2.5
Hungary	24.4	4.6
India	12.8	5.0
Indonesia	25.3	10.1
Korea	10.9	2.7
Malaysia	5.3	2.0
Mexico	30.2	7.1
Pakistan	26.8	9.2
Panama	10.1	5.0
Peru	42.8	16.7
Poland	20.9	5.2
Russian Federation	10.1	4.8
South Africa	10.0	3.2
Thailand	16.3	5.6

Source: World Bank, *Global Development Finance* (2002).
a. The numerator refers to 2002 data; the denominator, to an average of 1998–2000.

sense that at those levels of exports and debt, new lending and investment are zero and some of the old debt—whether private or public—is not being serviced. From that starting point the counterfactual is not full payment at the initial real exchange rate but less (probably substantially less) than that. In that situation, pesification of debt, coupled with a substantial change in relative prices, has the following effects: the IS shifts up as before, and the FC becomes steeper but now shifts down. The result is a potentially large recovery in output and investment, leading to a point such as A. There, debt can be serviced in full, but at a depreciated exchange rate.

Whether this situation is preferable or not to the counterfactual of no pesification and devaluation depends on a host of factors: how large was the share of debt that was not being serviced in the initial equilibrium, how sizable is the devaluation, and how much output rises in response. But pesification creates a scenario in which the output gain is potentially large. If lenders are capable of displaying a stiff upper lip, providing new funds even though their old loans are not being fully serviced, then the actual dollar value of debt serv-

Figure 12. Devaluation plus Pesification

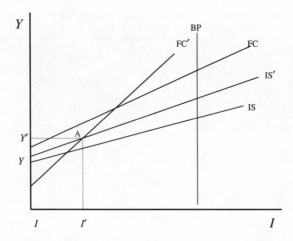

ice could well be higher than it would be if they just walked away from the country, refusing to accept pesification. In language that was popular in the late 1980s—when debt crises were the order of the day—there may exist a debt Laffer curve: by accepting a cut in the face value of the obligations owed them, creditors may well increase the value of debt service accruing to them.[34] Argentina was arguably in such a situation by the second half of 2000. Pesification plus floating might have helped, had it been done earlier and better.

Dollarization

The last of the simple and popular policy alternatives, advocated by former president Carlos Menem and central bank chief Pedro Pou, among others, was an outright abandonment of the currency. With no devaluation risk, dollarization advocates reasoned, country risk would also fall, capital flows would resume, and so would investment and growth. In this view, country risk is essentially bankruptcy risk, arising from the possibility that a real devaluation might render public and private dollar debts impossible to pay.

In contrast, in the story told here external shocks cause borrowing and investment to be constrained and output to fall, even if the real exchange rate does not move at all. All adjustment takes place via quantities, not prices, and it is precisely the fall in output that is associated with a tighter borrowing constraint. For dollarization to matter in this context one would have to believe

34. Krugman (1989).

that doing away with devaluation risk raises μ—that is, it increases the amount foreigners are willing to lend for every level of domestic output. Why that might be so, at least in the simple model, is unclear, since repayment capacity depends on output, which in turn is proportionate to future export capacity. The exchange rate plays no role.

This is not to say, of course, that it is impossible to come up with a conceptual framework in which dollarizing increases borrowing capacity. If bad states of the world are associated with real devaluations, and these in turn impair repayment capacity, then a risk averse investor might react to lower variance of the exchange rate by raising the average amount lent. But notice that this result only holds if lowering the variance of relative prices does not increase the variance of output, or of other variables relevant to repayment capacity.[35]

The scant empirical evidence in this regard is mixed at best. Panama has used the dollar for nearly a century, and its experience is no reason for optimism. Goldfajn and Olivares conclude: "The main conclusions drawn from the case of Panama are that . . . the elimination of currency risk does not preclude default risk or the high volatility of sovereign spreads."[36] Ecuador dollarized in 1999, and that experience does not encourage one to be hopeful either: its country risk spreads have remained among the highest in Latin America (second, after Argentina recently) and the country remains virtually cut off from international capital markets.

What We Do Not Know

One conclusion that emerges from the previous sections is that, given the magnitude of the shocks experienced in 1998–2000 and the inherited debt stocks, Argentina's policy options were very limited indeed. Monetary policy was unavailable by design, fiscal contraction and dollarization would not have helped much, and without pesification, depreciation was probably contractionary. All of which begs the obvious question: how could Argentina end up in such a dire situation? Were there things that could have been done earlier

35. Suppose (the log of) repayment capacity in dollars is proportional, say, to $y - e$, which are (the logs of) the real exchange rate and output. Then the variance of (the log of) repayment capacity is given by Var (y) + Var (e) + 2Cov (y, e). Hence reducing Var (e) brings down the volatility of repayment capacity only if there are no more-than-offsetting changes in Var (y) and Cov (e,y).

36. Goldfajn and Olivares (2001).

(in the mid-1990s, say) that might have prevented, or at least minimized the probability of, such a tragic outcome?

Our model helps organize the discussion. Starting in late 1998, and especially as of early 2001, Argentina found itself financially constrained: international markets were unwilling to provide the funds the economy needed to invest and grow. A key question, then, is how that constraint came to bind so tightly. Recall our FC schedule, which can be slightly extended to read

$$IE^{1-\gamma} < \alpha Y + \frac{\mu}{\beta}\frac{EX_1}{1+r} - (G-T) - (\delta+r)EF , \qquad (13)$$

so that, for a given output level Y, the value of investment is constrained. The addition is the parameter δ ($0 < \delta < 1$), which is the share of outstanding debt that has to be amortized in the current period. Clearly, the higher the average maturity of outstanding debt, the smaller is δ.

The extent to which this constraint binds and how much policy can loosen it depends on a long list of factors, among them export prospects and competitiveness; the currency denomination of debt; the performance of output growth; the size of outstanding debt, both gross and net; the tightness of fiscal policy; and the availability of financing coming from the Washington multilaterals. A discussion of each follows.

Mundell Lives

In a very basic sense, constraint equation (13) above binds because export prospects are too low, at least relative to accumulated debt. Why did this come to pass in Argentina? One answer is bad luck: adverse terms of trade, weakening capital flows, erratic performance in Brazil, and so on. But another unavoidable answer is bad policy—bad exchange rate policy, more precisely. What made the Argentine currency board ultimately unsustainable was not just that it involved a peg, but that it involved a peg to a strong dollar only. Add to that a weak *real* and you have the ingredients for a lethal noncompetitiveness brew. Perry and Servén of the World Bank estimate that by 2001 the Argentine peso was overvalued by more than 40 percent—and much of that was due to movements in the multilateral nominal exchange rate.[37] It is hard to envision a misalignment of that order of magnitude not affecting export performance, and in turn the country's creditworthiness. And as misalignment became long-lived and the perceived profitability of exporting fell, produc-

37. Perry and Servén (2002).

tivity-enhancing investments did not take place, making the situation worse over time.

None of this, of course, would have come to a surprise to the Robert Mundell of the early 1960s. Argentina is not Mexico. It satisfies few of the requirements of an optimal currency area with the United States. When Mexicans speak of the colossus to the north, they mean the United States; when Argentines do so, they increasingly mean Brazil. In the 1990s, Argentine exports to the United States never reached 20 percent of the total, and they were dwarfed by exports to Mercosur and the European Union. And, as events of the late 1990s made sufficiently clear, the Argentine business cycle could be woefully out of step with that of the United States.

Original Sin

A basic problem here is the existence of dollarized liabilities. With debts denominated in units of domestic goods, the real exchange rate would not multiply the inherited debt stock in equation (13). In that case, standard policy would work: a depreciation would move the FC (and the IS) in the right direction, stimulating both investment and output.

This is a problem of missing markets: South Africa has been the only so-called emerging economy to be able to borrow in its own currency, for reasons that have much to do with historical accident. The consequences are dire, for the co-movements work in exactly the wrong direction: regardless of the nominal exchange rate regime, the real exchange rate is likely to weaken in bad times, increasing debt service and reducing creditworthiness at precisely the time when a country most needs access to international capital markets. A second shock (lost ability to borrow) piles on top of the first one, paving the way to an eventual crisis.[38]

Whether there is anything Argentina could have done about this problem *ex ante* is debatable. The room for borrowing in an emerging market's own currency (or even in indexed units, as Chile has tried to do) is very limited indeed. But if new crises like this one are to be avoided, other kinds of debt—whose value in terms of home output need not rise in bad times—have to be found. An alternative is to rely less on debt and more on equity, which does not oblige the debtor to pay in bad times.

38. The theoretical literature on why countries have trouble borrowing in their own currencies is in its infancy, and there is no broadly accepted account of why this is so. See the recent work by Burnside, Eichenbaum, and Rebelo (1999), Schneider and Tornell (2000), Caballero and Krishnamurthy (2001), Jeanne (2001), and Chamon (2001).

There Are Many Ways to Die

Policymakers, analysts, and academics were well aware of the dangers of sharp movements in relative prices in the face of dollar liabilities. Therefore, during much of the 1990s policy efforts were focused on reassuring investors that there would be no wild swings in the exchange rate, and that therefore the solvency of domestic corporations and banks was well protected. The inception of the currency board was central to this effort to build credibility for Argentina, as were measures to make the central bank more independent, strengthen banks, improve their supervision, and so on. But Argentina showed that financing constraints—and, eventually, bankruptcy—can hit even if relative prices never move. For that, all you need is a deep enough decline in activity: as the FC curve above shows, if *Y* falls sufficiently the constraint will bind and investment will suffer, even if other variables do not move. In this sense, Argentina faced a trade-off between stabilizing the exchange rate and stabilizing output—at least until the endgame, when so much debt had been accumulated that real devaluation was arguably contractionary. This begs the question of whether early abandonment of convertibility—after overcoming the tequila crisis, say—might have saved Argentina. At the time, this option was unthinkable, as the economy was able to extricate itself from the crisis without the disruptions suffered by Mexico; in retrospect, it seems very much worth thinking about.

But one should not exaggerate this point. During a good part of the crisis and until the early summer of 2001, Brazil looked just as vulnerable as Argentina if not more, in spite of its flexible exchange rate (events in the summer of 2002 confirm this point). A weakening real in 1999 and 2001 was causing the domestic cost of the foreign currency debt service to jump, while the need to raise interest rates in order to maintain some semblance of a nominal anchor was raising the real cost of local-currency obligations. The sense of impending doom was aggravated by the fact that Brazil was so much less liquid than Argentina. The absence of a credible nominal anchor in Brazil severely shortened the duration of domestic-currency debt, which was to a large extent indexed to the overnight rate. This reduced the credibility of monetary policy by complicating the fiscal arithmetic of a monetary contraction. Seen from Argentina in early 1999, the Brazilian way did not seem like a panacea.

Liquidity Is Not All

After the run on the short-term Mexican tesobonos in 1994–95, avoiding self-fulfilling liquidity crises became another obsession of the policy community, in both Buenos Aires and Washington. Argentina took the lesson to heart both in fiscal management and in financial sector policies. On the fiscal front the most obvious thing to do was to lengthen the maturity of debt, and Argentina did this with a vengeance. After the tequila crisis the Menem administration deliberately focused on issuing long-term bonds. In 2001 Domingo Cavallo took this logic to the extreme, swapping debts coming due for longer maturity (and higher yielding) obligations, in the controversial *mega-canje*. Did it all help? In a sense, yes. As the FC schedule in equation (13) shows, the smaller is δ (the share of debt coming due), the less likely the constraint will bind in the current period. But this policy alone could not cure Argentina's ills: at the low levels of output and profits that resulted after three years of recession, the debt simply became impossible to pay, regardless of maturity. Argentina's agony began, in retrospect, with the Brazilian devaluation in February 1999 and ended with de la Rua's resignation in December 2001. The earlier policy of maturity lengthening could delay the eventual and painful denouement, but beyond giving time to the rest of the world to right itself, it did not generate the incentives for the economy to avoid the crisis.

Too Much Debt?

The last three points suggest that it was the size of the debt, both private and public, that did it. But was total external debt actually so large? Enough to sink a nation that half a decade earlier had been the toast of Wall Street? A first glance does not suggest so. By the end of 2001, total external debt stood at 55 percent of output, not unlike the situation of other emerging market economies. In the eight years from 1993 to 2000, the cumulative current account deficit was 29 percent of 2001 GDP.[39] Again, not tiny, but not at all out of line for an economy whose capital-labor ratio is far below that of rich nations, and that should naturally be a capital importer. But Argentina sank nonetheless, which seems to suggest that traditional standards for measuring debt sustainability may be sorely inadequate for countries with dollarized liabilities and potentially large real exchange rate swings.

In retrospect, then, perhaps Argentina should have accumulated less external debt. How to have achieved this, however, is not clear. A simple answer is that the government should have borrowed less. But much of the foreign debt was private, and private sector borrowing decisions are made without consulting government bureaucrats. One possibility was a strongly countercyclical fiscal policy, which would have increased the government surplus every

39. Ministerio de Economía, Republica de Argentina, www.mecon.gov.ar.

time the private sector borrowed, so as to leave the current account unchanged. But notice this is exactly the opposite of what the Barro principles of optimal debt management call for. An alternative is to meddle with private borrowing directly, perhaps taxing it to discourage excessive debt accumulation. Some countries have done this, arguing that there is an externality in private borrowing decisions. But Argentina's strategy in the mid-1990s was to increase integration into world capital markets, not to limit it.[40] At the time, taxes on foreign borrowing were also unthinkable.

Gross or Net Debts?

Private Argentine citizens and corporations borrowed heavily abroad, but also accumulated a large stock of assets overseas. This makes the point that Argentina arguably did not have a private external debt problem. Once you subtract over $90 billion in foreign assets held by Argentine residents, the overall external private net debt burden was negative.[41]

But is such netting out reasonable? In a standard model with well-functioning financial markets, of course it is: it has to be net, not gross, debt that matters for the ability to repay. But in a world with market segmentation and under-the-counter transactions, the answer is more complicated. In constraint equation (13) it is not explicit whether F stands for gross or net liabilities. But suppose that it is domestic corporations and banks that do the bulk of the gross borrowing (as happened in Argentina), while their stockholders and uncles keep personal deposit accounts in Miami. Could (or should) foreign creditors net out these assets in determining how much they want to lend to Argentina-based banks and companies? The answer is probably no.

This suggests that financial globalization may bring its discontents. A country, like Argentina, that tries to integrate itself fully into international markets will doubtless see gross flows increase even if net flows stay put. Once you are fully integrated (think Switzerland) this is just fine. But if you are still

40. Argentina did impose liquidity requirements on all bank liabilities, including foreign borrowing. This was seen as part of its liquidity policy and was perceived at the time as addressing what was thought to be the fundamental externality, that is, the multiple equilibria associated with bank runs.

41. Argentina's balance of payments for 2000 shows $6.5 billion in interest earned on foreign assets. This represents 52 percent of the national external debt payments. Assuming an improbably high interest rate of 7 percent, this amounts to some $93 billion in interest-earning assets. In addition, the balance of payments reports a further $1 billion in profits and dividends earned abroad by Argentine residents. Ministerio de Economía, Republica de Argentina, www.mecon.gov.ar.

credit constrained and crisis prone, this can be problematic. The fact that Argentines or Venezuelans had massive dollar holdings abroad did not make international lenders any more willing to lend to those countries during the debt crisis of the 1980s, and the same has been true this time around. And the fact that those Miami accounts cannot be taxed does not help the fiscal solvency of cash-strapped governments.

And once a crisis erupts, the funds held abroad are not much help either. In a pinch, an Argentine businessman may repatriate a few dollars to prop up his own consumption or to keep his company running over the short term. But the incentives not to spend or even disclose those dollar holdings are huge. The helping hand of the fisc only helps those companies that claim to be unable to help themselves. Indeed, in today's Argentina many of the same people who held dollars abroad have seen their domestic debts pesified while the exchange rate depreciates massively—that is, they have gained on all sides.

Making Implicit Debts Explicit

One interesting issue that is raised by this experience is the question of whether documenting a preexisting debt or transforming an implicit Social Security liability into negotiable bonds affects in some fundamental way the fiscal stance. This is an important issue, as so much of the increase in net debt between 1995 and 2000 can be attributed to these changes (see table 3). Does it matter whether the debt of the pension system is just a pay-as-you-go obligation or is a bond instead? Will the market see through the equivalence?

One could think of pay-as-you-go debt has having Arrow-Debreu characteristics. In Argentine history, the government paid it in good states of nature but not in bad (a common trick was to let nominal pension readjustments lag and then let inflation do its dirty deed). This is extremely convenient for a government that finds itself financially constrained in bad states: pensioners are de facto lenders of last resort to the fisc. In this setup all risk is borne by pensioners, who have little bargaining power and do not get to set the rate of interest. Hence the government does not have to compensate them for bearing that risk, as implicit actuarial debt is nonnegotiable and uncertainty over the ability of the government to pay the pension obligations is borne solely by the prospective retiree. The same is true of implicit bank debt and other kinds of skeletons in the closet, which have been turned into explicitly and tradable debt in Argentina and elsewhere.

Aside from enlarging the stock of explicit debt, which in itself may scare some actual and potential creditors, documenting implicit obligations changes the risk profile of the obligations. The bond issued is no longer a state-contingent liability, and the question arises of who will bear the risk of non-payment. Conceivably, the government will have to issue negotiable interest-bearing debt that pays a higher interest rate in order to compensate bond-holders for the risks previously borne by the trapped creditors. This means that the reform will lead to an increase in the interest burden of the obligation that will be larger the greater is the country risk. In Argentina, the Social Security reform and the documentation of debt probably had the effect of increasing the total real interest burden of the debt and weakened fiscal balance significantly.

Another Role for Fiscal Policy?

In a trivial sense, equation (13) shows that fiscal policy matters for credit-worthiness: the less is the government borrowing (the smaller is $G - T$), the less tight the constraint on investment and growth. But in a more complicated sense, a lesson from this paper's analysis above is that fiscal policy in finan-cially constrained economies may be much less effective than is often thought. True, some countries have been able to adjust their fiscal accounts in a reces-sion: Turkey, Russia, and even Brazil were able to adjust their primary fiscal deficits in a significant manner and were rewarded by the markets via lower country risk. For example, on April 24, 2002, the EMBI spread of formerly bankrupt Russia amounted to a mere 468 basis points, while that of still trou-bled Turkey reached only 581.[42]

Is this not an indication that fiscal adjustment works? Not really, if what one has in mind is that fiscal adjustment should allay sustainability fears and increase the country's access to external finance. The EMBI spread data do not show that the supply of funds to these countries increased. On the con-trary, at the time of this writing both Turkey and Russia exhibit large current account surpluses, which suggests that the overall flow of funds to those economies has declined. In some sense, the lower country risk just indicates that the economy was able to adjust to a collapse in capital flows through reces-sion and real depreciation, not that it was able to displace the FC curve so as to run larger deficits.

Yet this is what was hoped for from fiscal policy in Argentina. As the sim-ulation presented in figures 3a, 3b, and 3c indicate, given the international

42. UBS Warburg.

context, what Argentina required to achieve moderate growth was a sustained current account deficit of 5 percent of GDP (and that, in itself, would have gone a long way toward solving the perceived fiscal problem). This is far from the experience of Russia or Turkey. If anything, it resembles the experience of Brazil. In that country, fiscal adjustment and real depreciation did not cause a major shift in the current account deficit, which remained large. But note that even in Brazil the current account deficit actually declined. From this perspective, it is really hard to see how Argentina could have extricated itself from its predicament through fiscal tightening alone.

Moral Hazard and the IMF's Role

If imperfections in world capital markets are at the heart of the crisis story in Argentina and elsewhere, what is the international community doing about it? After the East Asian and Russian crises, support for large financial rescue packages among the G-7 nations dwindled. Talk instead moved to bail-ins, burden sharing, and the more euphemistic concept of private sector involvement. The arguments against financial rescues were based on moral hazard: each bailout might be locally successful, but to give the wrong sense of confidence to markets would lead to more imprudent lending and additional crises down the road. Conservatives often argued at the time that the cause of the East Asian crisis was the moral hazard generated by the Mexican bailout.

But there is scant evidence that moral hazard is that big a deal, so the justification for the policy shift away from large rescue packages was debatable.[43] Worse, there was no clearly articulated new policy to replace the old policy. Disagreements between the United States and Europe as to whether they should adopt a set of rules for dealing with troubled countries or instead adopt a case-by-case approach have not been resolved. Dozens of meetings with the private sector have led nowhere.

In this context, the perception that the public sector was abandoning a coordinating role in crisis resolution almost surely lead to the perception of increased systemic risk in emerging markets. After Russia, capital flows to developing countries collapsed: the current account deficits on non-fuel-exporting developing countries declined continuously from $105.5 billion in 1996 to $28.8 billion in 2001.[44]

The new approach reduced the amount foreigners were willing to lend for any set of local macroeconomic conditions. In the context of this paper's

43. See, for example, Eichengreen and Hausmann (1999); Fischer (2000).
44. IMF (2002).

model, this can be interpreted as a decline in μ, leading to a downward movement in the FC curve, less investment and less growth. The sequence of blowups that followed in several countries is arguably the local consequence of the new systemic policy. The U.S. Treasury and the IMF may have tried to make the world safe for capital flows. In practice, they rendered the world safer for crises.

Appendix: Extended Model

The only change to the model is to introduce a nonunitary demand for exports, so that in the final period dollar output is not uniquely pinned down by exogenous X_1. In that period market clearing is now

$$\beta Y_1 = E_1^{1/\sigma} X_1, \qquad (A\text{-}1)$$

where $\sigma^{-1} > 1$ is the price elasticity of export demand. From the production function and equilibrium labor supply, we have $Y_1 = I^\alpha$. Using this in equation A-1 and rearranging, we find the real exchange rate in the final period is

$$E_1 = \left(\frac{\beta I^\alpha}{X_1}\right)^\sigma. \qquad (A\text{-}2)$$

Recall the borrowing constraint is $(1 + r)E_1 F_1 \leq \mu Y_1$, which, using equation A-2, becomes

$$(1+r)F_1 \leq \mu \beta^{-\sigma} I^{\alpha(1-\sigma)} X_1^\sigma. \qquad (A\text{-}3)$$

Hence substituting in for the value of F_1, the FC schedule can be written as

$$\alpha Y \geq G - T + (1+r)EF + \left\{ IE^{1-\gamma} - \mu \beta^{-\sigma} I^{\alpha(1-\sigma)} \frac{EX_1^\sigma}{1+r} \right\}. \qquad (A\text{-}4)$$

In turn, using equation A-2 the BP schedule can be easily shown to be

$$I^{1-\alpha(1-\sigma)} = \beta^{-\sigma} \frac{E^\gamma X_1^\sigma}{1+r}. \qquad (A\text{-}5)$$

Finally, the IS schedule is now just as before, but with the real exchange rate raised to the power σ^{-1} in front of export demand

$$\beta Y = \gamma I E^{1-\gamma} + G - \gamma T + E^{1/\sigma} X. \qquad (A\text{-}6)$$

These last three equations complete the description of the extended model.

It is straightforward to show that the FC is now nonmonotonic and convex, with a minimum at

$$I^{1-\alpha(1-\sigma)} = \alpha(1-\sigma)\mu\beta^{-\sigma}\frac{E^{\gamma}X_1^{\sigma}}{1+r}, \tag{A-7}$$

which is smaller than the unconstrained level of investment shown in equation A-5. Notice also that the slope of the FC is

$$\frac{\partial Y}{\partial I} = \alpha^{-1}E^{1-\gamma}\left\{1 - \alpha(1-\sigma)\mu\beta^{-\sigma}I^{\alpha(1-\sigma)-1}\frac{E^{\gamma}X_1^{\sigma}}{1+r}\right\}, \tag{A-8}$$

so that as investment becomes arbitrarily large, this slope converges to $\alpha^{-1}E^{1-\gamma}$, precisely the slope of the FC in the simpler model presented in the text.

Finally, notice that the intercept of the FC is $[G - T + (1 + r)EF]\alpha^{-1}$, while the intercept of the IS is $[G - \gamma T + E^{1/\sigma}X]\beta^{-1}$. Hence the IS cuts the vertical axis above the FC if

$$G(1-\alpha) - T < \left[\alpha E^{\frac{1}{\sigma}}X - \beta(1+r)EF\right](1-\gamma)^{-1}, \tag{A-9}$$

which is the same as the condition for the IS to cut above the FC in the simpler model, except that now E is raised to the power σ^{-1}. It follows that sufficiently large G causes this condition to be violated, bankrupting the economy in a crisis where investment goes to zero.

References

Aghion, Philippe, Philippe Bacchetta, and Abhijit Banerjee. 2001. "Currency Crises and Monetary Policy in an Economy with Credit Constraints." *European Economic Review* 45 (7): 1121–50.

Burnside, Craig, Martin Eichenbaum, and Sergio Rebelo. 1999. "Hedging and Financial Fragility in Fixed Exchange Rate Regimes." Working Paper 99-11. Federal Reserve Bank of Chicago.

Caballero, Ricardo, and Arvind Krishnamurthy. 2001. "Excessive Dollar Debt: Financial Development and Underinsurance." Mimeo. Northwestern University, Finance Department.

Calomiris, Charles W., and Andrew Powell. 2000. "Can Emerging Market Bank Regulators Establish Credible Disciple? The Case of Argentina, 1992–99." Working Paper 7715. Cambridge, Mass.: National Bureau of Economic Research (May).

Calvo, Guillermo, Alejandro Izquierdo, and Ernesto Talvi. 2002. "Sudden Stops, the Real Exchange Rate, and Fiscal Sustainability: Argentina's Lessons." Mimeo. Inter-American Development Bank.

Céspedes, Luis Felipe, Roberto Chang, and Andrés Velasco. 2000. "Balance Sheets and Exchange Rate Policy." Working Paper 7840. Cambridge, Mass.: National Bureau of Economic Research (August).

Chamon, Marcos. 2001. "Why Can't Developing Countries Borrow in Their Own Currencies?" Mimeo. Harvard University.

Eichengreen, Barry, and Ricardo Hausmann. 1999. "Exchange Rates and Financial Fragility." Working Paper 7418. Cambridge, Mass.: National Bureau of Economic Research.

Fernandez-Arias, Eduardo, and Ernesto Talvi. 2000. "Devaluation or Deflation? Adjustment under Liability Dollarization." Mimeo. Inter-American Development Bank.

Fischer, Stanley. 2000. "On the Need for an International Lender of Last Resort." *Essays in International Economics* 220. Princeton University, Department of Economics (November).

Goldfajn, Ilan, and Gino Olivares. 2001. "Full Dollarization: The Case of Panama." *Economía* 1 (2).

International Monetary Fund. 2002. "Statistical Appendix." *World Economic Outlook*. Washington (May).

Jeanne, Olivier. 2001. "Why Do Emerging Economies Borrow in Foreign Currency?" Mimeo. International Monetary Fund, Research Department.

Krugman, Paul. 1989. "Private Capital Flows to Problem Debtors." In *Developing Country Debt and the World Economy*, edited by Jeffrey Sachs. University of Chicago Press.

———. 1999. "Balance Sheets, the Transfer Problem and Financial Crises." In *International Finance and Financial Crises*, edited by Robert Flood and others. Kluwer Academic Publishers.

Mussa, Michael. 2002. "Argentina and the Fund: From Triumph to Tragedy." *Policy Analysis in International Economics* 67. Washington: Institute for International Economics.

Perry, Guillermo, and Luis Servén. 2002. "The Anatomy of a Multiple Crisis: Why Was Argentina Special and What We Can Learn From It." Mimeo. World Bank.

Schneider, Martin, and Aaron Tornell. 2000. "Balance Sheets Effects, Bailout Guarantees, and Financial Crises." Working Paper 8060. Cambridge, Mass.: National Bureau of Economic Research (December).

Tejeiro, M. 2001. "Una Vez Más, La Política Fiscal." Mimeo. Centro de Estudios Públicos, Buenos Aires.

Comments and Discussion
on the Argentine Papers

Joyce Chang: I concur with Andrew Powell's conclusions on the roots and causality of the Argentine crisis. Powell points out convincingly that the scope of the crisis is clearly multidimensional. He also demonstrates that fiscal mismanagement and the deteriorating trend in debt dynamics, exacerbated by messy politics, provided the best forewarning of the crisis. Powell presents a thoughtful analysis of why the balance of payments and size of the current account deficit are less relevant sources of the country's crisis.

I fully agree with Powell's assessment that the fiscal adjustment did not need to be so large in the first year of former president de la Rua's administration. The biggest disappointment was that the government was not able to take the initial small steps necessary on the fiscal side to embark on a path of debt stabilization. I would argue that if the de la Rua government had posted a relatively modest increase in the primary surplus in 2001, bringing the primary surplus up to 1.5 percent of gross domestic product (GDP) in 2001 from 0.4 percent of GDP in 2000, this would likely have been sufficient to gain market credibility. By the time the de la Rua administration realized the magnitude of the crisis and called for a zero deficit, it was too late to regain market credibility. Much larger spending cuts were necessary, in the order of 25 percent, not the 13 percent announced.

Powell references a JP Morgan research report written in 2000 (before the JP Morgan Chase merger), which illustrates that the initial fiscal adjustment necessary for Argentina was not that large, and the failure to deliver that adjustment was a key cause of the crisis.[1] I would like to point out that JP Morgan's paper was revised in 2001 (postmerger) by a new research team under my

1. JP Morgan (2000).

leadership to account for several factors that we felt were missing from the original exercise.[2]

In the revised debt dynamics exercise, JP Morgan first questioned examining debt as a percentage of GDP. Powell argues *ex post* that a country with Argentina's characteristics should maintain debt-to-GDP levels lower than 45 percent. Most emerging markets countries have ratios of public sector debt to GDP that are larger than 45 percent of GDP, and this is not in itself so worrisome. In my view, debt-to-GDP ratios are imperfect measures because nominal GDP is very sensitive to the exchange rate. (Why not measure debt ratios in terms of exports?) At a different peso value, the ratio of debt to GDP ballooned to unsustainable levels. Moreover, the debt trends matter more than the stock. If Argentina's growth and fiscal adjustment prospects had been encouraging, the debt dynamics would not have been threatening.

Second, JP Morgan revised the debt dynamics exercise based on consolidated public sector balances, rather than relying only on central government data. As a result, on a consolidated basis the primary balance looks significantly worse, making the starting point, for example, a consolidated public sector primary surplus of 0.4 percent of GDP, rather than a primary surplus for the central government of 1.2 percent of GDP for 2000.

Third, the revised JP Morgan debt dynamics exercise used more conservative growth assumptions. The original report assumed average nominal 4.4 percent GDP growth, although average nominal growth for the 1994–2001 period was only 1.7 percent.

We also questioned the assumption that if GDP growth improved tax revenues would improve, therefore making it easier to post larger fiscal surpluses. This was a flaw in most of the debt dynamics exercises on Argentina. The historical data for Argentina do not point to a strong linkage between higher growth and the generation of a more substantial primary surplus. This goes back to the question of the capacity and willingness of Argentina's political class to cut spending and the long-standing challenges to collecting taxes in Argentina. I do agree with Powell that increasing taxes in the midst of a recession is a suboptimal strategy to reduce the fiscal deficit, and expenditure cuts were more appropriate. However, Argentina's tax collection amounts to only 17 percent of GDP, and some sort of tax reform to increase revenues is also necessary over the longer term.

I would only add to Powell's arguments that some negative developments during the early years of the Menem administration set the stage for Argentina's

2. JP Morgan (2001).

fiscal woes. Specifically, privatization proceeds were not saved or used to retire debt, but were spent as part of the public sector current revenue. In addition, privatization revenue was booked in the public sector accounts above the line (as current revenue), meaning that fiscal results in those years were distorted and showed better results. The government only started reporting privatization revenues below the line (as financing) after 1995, after the International Monetary Fund (IMF) changed the accounting procedures. I would also argue that the reform process essentially halted in 1995, not in mid-1998 as argued in Powell's paper. From my perspective, the labor reform passed in the first year of the de la Rua administration was massively watered down.

Expanding on Powell's point that politics exacerbated the crisis, it is important to note that political reform did not follow economic reform. Menem's authority was very much influenced by his ability to provide goods in exchange for favors. Once privatization proceeds were exhausted, the power of the executive branch was severely weakened. By the time de la Rua took office, there was relatively little in the way of goods to distribute to political leaders. Menem was in a position to "give and splurge," while de la Rua was left with the task of attempting to "take back and save."

The arguments in Powell's excellent piece that were less persuasive centered on some of the market observations, such as the argument on "common knowledge." Similarly, while Powell's game to understand the strategic interactions between the IMF and creditors demonstrates why additional mechanisms to address country crisis resolution are necessary, it is not clear to me why the best alternative could be the introduction of sovereign bankruptcy procedures. The absence of a formal framework for negotiations has not been a decisive factor in past debt restructurings; domestic economic and political conditions are more important. In my view, the key factor that drives sovereign debt workouts is the capacity of the government to negotiate with creditors.

Liliana Rojas-Suarez: It is not a surprise that the number of papers aiming to explain the recent Argentine crisis is growing.[3] There are two major reasons why this event has attracted research. First, there is the magnitude of the crisis. After all is said and done, resolution of this crisis may well prove to be one of the most costly in Latin America's recent history, in terms of both output loss and fiscal costs. Second, in contrast to many other previous crisis

---

3. To cite a few, see Calvo and others (2002); Krueger (2002); Mussa (2002); Perry and Servén (2002).

episodes, there is consensus neither on the origins of the crisis nor, at the time of this writing, on its solution.

The papers by Hausmann and Velasco as well as Powell are important contributions to the literature and share some common features. First, both discuss the alternative hypotheses that have been advanced in recent literature to explain the emergence of the crisis. Second, both papers develop an analytical framework to examine the alternative hypotheses. While Hausmann and Velasco develop a model with the prominent feature that firms and the government faced severe borrowing constraints, Powell conducts an empirical assessment of competing theories using vector autoregression analysis. The papers, however, differ significantly in their conclusions. The Hausmann and Velasco analysis suggests that the crisis was inevitable, given the shocks of 1998–2000 in the context of convertibility along with the inherited stock of debt. In contrast, Powell specifically argues that the crisis could have been avoided if Argentina had taken the necessary fiscal measures and political circumstances had been less messy. In Powell's view, the adverse effects particular to Argentina generated a vicious cycle that ended in economic and political collapse. Powell's statistical analysis does not discard the possibility of multiple equilibria. Hausmann and Velasco's paper gives little weight to this explanation of the crisis.

This comment addresses the specific interpretation of events in both papers and discusses the papers' differing views. In addition, this comment identifies an important omission: neither paper takes into account the large fiscal contingent liability that arose from the government's offer of a free guarantee to the banking system. The free guarantee derived from the promise of keeping the convertibility law without charging the banks a premium for the risk that the exchange rate might eventually move. If the contingent liability had been properly accounted in the fiscal balances, it would have shown that the fiscal stance was significantly more deteriorated than recognized in either paper.

Interpretation of Events and Ensuing Conclusions

Both papers do a comprehensive job of assessing the multiple dimensions of the Argentinean problems in the period before the crisis erupted. Both emphasize the complexity of the situation and recognize the limitations of their chosen framework of analysis. However, because of their different interpretations of events, the papers derive significantly different conclusions. An expansion of these differences follows.

Why did Hausmann and Velasco argue that "the catastrophe proved impossible to avoid"? Their argument is based on three key interpretations of events: an overvalued exchange rate, the country's lack of access to international capital markets, and the endogeneity of the fiscal stance; that is, fiscal imbalances are interpreted as a "consequence rather than as a cause of the crisis," largely attributed to the recession and the preexisting stock of debt.

In their view the government could not devalue, in spite of the large misalignment of the real exchange rate. This was because of the devastating effect it would have had on the balance sheets of banks and firms due to the large amounts of dollar lending to borrowers with peso-denominated income sources. Moreover, as the overvaluation of the exchange rate sharply deteriorated exports prospects (and, therefore, the country's capacity to service its external debt obligations), investors in the international capital markets were not willing to finance the necessary current account deficit (over 5 percent, according to their calculations) consistent with the renewal of growth. The large current account deficit necessary to resume growth was, in turn, calculated using an estimated marginal propensity to import of about 0.2. Finally, because in their model investment has a larger component of imports than does government spending, a contractionary fiscal policy reduces net demand for domestic goods and, therefore, output.

In this context it is easy to understand why, in the Hausmann and Velasco view, there is no way out.[4] Simply put, the analysis implies that there were no policy tools that could be used effectively to deal with Argentina's problems. A devaluation would be counterproductive as it would cause corporations and banks to fall into bankruptcy, making a default unavoidable. Attempting to grow through increased investment was not possible due to the lack of financing for the current account of the balance of payments. Finally, attempting to restore fiscal balance would, under most conditions in their model, only exacerbate the recession, aggravating the problem.

Turn now to Powell's paper. His view, opposite to that of Hausmann and Velasco, is that the crisis was indeed avoidable, and is based on a different

4. The paper contains a brief discussion of a possible way out: pesification of financial assets and liabilities, combined with exchange rate flexibility. By eliminating the currency mismatch, it was expected that the exchange rate movement would correct for the misalignment without generating financial distress in banks and corporations. However, a forced pesification is equivalent to a default, since the public would have been obliged to hold certain kinds of assets against their will. In my view, this was not an appropriate way out of the problems.

interpretation of events. First, Powell argues that even if the exchange rate was overvalued, the current account had already adjusted by the end of 2000. Since Powell did not perceive the exchange rate misalignment as a major factor in the crisis, the implicit conclusion that derives from his analysis is that there was no need to abandon the convertibility regime. Second, and perhaps more important, in contrast to Hausmann and Velasco, Powell sees an effective role for fiscal policy. His analysis leads him to conclude that a moderate fiscal adjustment was required to attain debt sustainability. From his perspective, the problem was that the necessary adjustment was not done. Third, Powell stresses the role of political factors. Indeed, he argues that it was the lack of political will to undertake the required fiscal adjustment that was at the core of the crisis. In sum, in Powell's view, the crisis was not only avoidable, but the magnitude of the adjustment necessary to prevent the crisis was not large.

Missing Analyses:
Contingent Fiscal Liabilities and the Banking Sector

I agree with some of Hausmann and Velasco's interpretation of events as well as some of Powell's, but not with all interpretations in either paper. As a result, I derive a different assessment of the Argentina's crisis than these authors.[5] I agree with Hausmann and Velasco's assessment of an overvalued exchange rate, but disagree with their interpretation of the constraints imposed by balance sheet effects (see below). I agree with Hausmann and Velasco in that the country faced a lack of access to the international capital markets, but argue that this resulted because the market did not see a viable and credible solution to the problem, including a solution to the unsustainable debt problem. Where I agree with Powell (and disagree with Hausmann and Velasco) is in the assessment that fiscal policy could have been used more effectively as a tool against the shocks, but I disagree with his assessment that the necessary fiscal adjustment was small. I also agree with Powell's conclusion that the crisis was avoidable, if one understands crisis as the debt moratorium, collapse in the payment system, and sharp output loss that occurred in late 2001 in Argentina. However, I disagree with the implication from Powell's analysis that the convertibility regime could have been sustainable.

---

5. This should not be a surprise. It is a common joke among practitioners that adding one more economist to the discussion invariably brings a different point of view.

My own view of the crisis is that Argentina had a severe fiscal problem that none of these authors recognized, as they did not use the appropriate concept of fiscal balances.[6] Both papers fully ignored the large fiscal contingent liabilities that accumulated as a result of the continuous weakening of the banking system in the years before the crisis.[7] The standard assessment of Argentina's banking system (including these authors') is that it was a very strong one and the management of the crisis led to its current difficulties. While I fully agree that the crisis management so far has been disastrous for the banks, I argue that the health of the banking system had been deteriorating long before the eruption of the crisis and that this situation was, in turn, increasing contingent liabilities to the government.

My main claim is that long before the crisis, severe problems in the pricing of risk in the Argentinean banking system started to develop and grew throughout the period that ended in the collapse of end-2001. Two arguments to sustain this contention follow.

First, take a closer look at the assertion that a devaluation in Argentina would have led to a massive increase in nonperforming loans in the banking system because a significant proportion of bank assets were dollar-denominated loans to sectors with peso-denominated sources of income. To many, this currency mismatch led to conclusions about the exchange rate regime. Some, including Hausmann and Velasco, argued that Argentina could not devalue unless it corrected for this currency mismatch through pesification of banks' assets and liabilities denominated in dollars. Others recommended the opposite policy prescription: full dollarization. I think that neither of those extreme proposals

6. I find the treatment of the fiscal issues in Hausmann and Velasco particularly problematic. For example, the paper does not recognize the crucial importance that the markets were giving to fiscal expenditure as a tool to react to the shocks. Indeed, to argue that the fiscal stance was not expansionary, they show that primary spending as percentage of GDP had "remained remarkably flat." But that is precisely a point that disappointed the market. With fiscal revenues adversely influenced by the recession and with increasing debt service payments, the only possible fiscal policy had to come from a tightening in fiscal expenditure as proportion of GDP. Moreover, as a further proof that the root of the crisis was not fiscal, they argue that both the primary surplus (excluding Social Security payments) and the provinces' fiscal balance improved. But again, what matters to assess the capacity of the government to meet its obligations is the primary balance of the consolidated public sector and, certainly since 1999, there was not consistent improvement (based on table 2 in the Hausmann and Velasco paper). Thus the authors' comparison between the fiscal adjustment in Argentina, excluding the Social Security system in the precrisis period, and that of the consolidated public sector in Brazil in 1999–2000 is simply incorrect.

7. Banking issues related to the Argentina crisis are also discussed in de la Torre, Levy Yeyati, and Schmukler (2002).

was necessary (or appropriate) and that most analysts have missed the essence of the problem: the lack of adequate provisioning when extending loans to the nontradable sector. From my perspective, the potential adverse effects on banks of a devaluation are clear indicators that bank loans to the nontradable sector were riskier than bank loans to the tradable sector. Exchange rate risk had transformed into credit risk for the nontradable sector. If the safety of the banking system were at the top of the authorities' priorities, why not put brakes on such credit expansion of loans to the nontradable sector? Why would banks' managers, aware of a devaluation risk (and it is impossible to assume that they were not aware after the stream of shocks that affected Argentina's competitiveness since the Russian crisis), not protect banks' portfolios sufficiently for the increased perception of risk?[8] Why did the percentage of dollar-denominated loans in total loans reach levels above 70 percent by end-2000, in spite of a significant slowdown in the tradable good sector?[9]

My explanation for the sustained increased relative exposure of banks to the nontradable sector—and, therefore, for excessive risk-taking behavior by banks—is that the government was offering a free guarantee to the banks; namely, the promise of a fixed exchange rate without charging the banks a premium for the risk that the exchange rate may actually depreciate. One can draw a parallel between this implicit guarantee and an implicit deposit insurance. As is well known, the problem with that practice is that it induces excessive risk taking by banks; that is, banks underprice the risk of their portfolios. But the implicit insurance also implies that if something goes wrong and banks run into severe difficulties, the government will have to absorb the costs associated with the banking crisis. In good times, when the difference between the market and the actual price of the guarantee is low, the system functions without apparent problems and the fiscal stance looks good. When difficulties in the banking sector materialize, however, the true fiscal contingency also materializes.

Powell talks about bad policy advice. I want to add another to his list of bad policy advice—the implicit constraint of policy choices for Argentina by advising policymakers not to increase the flexibility of the exchange rate system for the sake of the stability of the banking system, as if that were the only

8. The fact that the authorities and analysts never stop worrying about the adverse effects of a potential devaluation on the banks is proof that banks did not take sufficient precautionary measures against that risk.

9. According to Hausmann and Velasco's data, real growth of exports declined from an average of 13.6 percent in the period 1994–98 to an average of 1.4 percent in the 1999–01 period.

policy option to maintain bank soundness. That is bad advice. If a depreciation of the exchange rate may damage banks' portfolios but the country is not in a crisis (as it was indeed the case in the 1996–2000 period) is it not a better policy option to be stricter in provisioning requirements and, therefore, contain the expansion of risk? I am aware that this option would have further limited the access of credit to the nontradable sector; but since it would have contributed to preventing the crisis altogether, that problem would have been easier (relative to crisis circumstances) to tackle. Having contained the potential damage of an exchange rate depreciation to banks' portfolios, policymakers would have faced fewer restrictions when considering the option of a more flexible exchange rate system.

My second argument about the underpricing of risk in the Argentinean banking system relates to the treatment of government paper. While not as severely distorted as in many other emerging markets, the Argentinean banking regulations underestimated the risks to the banks associated with holding government paper by having lower capital requirements for government paper relative to private sector liabilities.[10] While considering government paper as a safer asset may be a good assumption in industrial countries, the long history of government default in many emerging markets, and particularly in Argentina, does not warrant extrapolating this treatment of risk from industrial countries to emerging markets.

Figure 1 shows the evolution of the share of government paper in banks' balance sheets in Argentina since 1990. While this share declined significantly up to 1994 (and found the banking system in good standing at the time of the tequila crisis), it increased afterwards and by end-2001 had reached a level close to that in 1990. This observation is a sad irony for Argentina, since a significant component of the efforts at financial sector reform undertaken in the 1990s aimed at decreasing the share of banks' claims on government. The idea was to free banks from any form of government interference. This is difficult to achieve when more than 30 percent of banks' portfolios are composed of government paper.

It can be argued that because of the recession, banks found themselves without good subjects of credit, and therefore the government was one of the few available clients. However, the market assessment of the quality of govern-

10. This distortion is extremely severe in most emerging markets. When estimating their capital requirements, most of these economies attach a 0 percent risk weight to their own government paper and a 100 percent weight to private sector liabilities. See the extensive discussion of the problems associated with this practice in Rojas-Suarez (2002).

Figure 1. Government Liabilities Held by Banks (as a Percentage of Total Assets), 1990–2001

Percent

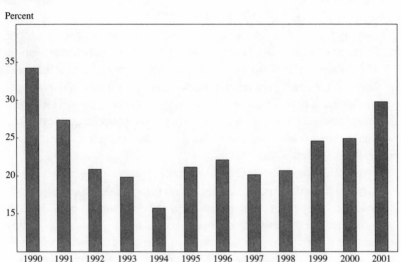

Source: International Monetary Fund, *International Financial Statistics*, various issues.

ment debt, as reflected by the international spread on sovereign paper, tells a different story. As shown in figure 2, banks' relative holding of government paper increased continuously in the year previous to the eruption of Argentina's crisis in spite of a sharp deterioration in the market assessment of the risk of these assets.

It can also be argued that the government forced the banks to increase holdings of government bonds in the months before the crisis. This is a correct argument. However, it is important to notice that banks had been increasing their relative holding of government paper since 1999 (see figure 1). In any case, an important lesson for bank regulators derived from the Argentinean crisis is that it is not appropriate to assume that government paper is safer than private sector debt, especially when compared with large export-oriented companies. Biasing the assessment of risk in favor of government paper just provides an easy territory for fiscal financing through the financial system.

Taken together, my two arguments about the underpricing of risk in Argentine banks imply that the banking system was extremely weak by mid-2001. Accounting assets by implied market prices would have shown undercapitalized banks long before the debt moratorium and devaluation. With such a weak asset position, the run on banks during 2001 was fully justified. Indeed, the

Figure 2. Sovereign Spread and Banks' Claims on Government, December 2000–December 2001

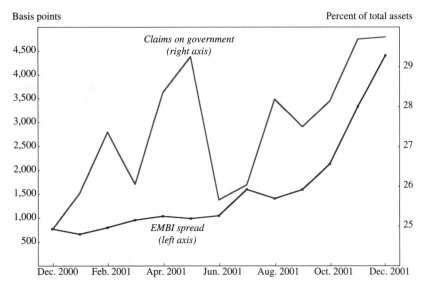

Source: International Monetary Fund, *International Financial Statistics*; Bloomberg.

moratorium-cum-devaluation simply materialized the contingent fiscal lia-bilities that the government had been accumulating from a debilitated (first) and bankrupt (finally) banking system.

Now, go back to compare the previous analysis with that of Hausmann and Velasco along with Powell. As I mentioned before, I believe that this crisis was avoidable. With the benefit of hindsight, I argue that the crisis could have been prevented if the authorities had taken two steps soon after the Russian shock. The first step would have implied taking the necessary measures to minimize the adverse effects of an exchange rate depreciation on the banks' balance sheets. This could have been achieved, at least partially, via adequate provisioning requirements on loans to the nontradable sector. More likely, how-ever, insulating the banking system would have also required a government offering of currency hedges, which would have increased further interest expenses in the budget. The second step would have required the containment of the overall fiscal deficit that, by being financed partially by the banking sector, transferred the default risk on government debt to a credit risk in the banking sector. Because the first step had brought an increase in interest expenses, the overall fiscal adjustment would have had to compensate for such expansion.

If the potential fragilities of the banking sector resulting from government actions had been minimized, Argentina could (and should) have abandoned the convertibility law sometime in late 2000 or early 2001. It was clear that the peso was severely overvalued and the resumption of growth needed a correction of the misalignment. This, of course, does not mean that a devaluation would have been sufficient. A comprehensive package, including a credible fiscal program that incorporated a renegotiation of the tax-sharing agreement between the provinces was necessary. All that my analysis suggests is that without the threat of severe banking problems, Argentina would have had more options.

Policymakers in Argentina and the country's advisers rested too long on the belief that the Argentine banking system was profoundly strong. It was indeed strong in the period 1996–98. And it could have continued on its strong path if the government and its advisers early on had recognized the sources of fragilities and corrected for them. After the Asian and Russian shocks most countries in Latin America understood that the adverse effects of the shocks on their economies could be minimized through a depreciation of their exchange rates. Argentina and its advisers got caught in a trap: rather than planning on initiatives to minimize the costs of a devaluation, they focused on how to keep convertibility in place.

It is my view that one of the essential ingredients of resolving Argentina's crisis (and, at the time of this writing, the solution did not seem to be in the near future) lies in recognizing that resolving the banking crisis is indeed a fiscal problem. Unfortunately, the longer the government takes to recognize this, the more expensive crisis resolution will be. Over the last three to four years, Argentina has had a number of opportunities to correct for the weaknesses in the banking system derived from the promise of a fixed exchange rate system that ceased to be fully credible after the large number of external shocks. But correcting for those fragilities would have implied increased expenses in the budget, and therefore larger fiscal adjustments to offset the fiscal deterioration. Here, I fully agree with Powell: in Argentina there was no political will to undertake the necessary fiscal adjustment. Eventually, such political consensus will develop. History shows that sooner or later such a consensus will be achieved. Unluckily for Argentina's citizens, the costs of resolving the crisis keep increasing by the day.

Discussion: There was an active and lengthy discussion of the issues raised by the two papers and the invited discussants in this session. The main points are summarized below.

Kristin Forbes began the discussion by asking conference participants why Argentina's crisis turned into such a severe financial meltdown. She argued that, unlike the experiences seen elsewhere (including Mexico in 1999), Argentina is unlikely to have the relatively rapid turnaround typically known as a V-shaped recovery. In Forbes's view, answers are better understood to two other questions raised in the papers: what caused Argentina's three-year recession, and what caused the July 2001 crisis? Responding to her question, John Williamson identified three factors. First, the collapse of the currency board likely had a bigger negative impact on confidence than a regular devaluation would have. Second, he believed that Argentinians have an unusual degree of distrust of their government. And finally, he argued that the government's policy response was seen as incoherent. Eliana Cardoso added to Williamson's list. She noted that Argentina did not have a package of international financial assistance comparable to the ones put together for Mexico and Brazil. These two countries had not been dollarized to the same extent as Argentina. Another key difference was the political situation, which meant that Argentina was unable to achieve a primary budget surplus, unlike Brazil. Finally, she noted that in Brazil and Mexico devaluation had a positive impact on government accounts through revenues related to petrogas and oil, respectively.

Some of the discussion focused on the finding (in both papers) that the fiscal adjustment that would have been required for Argentina's situation to remain sustainable was relatively small. Eduardo Fernandez-Arias asked why it was so difficult for this adjustment to be achieved and argued that this failure was interpreted as a very negative signal by financial markets. Fernandez-Arias also expressed the view that the government played a somewhat unusual role in Argentina's crisis. He noted that the way out of a banking crisis typically involves the government footing the bill. In contrast, in Argentina the government got into trouble first, bringing down the banks. Ted Truman and other participants seconded the view, expressed by Joyce Chang in her discussion, that to regain investor confidence, the government needed to change policies enough to get out in front—or to "overshoot." Many agreed that this was difficult because of political constraints and a relatively limited set of policy instruments.

Jose Luis Machinea took issue with some of the points that had been made in the papers and in the discussion. He argued that the magnitude of the fiscal deficits had been understated in places. In particular, he stressed the importance of including the provinces as well as the central government, which was done in the revised versions of the papers. He noted that less than half of the increase in Argentina's Social Security deficit was attributable to the reforms undertaken. Roughly 60 percent (1.5 percent of GDP) was due to reductions in taxes on labor that occurred during 1995–96 and 1998–99. He also disagreed with the characterization of the fiscal adjustment that did occur as coming primarily from tax changes, stating that the major changes came instead from expenditure reductions. Machinea wondered whether the regressions presented overstate the responsiveness of Argentina's imports to GDP because they do not fully account for changes in import prices.

Machinea also disagreed with the view expressed by the authors and others that the fiscal adjustment required in Argentina was relatively small and comparable to adjustments achieved elsewhere. He argued that the situation was very different because Argentina was in the midst of a deflation. This meant that the government would have been required to make sizable nominal cuts in wages and pensions. This is politically much more difficult than achieving reductions in government spending as a share of GDP in an economy with price inflation.

A number of participants agreed that the role of deflation has received less attention than it deserves in analyses of Argentina's experience. Truman suggested that Argentina could be thought of as being in a similar situation to Japan, but without three important freedoms. Unlike Japan, Argentina did not have a flexible exchange rate, a large stock of foreign exchange reserves, or a current account surplus. These factors severely limited the policy instruments available.

Truman also expressed curiosity about the role that foreign banks played as the crisis unfolded. He argued that their reactions most likely reflected their relatively poor risk assessments a priori. Others seconded his interest in additional information.

Participants disagreed about the degree to which Argentina's currency was uncompetitive and the implications of the exchange rate for Argentina's exports. Michael Gavin presented his analysis, which found that Argentine export performance during 2000–01 was similar to that of Brazil, despite the fact that Argentina had not devalued. Williamson questioned this result, preferring a volume indicator of exports. Truman described his own work, which concludes that Argentina's exports grew more slowly in real terms than those of any other emerging market economy during the second half of the 1990s. Andrés Velasco cautioned against being too pessimistic about export behavior looking forward. In his view, a significant devaluation will encourage increased investment in exports and will generate significant export growth, though perhaps with some lags.

Finally, Velasco reiterated the view he shares with Ricardo Hausmann that small fiscal adjustments in Argentina would have been unlikely to restore confidence automatically but likely to deepen the recession. He also noted that the VAR in Powell's paper finds that interest rates on emerging market bonds tend to react to growth rates, but not to changes in government spending. If this is true, it suggests that a cut in spending that improves the fiscal situation but causes a recession will tend to raise bond rates and not to restore market confidence or generate capital inflows.

References

Calvo, Guillermo, and others. 2002. "Sudden Stops, the Real Exchange Rate, and Fiscal Sustainability: Argentina's Lessons." Mimeo. Inter-American Development Bank

De la Torre, Augusto, E. Levy Yeyati, and Sergio Schmukler. 2002. "Argentina's Financial Crisis: Floating Money, Sinking Banking." Mimeo. World Bank and Universidad Torcuato Di Tella.

JP Morgan. 2000. "Argentina's Debt Dynamic: Much Ado about Not Very Much." Market Brief. New York (September 6).

————. 2001. "Argentina, Back to Basics: A Real (Old Economy) Adjustment Is Needed." New York (February 26).

Krueger, Anne. 2002. "Crisis Prevention and Resolution: Lessons from Argentina." Speech prepared for National Bureau of Economic Research Conference on the Argentina Crisis. Cambridge, Mass. (July 17).

Mussa, Michael. 2002. "Argentina and the Fund: From Triumph to Tragedy." Policy brief prepared for the Institute for International Economics (July).

Perry, Guillermo, and Luis Servén. 2002. "The Anatomy of a Multiple Crisis: Why Was Argentina Special and What We Can Learn From It." Mimeo. World Bank.

Rojas-Suarez, Liliana. 2002. "Can International Capital Standards Strengthen Banks in Emerging Markets?" Working Paper 01-10. Washington: Institute for International Economics (November).

FATIH ÖZATAY AND GÜVEN SAK
Central Bank of Turkey and Ankara University

Banking Sector Fragility and Turkey's 2000–01 Financial Crisis

The Turkish economy was hit by two crises in the last decade. The first one, which attracted surprisingly limited international interest, occurred at the beginning of 1994, at which time there was a managed float.[1] The second crisis, preceded by financial turmoil, erupted in the second half of November 2000 in the midst of a stabilization program based on the exchange rate. In response to the turmoil, a new letter of intent was presented to the International Monetary Fund (IMF) by the government, which calmed market pressure. However, at the end of December average interest rates—both the overnight and secondary market bond rates—were almost four times higher than levels at the beginning of November and more than five times higher than the preannounced (at the outset of the 2000–02 program) year-end depreciation rate of the lira. This unsustainable situation ended on February 19, 2001, when Prime Minister Bülent Ecevit announced that there was a severe political crisis (without naming a specific cause), which had ignited an equally serious economic crisis in the highly sensitive markets. The markets were already jittery due to what had happened at the end of the preceding year. On that February day, overnight rates jumped to unprecedented levels of 6,200

The views expressed in this paper are the authors' and do not necessarily represent those of the Central Bank of the Republic of Turkey. The authors are grateful to Erdal Özmen and this paper's discussants, Peter Garber and Atish Ghosh, as well as participants of the Brookings Trade Forum 2002 and an anonymous referee, for helpful comments for an earlier version of this paper. The usual disclaimer applies. This paper focuses on the January 1995 to February 2001 period. The appendix briefly discusses the developments in the postcrisis period, March 2001 to July 2002.

1. Özatay (2000), which analyzes the 1994 crisis, argues that despite the weak fundamentals of the period preceding the crisis, it could have been avoided. Turkey could have escaped the turmoil had there not been policy mistakes—mistakes that played a role in a series of shocks in the second half of 1993.

121

percent in uncompounded terms. Three days later the exchange rate system collapsed, and Turkey declared that it was going to implement a floating exchange rate system.

The crisis of 2000–01, which was more severe than that of 1994, raises a multitude of questions. What were the reasons behind the events of 2000–01? Why did the crisis erupt in the midst of the IMF-supported stabilization program? What are the lessons that can be drawn? By answering these questions, this paper concludes that the root cause of the crisis was the combination of a fragile banking sector and a set of triggering factors that made this fragility crystal clear.

The banking sector's weakness is noted in other studies of the recent Turkish crises. Akyüz and Boratav point to shortcomings in the design of the 2000–02 stabilization program and the inadequacy of crisis management policies.[2] They emphasize the dependence of the banking sector's earnings on high-yielding Treasury bills, thus rendering this sector highly vulnerable to disinflation. They further argue that since much of the fiscal adjustment was predicated on declines in nominal and real interest rates, the program was not compatible with this feature of the banking system. Alper focuses on the events that occurred at the end of 2000.[3] He argues that three factors were responsible for the crisis: the inability of the Turkish government to maintain the stream of good news and sustain capital inflows; not enough backing for the IMF program; and the "no sterilization" rule of the program, which led to interest rate undershooting in the first phase of the 2000 program. The banking sector's fragility is a major theme of the analysis presented in Alper's work.

Unlike the two studies mentioned above, this paper analyzes the structural characteristics of the Turkish banking system and provides a precise definition for banking sector fragility in the context of Turkey right before the crisis. This paper demonstrates that pressure in the markets increased at the end of 2000. It shows that although the macroeconomic fundamentals were rather weak in 2000, the prerequisites of the first-generation crisis models were absent (see table 1 for descriptions of crisis model features). The role of self-fulfilling prophecies is discussed, and an analysis of the performance of the economy in the aftermath of the crisis is presented.

Was the principal cause of the Turkish crisis a prospective deficit associated with implicit bailout guarantees to a failing banking system? Or was the root cause of the problem financial fragility in the banking sector in the sense

2. Akyüz and Boratav (2001).
3. Alper (2001).

Table 1. Salient Features of Crisis Models

Crisis model	Features
First generation	a. Controlled exchange rate. b. Loose fiscal policy, budget deficits are financed by printing money. c. Investors act on an unsustainable situation due to inconsistency between macroeconomic policies and the exchange rate regime. d. Efficient markets are assumed, and the regulatory and institutional structures of financial markets are not considered. e. No output decline in the postcrisis period. f. Leading indicators available; gradual decline in reserves and gradual increase in the interest rate differential. g. Natural collapse, given the policy framework; government is the culprit.
Second generation	a. Controlled exchange rate. b. Macroeconomic policies and the exchange rate regime are not neccesarily inconsistent, but some domestic concerns (unemployment and so on) on the part of policymakers may lead them to change the existing policy framework. c. Despite sound monetary and fiscal policies, investor pessimism and the resultant portfolio shift from domestic currency–denominated assets to foreign currency bring an end to the exchange rate regime. d. Efficient markets are assumed; the regulatory and institutional structures of financial markets are not considered; balance sheets do not necessarily matter. e. Faster growth potential after the collapse. f. No leading indicators available. g. No natural collapse; speculators are the culprits.
Third generation	a. Controlled exchange rate. b. Macroeconomic policies and the exchange rate regime are not necessarily inconsistent. c. Despite sound monetary and fiscal policies, investor pessimism regarding financial soundness of banks and corporate sector lead to a portfolio shift from domestic currency–denominated assets to foreign currency that brings an end to the exchange rate regime. d. Informationally inefficient markets are assumed; weak regulatory and institutional structures are considered for the country, allowing risk accumulation in bank and corporate sector balance sheets; balance sheets do matter. e. Slower growth potential after the collapse due to damage done in banking and corporate sector balance sheets. f. No leading indicators available; possible to follow accumulation of risks in balance sheets, but change in risk perception of investors is hard to specify. g. No natural collapse.

Source: Authors' notes.

of a third-generation crisis model? This paper analyzes the banking sector structure in the period preceding the crisis and provides strong evidence that points to the weakness of the banking sector. Furthermore, this paper identifies two types of dichotomy in the banking sector: between private and state banks and within the private banks.

What were the major distinctions between 1999 and 2000?

—As opposed to the managed floating exchange rate system of 1999, there was a pre-announced crawling peg system in 2000.

—The current account registered a record high level of deficit in 2000.

—Given a weak banking system, delays in reforming the banking sector increased tensions in the markets in the second half of 2000.

—A takeover of some of the private banks, starting in October 2000—and, at the same time, sensational criminal investigations of some bankers—made it clear that the banking system was not homogenous, but rather dichotomized as "good" and "bad" banks. This intensified rumors about which banker or bank was next in the line for investigation. As a result, in the second half of November 2000 good banks closed their credit lines to bad banks. This paper argues that the first two differences listed above were not sufficient to trigger the crisis. The main igniting factors were the delays in reforming the banking sector and the actions that caused the dichotomy in the banking sector to come to the surface.

Identifying the Crisis

In February 1990 Turkey applied to the IMF for full convertibility of the lira. Up to January 2000, a managed floating exchange rate system was operative. At the end of 1999, Turkey signed a standby agreement with the IMF and started to implement a stabilization program, a pillar of which was a preannounced, crawling peg exchange rate regime. The novelty of this exchange rate regime was that both the exit strategy and date of exit were known publicly at the very beginning of the program. It was announced at the agreement's signing that after eighteen months the exchange rate would be allowed to fluctuate in a continuously widening band. However, after a sky-high overnight rate (as high as 6,200 percent in uncompounded terms) and a huge decline in the foreign exchange reserves of the Central Bank of Turkey, on February 22, 2001 (just four months before the exit day) the exchange rate system collapsed and the central bank declared that it would allow the lira to float freely. By this announcement, the dollar rate jumped from a level of 685,000 liras to 958,000 liras in one day.

Figure 1 shows the pressure in the markets based on an ad hoc exchange market pressure index, along with its mean and mean plus two standard deviations, which are indicated by horizontal lines. As advocated by Eichengreen, Rose, and Wyplosz as well as Sachs, Tornell, and Velasco, this pressure index is a weighted average of monthly rates of changes of exchange rate, (the negative of) official reserves, and overnight rates for the January 1990 to December 2001 period.[4] The monthly percentage change of each variable is weighted by the inverse of its variance. There are two instances at which the index exceeds its mean plus two standard deviations: the first one is the February to April 1994 period and the second is the February to April 2001 period. This result is robust to the types of weight used. Figure 1 does not indicate the first attack against the lira, which occurred at the end of November 2000, since the central bank's defense of the lira was successful at that time. However, as a result of this attack, the central bank lost almost 20 percent of its foreign exchange reserves, while the average overnight rate jumped to 873 percent, again in uncompounded terms. To highlight the severity of this attack, the evolution of the individual items of the market pressure index is provided in figures 2 to 4. Figure 2 presents the dollar-lira rate from the first working day of 1999 to the last working day of 2001. Figure 3 shows the evolution of the weighted average overnight rates in the same period. Finally, the time path for the weekly foreign exchange reserves of the central bank is demonstrated in figure 4.

Fundamentals and Self-Fulfilling Prophecies

The first- and second-generation models of currency crises may shed some light on the 2000–01 crisis but cannot fully explain what happened. For example, on the one hand, in the period preceding the crisis, the public sector borrowing requirement was very high. This brings to mind a first-generation type crisis. On the other hand, the public sector borrowing requirement was mainly financed by issuing domestic debt rather than by inflation tax, which is at the core of such models. Moreover, corrective fiscal measures had already been taken. On the one hand, high levels of short-term public debt and a weak banking sector might have set the stage for a self-fulfilling attack, inducing

4. Eichengreen, Rose, and Wyplosz (1995); Sachs, Tornell, and Velasco (1996a).

Figure 1. Exchange Market Pressure Index, 1990–2001[a]

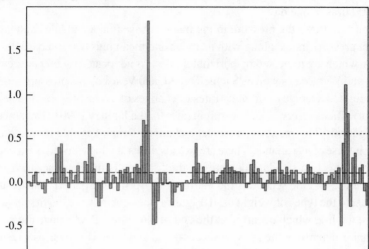

Source: Authors' own calculations based on data obtained from Central Bank of Turkey, Electronic Data Delivery System, www.tcmb.gov.tr.

a. Dashed lines indicate mean and mean plus two standard deviations.

Figure 2. Daily Exchange Rate, Lira-Dollar, 1999–2001

Thousands

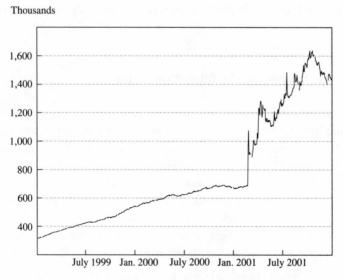

Source: Central Bank of Turkey, Electronic Data Delivery System, www.tcmb.gov.tr.

Figure 3. Weighted Average Overnight Rate, Daily Data, 1991–2001

Percent (logarithmic scale, uncompounded)

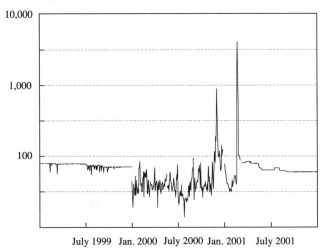

Source: Central Bank of Turkey, Electronic Data Delivery System, www.tcmb.gov.tr.

Figure 4. Foreign Exchange Reserves of the Central Bank, Weekly Data, 1999–2001

Billions of dollars

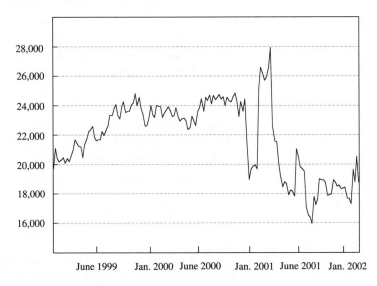

Source: Central Bank of Turkey, Electronic Data Delivery System, www.tcmb.gov.tr.

speculators to anticipate that the government would not dare to increase interest rates to defend the currency. On the other hand, despite corrective measures the fundamentals were weak, output contracted sharply, and the fiscal policy was not expansionary in the aftermath of the crisis, contrary to what the second-generation models envisage.

First-Generation Type Crisis?

Early models of balance of payment crises, following Krugman as well as Flood and Garber, emphasize continuous deterioration of macroeconomic fundamentals—which depletes international reserves of central banks—as the main cause of currency collapses.[5] This generally materializes through reliance upon seigniorage revenue to finance public sector deficits. There comes a point in time when a rational economic agent will realize that a gradual depletion of international reserves is an indicator that the prevailing exchange rate regime will not survive. This anticipation triggers a sudden speculative attack on the currency to prevent excessive capital losses. The collapse of the exchange rate system is inevitable due to its incompatibility with loose monetary policy. Table 2 provides information on how consolidated budget deficits were financed in the 1995–2001 period.[6] As table 2 indicates, the Central Bank of Turkey's lending was zero since 1997. Moreover, in the same period base money creation was entirely through foreign exchange reserve buildup, except during the 1998 Russian crisis. Table 3 documents the evolution of the three main items of the central bank's balance sheet (namely net domestic assets, net foreign assets, and base money), along with the bank's reserves. Hence the central bank's resources did not finance the budget deficits in the period preceding the crisis. That is, the central element of the first-generation models was not on the stage. Two additional points should be noted. First, during the period analyzed, only in 1999–2000 was net foreign borrowing positive. Second, domestic debt maturity was considerably increased again in these last two years (see table 4). These two phenomena do not fit in a scenario where economic conditions are continuously deteriorating and the risk is continuously rising.

It is evident from figures 3 and 4 that neither the increases in interest rate nor the reserve fall were gradual, but rather were sudden. The overnight rate

5. Krugman (1979) and Flood and Garber (1984).
6. The consolidated budget is a part of the public sector. In addition to the consolidated budget, the public sector covers state economic enterprises, special funds, and municipalities. Note that consolidated budget deficits have accounted for an important part of the public sector deficits since the early 1980s.

Table 2. Financing of the Consolidated Budget Deficit, 1995–2001[a]

Percent of GNP

	1995	1996	1997	1998	1999	2000	2001
Public sector borrowing requirement	5.0	8.6	7.7	9.4	15.6	12.5	15.9
Consolidated budget borrowing requirement	3.7	8.5	7.6	7.1	11.6	10.2	17.9[b]
Net domestic borrowing	3.6	7.1	8.5	8.6	12.4	7.4	12.9
Net foreign borrowing	–1.0	–0.9	–1.5	–1.9	0.6	2.1	–2.5
Central bank advances	1.2	1.5	0.0	0.0	0.0	0.0	0.0
Other[c]	0.0	0.7	0.6	0.5	–1.4	0.6	7.4[b]

Source: Turkish Treasury, various issues of Main Economic Indicators.
a. Consolidated budget is a part of the public sector. In addition to the consolidated budget, public sector covers state economic enterprises, special funds, and municipalities.
b. Includes interest liability of the Treasury to the state-owned banks that is partly rolled over.
c. Includes such "financing" items as deferred payments.

was highly volatile throughout the first eleven months of 2000, in sharp contrast to what had happened in the year before, and no upward trend was observed in 2000. At best, it can be said that overnight rates fluctuated around a constant mean of 40 percent, reaching 82 percent on November 15 and 873 percent on December 1. The evolution of the price of the Turkish Treasury thirty-year eurobond, which was issued on January 11, 2000, with an initial price of $98.45, is also illuminating in this respect. The downward trend

Table 3. Balance Sheet of the Central Bank, End-of-Period Values, 1995–2001

	Net domestic assets[a] (trillions of lira)	Net foreign assets[b] (trillions of lira)	Base money[c] (trillions of lira)	Reserves[d] (millions of dollars)
1995	323	–6	317	12,391
1996	335	275	610	16,273
1997	142	988	1,130	18,419
June 1998	–1,778	3,331	1,553	26,377
1998	625	1,486	2,111	19,721
June 1999	–899	3,526	2,627	21,521
1999	-938	4,818	3,880	23,177
June 2000	–1,741	6,372	4,631	24,547
October 2000	–1,815	6,710	4,895	23,545
2000	2,485	3,303	5,788	22,172
2001	20,475	–12,672	7,803	18,787

Source: Central Bank of Turkey, Electronic Data Delivery System, www.tcmb.gov.tr.
a. Net domestic assets equals credit to public sector + government securities + credit to banking sector – public sector deposits + other.
b. Net foreign assets equals foreign assets – foreign exchange liabilities to nonresidents – foreign exchange liabilities to banking sector.
c. Base money equals net domestic assets + net foreign assets.
d. International reserves.

Table 4. Main Fiscal and Economic Indicators, 1995–2001

Percent of GNP, except as indicated

	1995	1996	1997	1998	1999	2000	2001
Public sector borrowing requirement (PSBR)	5.0	8.6	7.7	9.4	15.6	12.5	15.9
Duty losses of state banks	2.2	4.2	5.2	7.5	13.3	12.0	0.0
PSBR + duty losses of state banks	7.2	12.8	12.9	16.9	28.9	24.5	15.9
Primary surplus	2.1	1.3	0.0	2.1	–1.9	3.8	6.7
Consolidated budget deficit	3.7	8.5	7.6	7.1	11.6	10.2	17.9
Consolidated budget interest payments	7.4	10.0	7.7	11.5	13.7	16.3	22.9
Domestic	6.1	8.9	6.7	10.5	12.6	15.0	20.9
Foreign	1.3	1.1	1.0	1.0	1.1	1.3	2.0
Public debt[a]	37.6	40.3	40.5	41.3	51.8	53.4	99.6
Domestic	14.6	18.5	20.2	21.7	29.3	29.0	68.1
Foreign	23.0	21.8	20.3	19.6	22.5	24.4	31.5
Short-term public debt	8.0	10.2	8.1	10.9	4.1	2.1	11.1
Treasury auction borrowing rate, average (percent)	124.2	132.2	107.4	115.5	104.6	38.2	99.6
Consumer inflation (percent)							
Average	89.0	80.2	85.7	84.6	64.9	54.9	54.4
End-year	76.0	79.8	99.1	69.7	68.8	39.0	68.5
GNP growth rate (percent)	8.0	7.1	8.3	3.9	–6.1	6.3	–8.5
Average maturity of borrowing in auctions (days)	188.0	186.6	393.5	235.1	502.3	426.8	146.3

Source: Turkish Treasury, various issues of Main Economic Indicators; Central Bank of Turkey, Electronic Data Delivery System, www.tcmb.gov.tr.

a. Debt stock figures are for the end of the year. Foreign debt is converted to domestic currency by means of the average annual exchange rate. Foreign debt stock for 2001 is for the third quarter.

in price began as late as September 6, after reaching a maximum level of $108.7 (see figure 5).

A similar, sudden movement for reserves was also observed. The record high level for foreign exchange reserves was $26.4 billion at the end of June 1998. The impact of the Russian crisis drove down reserves to $19.7 billion at the end of the same year. After that the reserves followed an upward trend to the end of 1999, reaching a level of $23.2 billion. This trend was replaced by a fluctuation around a level of $24 billion in the second half of 2000, which in turn was halted by the eruption of Turkey's financial turmoil. Just two days before the turmoil erupted, that is on November 17, 2000, the reserve level was $24.4 billion, which was almost equal to the maximum level observed since before the Russian crisis.[7] Hence in the periods preceding the crisis, pre-

7. For the evolution of daily international reserves, see table 12.

Figure 5. Price of the Turkish Thirty-Year Eurobond, Daily Data, 2000–01

Dollars

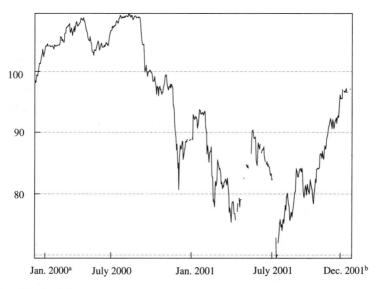

Source: Bloomberg System.
a. As of January 11, 2000.
b. Close of business, December 28, 2001.

requisites of the first-generation models were absent. Namely, the public sector borrowing requirement was never met through the central bank's resources, and no evidence existed that the crisis had been expected.

This does not change the fact that the fiscal fundamentals, examined in isolation, were indeed weak. However, one should note that the IMF-supported program aimed—and indeed succeeded, to some extent—at providing an end to the then unsustainable fiscal policy. The program did this by mainly reversing the upward trends in the real interest rate on government securities, public sector borrowing requirement, and domestic debt stock. Moreover, an important amount of primary surplus was registered in 2000 (see table 4). As evident in almost all economic dimensions, the 1999 fiscal performance was the worst in the 1995–2001 period. Then, why did the crisis erupt at the end of 2000, instead of in 1999?

Clearly, an analysis of fiscal indicators will not provide answers on the timing of the crisis. This should come as no surprise, since fiscal laxity does not necessarily end with a currency crisis. Eichengreen, Rose, and Wyplosz, using data from the Organization for Economic Cooperation and Development

(OECD) countries for the postwar period, state that they do not detect any link between lack of fiscal discipline and exchange market turbulence.[8] Frankel and Rose, using annual observations for the 1971–92 period for 105 countries, analyze 117 different crashes. They report that "neither current account nor government budget deficits appear to play an important role in a typical crash."[9] Sachs, Tornell, and Velasco examine financial events following the devaluation of the Mexican peso for a set of twenty emerging markets. They state, "as important as a country's fiscal stance may be in theory, however, it is important to notice that irresponsible fiscal behavior was not among the central causes of recent troubles."[10] Do these observations suggest that there is no correlation between poor fiscal fundamentals and a currency crisis? Sachs and others emphasize that countries with better fiscal performance had the chance to escape from any crisis.[11] Eichengreen and others state (as one of the plausible interpretations of their results) that only money-financed deficits may matter.[12] This is the crucial point, as demonstrated above, since the 1997 deficits were not financed by the central bank's resources.

Looking at table 5, it is evident that the lira was in an overvaluation trend against a basket of currencies from 1995. As of the end of September 2000, the real appreciation relative to 1995 was 14 percent, while for year-end 2000 it was 18 percent. Sachs, Tornell, and Velasco as well as Frankel and Rose demonstrate that one of the predictors of currency crises is real appreciation of domestic currency.[13] Note first, however, that at the start of the program it was publicly announced that the crawling peg system would be replaced in July 2001 by a relatively flexible exchange rate system, with increasing flexibility as time passed.[14] Second, the growth rate of the Turkish economy was, on average, very high in the 1995–97 period (that is, 7.8 percent), when half of the real appreciation was realized. The average growth rate of the 1995–2000 period was 4.6 percent. Hence the standard Balassa-Samuelson effect might be one of the reasons for the real appreciation.

8. Eichengreen, Rose, and Wyplosz (1995).

9. Frankel and Rose (1996, p. 365).

10. Sachs, Tornell, and Velasco (1996a, p. 180).

11. Sachs, Tornell, and Velasco (1996a).

12. Eichengreen, Rose, and Wyplosz (1995).

13. Sachs, Tornell, and Velasco (1996a); Frankel and Rose (1996).

14. However, there are some skeptical views on this exit strategy. For a discussion of the role of the exit strategy in the crisis, see the meeting summary of "NBER Program on Exchange Rate Crises in Emerging Markets: Turkey," held on July 18, 2001, www.nber.org/crisis/turkey_report.html.

Table 5. Balance of Payments and Real Exchange Rate, 1995–2001

Percent of GNP

	1995	1996	1997	1998	1999	2000	2001
Current account balance	−1.4	−1.3	−1.4	1.0	−0.7	−4.9	2.4
Net capital inflows	2.7	3.0	3.7	−0.4	2.5	4.7	−9.8
Short term	2.2	1.5	0.0	0.7	0.4	2.0	−7.9
Direct investment	0.5	0.3	0.3	0.3	0.1	0.1	1.9
Portfolio investment	0.1	0.3	0.9	−3.4	1.8	0.5	−3.1
Other long term	−0.1	0.9	2.5	1.9	0.2	2.1	−0.8
Real exchange rate[a]	96.9	100.0	110.5	107.8	108.7	118.2	107.0

Source: Central Bank of Turkey, Electronic Data Delivery System, www.tcmb.gov.tr.
a. Year-end values, 1995 average equals 100. An increase denotes real appreciation. Value for September 2000 is 114.0.

Was the record high level of current account deficit the major reason behind the crisis? The literature on the sustainability of current account balance stresses that in steady state the current account deficit should be less than the average growth rate of the economy times its net international debt as a share of gross domestic product (GDP). Calvo and Végh suggest that a maximum level of indebtedness is 80 percent of GDP, above which capital markets are reluctant to further extend credit to developing countries.[15] Multiplying 80 percent by the average growth rate of the Turkish economy in the 1969–2000 period (4.4 percent) results in 3.5 percent, which is lower than the ratio of current account deficit to GDP registered in 2000. Hence based on this measure, the current account deficit was high. However, note that the deficit was a one-off. In the preceding two years the current account was almost balanced. In addition, five other key points should be noted. First, long before the end of 2000, the government had announced that it was going to tighten its 2001 budget to reduce the current account deficit. Second, one of the underlying reasons for the high deficit was real appreciation of the lira. As discussed above, Turkey was planning to pass to a more flexible exchange rate regime in July 2001. Third, a major cause of the deficit was the rise in crude petroleum prices. Fourth, the U.S. dollar value of Turkish exports declined due to the appreciation of U.S. dollar against major European currencies, as Europe is a main trading partner of Turkey. Fifth, among others, Sachs, Tornell, and Velasco, along with Frankel and Rose, find that the current account is a poor predictor of currency crises.[16]

To summarize, in the five-year period preceding the crisis, the macroeconomic fundamentals of the last two years of the period were the worst. However,

15. Calvo and Végh (1999).
16. Sachs, Tornell, and Velasco (1996a); Frankel and Rose (1996).

despite a record high level of current account deficit for 2000 and real appreciation of the lira, almost all of the indicators displayed a positive stance in 2000 compared to 1999. This positive stance may be attributed to the IMF-supported stabilization program. Again, one must ask why the crisis erupted at the end of 2000 and not in 1999. The absence of the leading indicators of a first-generation type crisis, coupled with the vulnerability of the economy (despite an improving stance in macroeconomic fundamentals), suggests the possibility of a self-fulfilling crisis.

Second-Generation Type Crisis?

One of the main reasons the Turkish 2000–01 crisis is an interesting case study is that the high public sector borrowing requirement was mainly financed by the issuance of domestic debt in the period preceding the crisis. This financing mechanism, by limiting excess money supply, prevented both a jump in the rate of inflation to higher levels and a continuous depletion in international reserves, leading to a first-generation type crisis. As is well documented elsewhere, domestic borrowing masks foreign exchange losses. The most important point, however, is that if the real interest rate exceeds the real growth rate of the economy and there is no offsetting primary surplus, then domestic debt financing is not stable. Sooner or later this process will come to an end, but the timing depends on actions of the debt market's main actors, rendering the economy open to self-fulfilling attacks.

One can imagine a situation where a government aims to implement a stabilization plan, but, for example, postpones the plan due to a forthcoming election and continues domestic debt financing. Or the country already may be implementing a stabilization plan that addresses fiscal imbalances, but the initial level of the deficit is at such a high level that it may only be feasible to realize the fiscal discipline gradually, which means that debt financing should continue. Based on fundamentals, there is no natural collapse and hence such an economy does not deserve a first-generation type crisis. In the absence of speculative attacks, the prevailing exchange rate system can survive. However, second-generation models argue that exchange rate systems can collapse, because of the attack of speculators who anticipate that the government would abstain from taking necessary measures to defend the currency against an attack. A high public debt or high unemployment may lead to such anticipations.

Does the scenario described above fit the Turkish case? Although it is difficult to answer this question based on what happened in the postcrisis period, an answer can still be provided. There should not be an output decline in the aftermath of a crisis. As Krugman puts it, "if a speculative attack drives a currency off its peg, this does not imply a negative shock to employment and output. Indeed, in this case the contrary should be true: because the policy constraint of a peg is removed, the result is actually positive for short-run macroeconomics."[17] Evidently, this did not happen in Turkey. The economy sharply contracted by 8.5 percent in 2001, after 6 percent growth in 2000. In a similar vein, Flood and Marion note that second-generation crisis models require that in the postcrisis period there should be expansionary policies that validate anticipations of speculators.[18] However, postcrisis policies in Turkey were not expansionary. On the contrary, in May 2001 the Turkish authorities signed a new standby agreement with the IMF, and the primary budget balance registered a record high level of surplus (see table 4).

The discussion in this paper so far reduces the possibility of a second-generation currency crisis, thus necessitating a discussion of other explanations. Was the principal cause of the Turkish crisis a prospective deficit—in this case an additional deficit on top of the existing one—associated with implicit bailout guarantees to a failing banking system? Or was the root cause of the problem financial fragility in the banking sector in the sense of a third-generation model? Note that third-generation models give special importance to self-fulfilling prophecies, just as do second-generation models. Due to triggering events capital flows out of the country, domestic currency depreciates, and either the banking or the corporate sector—or both—collapse, pushing the economy into a deep recession. The collapse in the banking or the corporate sector (or both) is due to financial weakness in balance sheets.

Banking Sector

There is plenty of evidence regarding risk accumulation in Turkish commercial bank balance sheets. It has been shown in this paper that in the period preceding the crisis, the nature of risk accumulation in the banking system

17. Krugman (2001, pp. 6–7).
18. Flood and Marion (2000).

was not homogeneous throughout the system. Two different types of dichotomy were observed: first, the dichotomy between private and state banks, and second, the dichotomy within the private banking industry.

Banking Sector Vulnerability

During a crisis period, a central bank will find itself a lender of last resort for banks and hence its foreign exchange reserves should be compared with liquid liabilities of the banking sector. This is especially important during an exchange rate–based stabilization program. Sachs, Tornell, and Velasco emphasize that even if fundamentals are wrong, a speculative crisis is less likely to occur when there is no problem with international liquidity.[19] This paper uses two alternative definitions of total liquid liabilities of the banking sector. The first one is M2YR, which is the sum of currency in circulation, domestic currency–denominated deposits, foreign currency–denominated deposits, and repurchase agreements (repos) of commercial banks.[20] In the second definition, M1YRS, instead of all deposits regardless of their maturity, only deposits with maturity less than or equal to one month are considered. Two alternative reserve definitions are used. The first one is the official reserves, whereas the second one is the sum of the official reserves and the reserves of the commercial banks.

The first four rows of table 6 provide data for alternative definitions of the ratio of total liquid liabilities of the banking sector to foreign exchange reserves. No matter which definition is used, the conclusion remains the same. Liquidity ratios were stable up until November 2000 and only a slight deterioration materialized before February 2001. Moreover, the magnitudes of alternative ratios are small compared to those of crisis countries. For example, Sachs and others report that a similar ratio took a value of 7 in Mexico in mid-1994 and a value of 10 just before the Mexican crisis.[21] Calvo notes that the ratio was in the range of 2 to 3 for noncrisis countries such as Argentina, Chile, Colombia, and Uruguay.[22] Chang and Velasco argue that the Asian-5 countries— Indonesia, Korea, Malaysia, the Philippines, and Thailand—had a problem of international illiquidity when the Southeast Asian

19. Sachs, Tornell, and Velasco (1996a).
20. In Turkey repos are widely used by commercial banks as a retail instrument for government debt instrument portfolios. Average maturity of repos is rather short, usually less than a month. Their importance in the liability structure of banks is discussed below.
21. Sachs, Tornell, and Velasco (1996b).
22. Calvo (1994).

Table 6. Banking Sector Short-Term Liabilities as a Multiple of International Reserves and the Evaluation of Credit Stock

	1995	*1996*	*1997*	*1998*	*1999*	*2000*[a]	*2000*	*2001*
M1YRS / central bank reserves[b]	1.85	1.76	1.81	1.75	1.49	1.87	2.22	1.78
M1YRS / total reserves[c]	1.04	1.21	1.28	1.21	1.05	1.28	1.46	1.04
M2YR / central bank reserves[d]	3.57	3.48	3.39	3.64	3.53	3.69	4.16	3.98
M2YR / total reserves	2.01	2.39	2.40	2.52	2.47	2.52	2.73	2.32
Credit / GNP (percent)	20.4	23.9	26.2	20.8	20.7	21.0	21.1	18.2
Real credit growth (percent)	18.6	24.6	7.7	−14.7	−13.6	17.4	17.4	−28.2
Consumer credit / total credit (percent)	3.7	4.4	5.6	6.3	6.2	17.5	17.4	7.1

Source: Central Bank of Turkey, Electronic Data Delivery System, www.tcmb.gov.tr.
a. Values for end of September 2000.
b. M1YRS = M1 + repos + foreign currency demand deposits + domestic and foreign currency saving deposits with maturity one month or less.
c. Total reserves = central bank reserves + reserves of commercial banks.
d. M2YR = M2 + foreign currency deposits + repos.

crisis started.[23] The ratio of M2 to reserves was stable at high levels (or increasing) in each of these countries except Thailand, which was a special case, as demonstrated by Chang and Velasco. According to their calculations, the ratio of M2 to reserves was 6.5 in Korea as well as Indonesia, and 4.5 in the Philippines. They also note that the same ratio was about 3.4 in the then noncrisis countries Argentina and Brazil.

Table 6 also provides data on the ratio of total loans of the banking sector to GNP, as well as the real growth rate of the loan portfolio. These indicators are sometimes used as proxies for the banking sector's credit quality. It is argued that rapid credit growth is a signal of increasing credit risk for the banks. It is clear from these data that credit growth in Turkey in 2000 was rather high. However, note that a similar phenomenon was also observed in the noncrisis years, especially in the 1995–97 period. Neither the liquidity ratios nor the credit growth figures justify a crisis. The values they attain are not significantly different than in the noncrisis periods. This necessitates a closer look at the banking sector and the Turkish policy experience after 1999.

This paper now turns to the evolution of more direct measures regarding the risk exposure of domestic commercial banks. Table 7 presents various indicators of the risk exposure of the banking sector in the December 1995–September 2001 period. The figures are reported in three groups, as indicators for the credit risk, foreign exchange risk, and interest rate risk. All of these indicators clearly show that the vulnerability of the banking sector to capital reversals increased throughout 2000.

23. Chang and Velasco (1998a).

Table 7. Ratios of the Commercial Banking Sector, 1995–2001[a]

Percent, except as indicated

	1995	1996	1997	1998	1999	2000[b]	2000[c]	2000[d]	2000	2001[e]
Nonperforming loans / total loans	2.8	2.2	2.4	7.2	10.7	9.8	9.7	9.3	11.6	18.6
Permanent assets / total assets	7.6	7.3	6.7	8.0	9.4	9.4	11.1	13.4	14.8	18.4
FX assets / FX liabilities[f]	90.6	93.6	89.6	84.9	79.4	74.3	73.0	71.6	75.9	81.0
FX liabilities – FX assets (billions of dollars)										
Excluding off balance sheet	3.0	2.5	5.0	8.4	13.2	17.2	19.2	20.9	17.4	12.4
Including off balance sheet	0.6	1.2	1.9	2.9	2.9	5.7	5.6	5.8	5.5	0.7
Liquid FX assets / FX liabilities	44.8	44.6	41.0	39.5	40.0	36.6	35.2	34.4	35.9	38.3
Liquid assets / total sources[g]	46.7	44.0	41.1	39.9	42.6	42.4	41.0	38.3	37.9	51.4
Assets / liabilities (with three months or shorter maturities)	n.a.	n.a.	45.8	45.7	46.3	40.8	41.8	43.9	39.9	43.9
Share of deposits with six months or greater maturity in total deposits	26.1	26.6	24.7	22.9	28.2	19.8	18.7	19.3	15.1	11.6
Repos / (liabilities + repos)[h]	5.1	8.1	12.8	10.4	9.6	12.0	11.4	10.9	11.3	6.1

Source: Central Bank of Turkey; Banks Association of Turkey.
n.a. Not available.
a. End of period figures.
b. Values for end of March 2000.
c. Values for end of June 2000.
d. Values for end of September 2000.
e. Values for end of September 2001.
f. FX denotes "foreign currency denominated".
g. Total sources = deposits + nondeposit funds.
h. Repos had been recorded off the balance sheet since 2002.

Table 8. Ratio of Nonperforming Loans to Loan Portfolio

Percent

Bank	Date of takeover by the SDIF[a]	1997	1998	1999	2000
Sümerbank	December 21, 1999	0.28	1.58	296.70	911.90
Egebank	December 21, 1999	0.56	2.35	211.11	205.30
Esbank	December 21, 1999	3.02	1.52	50.48	118.80
Yurtbank	December 21, 1999	0.22	5.66	1,723.40	7,554.60
Yasarbank	December 21, 1999	0.30	0.41	63.53	87.20
Etibank	October 27, 2000	0.95	0.67	0.00	14.13
Bank Kapital	October 27, 2000	0.95	6.25	6.76	1,115.10
Demirbank	December 6, 2000	0.58	1.74	1.52	5.44

Source: Banks Association of Turkey and Banking Regulation and Supervision Authority.
a. SDIF = Savings Deposits Insurance Fund.

The ratio of nonperforming loans to total loans started to increase in 1998. Table 7 gives figures for the whole banking system, taking public, private, Saving Deposits Insurance Fund (SDIF)-controlled, and foreign banks together. Due to the growing number of banks taken under the control of the SDIF, this ratio reached 10.7 percent in December 1999.[24] This increase in nonperforming loans of the banks taken under SDIF control raised doubts about the quality of both information disclosure and rule enforcement. Combined with the delays in banking reform, this discrepancy in figures immensely blurred the picture regarding the health of the private commercial banks. It was understood that the nonperforming loan ratio increases radically whenever a bank is taken under the control of the SDIF. This point is seen more clearly when the nonperforming loans of the SDIF-controlled banks are analyzed (see table 8).

In the period preceding the crisis, an open foreign exchange position was a structural feature of the Turkish banking system. This phenomenon is related to a long history of high inflation and the inability of domestic banks to borrow long term in their own currency, as is discussed for developing countries in general by Goldfajn and Rigobon.[25] Three different measures of currency risk are presented in table 7, namely, the ratio of foreign currency–denominated assets to foreign currency–denominated liabilities, the open foreign exchange position of the balance sheet, and the aggregated balance sheet, including off balance sheet items. They all point to a significant increase in the foreign exchange risk. While the total open foreign exchange position of the banking

24. Table 11 lists banks taken over by the SDIF.
25. Goldfajn and Rigobon (2000).

system was following an upward trend on the road to the crisis, the ratio of liquid foreign exchange–denominated assets to total foreign exchange–denominated liabilities was following the opposite trend. The latter made the system more vulnerable to sudden reversals.

Maturity mismatch is another structural feature of the banking system in Turkey, due to the inability of domestic banks to borrow long term in the domestic currency. The ratios of assets to liabilities with matching maturities are reported in table 7. The figures show that the liabilities are more of a short-term nature, while the maturities of assets are longer. For example, for one unit of three-month liability, there is a 0.5 unit of three-month asset at the end of 1999. The picture becomes even worse when repos are taken into account. Note also the declining trend in the average maturity of total deposits, especially in 2000.

Banking Sector Dichotomy: Private versus State Banks

Despite the fact that both private and state banks had accumulated risks on the road to the crisis, the nature of their respective problems was different. On the asset side, the increasing size of duty loss accumulation of the state banks and the need to finance duty loss by short-term domestic bank liabilities were the source of the problem.[26] On the liability side, the ratio of lira to foreign exchange liabilities shows one major difference between the two groups. The ratio was much lower and, moreover, was decreasing for private banks. While the state banks were more open to interest rate risk, private ones were more prone to exchange rate risk. This is why the November 2000 crisis hit the state banks hardest and the effect of the currency collapse in February 2001 hit private banks.

Table 9 gives a comparison of the balance sheet structures of private and state banks. In the case of the former, those that were taken under SDIF control in any of the periods reported are not taken into account. The figures are adjusted to include repos in the balance sheets. There are two major interest-earning assets in the Turkish banking system: commercial loans and

26. After 1992 growing government debt instruments outstanding and the increasing financing needs of the Treasury led the government to finance some activities through loans taken from state banks. Instead of repaying the principal and the interest accrued, the Treasury allowed these nonperforming loans to be treated as performing loans by the state banks. The Treasury was directly controlling these banks, since they were state economic enterprises. In addition the Treasury, at that period, was also the banking supervision authority. This conflict of interest might have been one of the most important factors that led to duty loss accumulation. See table 4 for the importance of duty losses relative to other fiscal indicators.

Table 9. Structural Characteristics of Private and State Banks, 1997–2001[a]

	Bank	1997	1998	1999	2000[b]	2000[c]	2000[d]	2000[e]	2001[f]	2001[g]
Loan / GDI[h]	Private	113.72	119.28	82.52	93.26	102.49	111.39	130.70	139.00	144.97
	State	86.24	87.86	66.27	n.a.	n.a.	n.a.	59.22	n.a.	n.a.
Repos / lira deposits	Private	123.36	83.27	106.61	95.23	93.73	105.41	53.48	23.62	25.37
	State	22.49	19.07	13.64	30.29	28.67	29.50	27.27	55.36	41.52
Foreign exchange / lira deposits	Private	212.20	201.63	274.65	285.07	279.99	299.90	209.24	205.37	237.54
	State	46.37	35.61	26.49	31.66	32.42	33.13	29.37	37.12	37.12
Share of foreign exchange loans	Private	14.01	13.97	15.91	16.28	16.51	17.10	19.84	20.02	19.55
	State	3.07	3.18	2.30	2.13	2.78	2.85	2.54	3.36	2.78
Share of interest earning assets	Private	67.80	63.66	63.22	60.79	61.88	60.92	58.05	53.95	52.73
	State	36.63	35.34	28.85	n.a.	n.a.	n.a.	31.88	n.a.	n.a.
Share of accumulated duty losses	State	27.07	27.59	32.01	n.a.	n.a.	n.a.	30.68	n.a.	n.a.
Share of net worth	Private	9.13	9.87	11.29	12.16	12.83	13.85	12.39	11.25	9.65
	State	5.38	3.85	3.80	3.78	3.50	3.20	2.69	3.78	3.50

Source: Central Bank of Turkey.
n.a. Not available.
a. End of period data.
b. Values for end of March 2000.
c. Values for end of June 2000.
d. Values for end of September 2000.
e. Values for end of December 2000.
f. Values for end of March 2001.
g. Values for end of June 2001.
h. GDI = Government debt instruments.

government debt instruments. At the end of 1999, for example, when Turkey launched its exchange rate–based stabilization program, the share of the government debt instruments portfolio in private commercial bank balance sheets was even greater than the loan portfolio. The quality of the government debt instruments portfolio is directly related to the expectations regarding debt sustainability. This feature was increasing the vulnerability of bank balance sheets to concerns about the rollover possibility of the outstanding government debt instruments. Note that the situation in Turkey is not directly comparable with the "bad" private loan problems of East Asian commercial banks. In the case of the health of the Turkish private banking industry, smooth debt rollover is much more important. This issue needs to be understood to follow the factors triggering the crisis in November 2000. It is also important in discussing the balance sheet effects after the currency collapse.

The ratio of loan portfolio to government debt instrument portfolio is systematically lower in the case of state banks, due to the smaller size of their commercial loan portfolios. Moreover, from 1997 to 2000, this ratio continued to decline. The ratio of interest earning assets to total assets shows that the size of the commercial loan portfolios of state banks was rather small. Notice that the ratio for state banks is about half of the ratio for private banks. The reason for this discrepancy lies in the share of loans granted to the Treasury by state banks and later treated as a duty loss by the Treasury. The share of duty loss accumulated reached more than 30 percent of total assets.

A liability feature of private commercial bank balance sheets is that it reflects the banks' inability to borrow long term in domestic currency. The high ratio of repos to Turkish lira deposits is an indication of this. Banks used repos as a retail instrument to carry government debt instrument portfolios indirectly. However, all of the interest rate risk remains with the bank selling the repo contracts. The maturity of repos was much shorter than the maturity of lira deposits, which was around three months in 1999. While the ratio was on a declining trend for private banks after the November crisis, a reverse trend is observed for state banks. This amounts to saying that before the November 2000 crisis, state banks could borrow at relatively longer maturities. With the interest rate hike after November, the growing ratio of repos to lira deposits raised the cost of funds to state banks enormously, requiring immediate action by the Treasury or bank regulators, or both, starting from May 2001.

Another distinguishing feature of the private banks was their heavy reliance on the foreign exchange–denominated deposits of residents. The ratio of foreign exchange to lira deposits captures this feature. However, the maturity of foreign exchange deposits was also short, as in the case of lira deposits. Heavy reliance of private banks on foreign exchange deposits made them more vulnerable to international illiquidity crisis. In the period preceding the crisis, private banks relied more on foreign exchange loans from international banks. This was an additional factor that rendered them more vulnerable to capital reversals.

Banking Sector Dichotomy: Private Banks

This paper now turns to the heterogeneity of the private domestic commercial banking system. Regarding the banking crisis in Turkey, Eichengreen argues that the problem was with "a number of mid-sized banks [that] had taken highly-leveraged positions in anticipation of continued declines in interest rates."[27] It is true that the events leading to the actual crisis in November started with a mid-size bank, Demirbank, which had taken a highly leveraged position. The problem was the very risky mode of carrying a government debt instrument portfolio, which dates back to 1995 and became more acute over time. This risky mode of financing could also be found in the balance sheets of all private banks, as noted earlier. However, in the case of Demirbank this risky mode of financing led to enormous risk accumulation in its balance sheet when compared to the rest of the system. In this sense Demirbank could be taken as a prime example of commercial banks carrying large government debt instrument portfolios. Demirbank was heavily concentrated in the government debt instrument business and was acting as a market maker to defend its position.

The sharp differences between Demirbank and private banks are reported in table 10. First, for Demirbank, the ratio of government debt instrument portfolio to total assets was about twice the size of other private banks. Unlike other private banks, this bank was not active in traditional banking business of collecting deposits and distributing loans.

Second, Demirbank was carrying its government debt instrument portfolio mainly through short-term repos. The ratio of repos to total government debt instrument portfolio was around 70 percent at year-end 1999 and 2000. While financing the government debt instrument portfolio—mainly by very short-term repos—the share of long-term government debt instruments in its total portfolio was also very high. This share jumped rather sharply just before

27. Eichengreen (2001, footnote 8).

the November 2000 crisis, increasing the vulnerability of the bank to an upward movement in interest rates.

Third, Demirbank was carrying a large, long-term, government debt instrument portfolio by financing its activities mostly through overnight borrowing from other banks, as table 10 demonstrates by the ratio of bank repos to total repos. Put differently, the fact that banks are more informed investors had made Demirbank more vulnerable. A potential cut of this short-term credit line would have jeopardized the viability of Demirbank. Indeed, this was what happened in November 2000.

Fourth, the ratio of foreign exchange to lira liabilities was lower in the case of Demirbank, as most of its activities were financed by lira repos. However, the sharp increase in this ratio at the beginning of 2000 and its sharp decline in the fourth quarter require further elaboration. The rise in the ratio of long-term government debt instruments to total government debt instruments juxtaposed this development. This seems to be related to the fact that structured financing products started to be used by the domestic banking system in general—and by Demirbank in particular. In the case of structured loans, Turkish lira–denominated government debt instruments were used as collateral against foreign borrowing, and were accounted for as long-term government debt instruments in the balance sheets. With increasing financing difficulties, Demirbank seems to have resorted to foreign exchange borrowing by using domestic currency–denominated government debt instruments as collateral. In the case of structured loan agreements, there is a prespecified stop-loss level of government debt instruments' interest rates to start the automatic sale of the collateral portfolio. This feature of structured loans was instrumental in the massive sell-off in the debt market, accompanied by a massive demand for foreign exchange, in November 2000—right after the financing difficulties of Demirbank. The latter feature gave the crisis a systemic character. In the end, difficulties at a single, midsize bank turned into a crisis for the whole debt market. The situation then exploded into a crisis for the whole domestic banking system, since government debt instrument portfolios were an important interest earning asset in domestic bank balance sheets.

Third-Generation Type Crisis?

This paper concludes that the Turkish financial system, which was dominated by banks, was vulnerable to spikes in both the exchange rate and the

Table 10. Dichotomy in the Private Banking Sector: Demirbank versus Others[a]

		1997	1998	1999	2000[b]	2000[c]	2000[d]	2000[e]	2001[f]	2001[g]
Total GDI[h] / total assets	Sector	31.72	29.03	34.64	31.45	30.56	28.82	25.16	22.57	21.52
	Demirbank	58.54	57.09	65.12	58.33	54.68	63.53	67.50	74.98	67.63
Repos / GDI + repos	Sector	60.24	48.51	38.66	37.51	38.06	40.94	33.04	17.73	20.75
	Demirbank	68.30	57.16	69.48	66.40	59.10	64.81	70.69	52.60	19.57
Bank repos / total repos	Sector	20.64	22.51	19.09	14.93	28.57	21.08	5.48	0.24	6.62
	Demirbank	29.02	24.08	41.97	32.49	33.25	23.93	48.31	0.15	20.73
Share of interest earning assets	Sector	67.80	63.66	63.22	60.79	61.88	60.92	58.05	53.95	52.73
	Demirbank	77.44	72.86	79.57	73.57	78.14	85.34	93.21	98.06	84.60
Long-term GDI / GDI	Sector	9.95	8.37	18.43	20.30	25.12	36.62	44.98	62.63	69.26
	Demirbank	23.49	27.15	27.15	28.83	36.41	45.33	12.79	22.38	27.43
Foreign exchange / lira liabilities	Sector	135.48	155.11	194.23	213.31	213.21	219.72	219.47	262.14	279.32
	Demirbank	43.59	109.89	69.41	88.14	112.63	73.78	36.91	53.08	91.62

Source: Central Bank of Turkey.
a. End of period values.
b. Values for end of March 2000.
c. Values for end of June 2000.
d. Values for end of September 2000.
e. Values for end of December 2000.
f. Values for end of March 2001.
g. Values for end of June 2001.
h. GDI—Government debt instruments.

interest rate that a sudden capital reversal could cause. Moreover, this weakness sharply increased in 2000.

Turkey's banking sector problem was basically a result of the mechanism chosen to finance a very high public sector borrowing requirement. First, this led to an increase in government debt instruments, especially in the balance sheets of private banks. Second, it caused a significant deterioration in state-owned banks by accumulating duty losses. Risk accumulation in bank balance sheets, in order to carry the domestic debt stock, is an important element of crisis dynamics. Due to excessive risks accumulated in their balance sheets, credit lines were cut off to some banks that were specifically acting as market makers in the government debt instruments market (and hence accumulating larger than average GDI portfolios). Thus the banking sector problem turned into a debt rollover problem, increasing interest rates. The rise in interest rates changed the nature of the problem into a debt sustainability issue directly making rollover impossible. This happened despite the continuing fiscal discipline policy under an IMF-supported program.

At the core of some variants of the third-generation crisis models there is the vulnerability of the financial system.[28] Despite similarities, the Turkish crisis has some features that do not fit third-generation models, most notable being the high budget deficit, which was mainly financed by domestic debt. This feature renders useless one of the prescriptions of the variant of a third-generation model introduced by Krugman.[29] Krugman stresses the corporate sector balance sheet implications of a currency crisis, and the model he presents suggests fiscal expansion as one of the remedies to overcome the high exchange rate–low output equilibrium of the postcrisis period. This is hardly a solution in an economy where the main concern of the economic agents was the sustainability of domestic public debt, as at least in the first ten months of 2001 in Turkey.

Burnside, Eichenbaum, and Rebelo argue that a principal cause of the 1997 Asian crisis was large, prospective deficits associated with implicit bailout guarantees to failing banking systems.[30] Economic agents expect that these future deficits are going to be financed by money creation, which leads to a collapse of the fixed exchange rate regimes. The Turkish case also has some similarities with prospective deficits models.

---

28. For example, see Chang and Velasco (1998b).
29. Krugman (1999a and 1999b).
30. Burnside, Eichenbaum, and Rebelo (2001).

Triggering Factors

What were the factors igniting the crisis, and what were the responses of commercial banks to these factors? The role of these triggering factors in the severe dichotomizations of the banking sector, which led to credit line cuts, is examined below, emphasizing that this dichotomy did not materialize overnight. There was already enough risk accumulated in bank balance sheets. The igniting factors worked as a catalyst, bringing this dichotomy to a severe conclusion, with credit line cuts as banks stopped trading with each other. Delays in structural reforms, especially the inability to design a transparent and viable banking reform strategy at the outset—and the unsystematic as well as piecemeal nature of the SDIF intervention in "bad" banks—exacerbated the problem.

Structural Reforms Delayed

Structural reforms constituted an important part of the standby agreement signed with the IMF. These reforms were collected under six headings in the letter of intent: Pension Reform; Reform in Agriculture Sector, Tax Policy and Administration, Fiscal Management and Transparency, Privatization and the Capital Market, Strengthening the Banking Sector, and Banking Regulation. Hence the issue of banking reform was already considered in principle right at the outset of the agreement.

The main problems were in the last three areas. Under the fiscal management and transparency heading, the government promised to close sixty-one budgetary funds to broaden the effective coverage of the budget in 2000, whereas only twenty-seven of these funds were actually closed. The markets paid special attention to the privatization of the telecom sector. The discussions on this privatization began as early as 1990, but several laws passed by the parliament since then were then rejected by the Supreme Court. The IMF insisted on passing a new law to enable Turk Telecom to act as a private entity by making it subject to the Turkish commercial code and establish a regulatory body for this sector. There were sharp differences of opinion between the members of the government on this issue, and as a result the law was not drafted. Finally, the board of the Banking Regulation and Supervision Agency should have been named by the end of March 2000 so it would have been in full operation by the end of August. This task was accomplished on August 31, after a five-month delay, increasing concerns about the government's intentions regarding manipulating the board and causing a credibility loss.

In addition to delays in implementation, the program's lack of political and administrative leadership also contributed to uncertainty. The details of the program did not become public knowledge in a systematic manner. Especially in terms of banking reform, this lack of public knowledge was detrimental, contributing to severe dichotomy in the banking system and leading to credit line cuts. The announcement that the banking system had a problem, without any detailed and systematic program to show how the authorities were thinking of solving the problem and with long periods of inaction exacerbated the problem of heterogeneity in the banking sector, leading to a halt in trading.

SDIF Takeovers and Unending Court Cases

Just before the 2000–02 program was put into action, five banks were taken over by the SDIF, on December 21, 1999. This action did not alleviate the banking system's problems. Two more banks were taken over by the SDIF on October 27, 2000. These last two takeovers materialized only a month after the Banking Regulation and Supervision Agency board was named. The last four months of 2000 were especially hard times for some bankers. In September 2000, police initiated a criminal investigation—code name "Hurricane"— and started to arrest the owners and executives of five of these seven banks (see table 11). News about the arrested bankers, accompanied by videotapes and photographs of their arrest, were covered extensively by the media. This news was not limited to the financial section of newspapers or business programming on television. Rather, the news made the front page and primetime. The media's intense coverage of the arrests on this operation intensified rumors about who was going to be arrested next. Bankers acquired the nickname "tunnelers," the idea behind which was the same as the "tunneling" concept used by Johnson and others regarding newly privatized enterprises in postcommunist countries.[31]

All of these developments strengthened the idea that there was an immense problem in the private banking industry, and that the program to tackle the issue was not completed. The extensive press coverage of arrested bankers itself contributed to the uncertainty regarding the future of the banking industry. It also raised doubts about the possible costs that would be incurred very shortly. Considering the cost of banking reform to the public purse and the

31. Johnson and others (2000). The term tunneling, as used by Turkish media, refers to related lending much above regulatory limits and favorable treatment of companies that are owned by the owners of the banks.

Table 11. Banks Taken Over by the SDIF, 1999–2001[a]

Bank	Date of the takeover	Share in total assets as of the takeover year	Were any of the owners or the executives arrested?
Sümerbank	December 21, 1999	0.6	Yes, October–November 2000
Egebank	December 21, 1999	0.6	Yes, October–November 2000
Esbank	December 21, 1999	0.8	No
Yasarbank	December 21, 1999	0.5	No
Yurtbank	December 21, 1999	0.6	Yes, October–November 2000
Etibank	October 27, 2000	1.2	Yes, October–November 2000
Bank Kapital	October 27, 2000	0.3	Yes, October–November 2000
Demirbank	December 6, 2000	2.4	No
Ulusalbank	February 28, 2001	0.1	No
Iktisat	March 15, 2001	0.7	No
Bayındırbank	July 10, 2001	0.2	No
EGS Bank	July 10, 2001	0.5	No
Sitebank	July 10, 2001	0.1	No
Kentbank	July 10, 2001	1.0	No
Toprakbank	November 30, 2001	1.0	No

Source: Banks Association of Turkey, Banking Regulation and Supervision Authority, and various daily newspapers.
a. SDIF = Savings Deposit Insurance Fund.

use of government debt instruments to recapitalize banks, concerns about future debt sustainability increased. These concerns intensified on the road to the crisis. And the environment also contributed to severe polarization in the banking system between allegedly good and allegedly bad banks.

Turbulence in November 2000

The banking sector fragility made life very difficult for those banks that had desperately chosen to borrow in short-term maturity and lend to the government in relatively longer terms. Adding to the problem was the fact that state banks were suffering from duty losses. These state banks had been heavily dependent on overnight funds and found themselves in a position where they could not conduct business as usual. Demirbank could not borrow in the overnight market on October 20. So as not to exceed the IMF ceilings on net domestic assets, the Central Bank of Turkey did not lend to Demirbank. This forced Demirbank either to sell part of its government securities portfolio or stop acting as a market maker in the government debt instrument market on the buying side (both of which led to similar market repercussions), causing an increase in secondary market interest rates. This marked the start of the first period in the crisis. The rise in interest rates to the "stop-loss" levels in structured foreign exchange–denominated loans started a new wave of sell-offs of government debt instruments. Consequently, demand for foreign currency increased sharply as lira-denominated government debt instruments were used as collateral for foreign exchange borrowing. Due to this sell-off, secondary market interest rates increased, further raising doubts about debt sustainability and the stability of the exchange rate–based stabilization program.

This paper divides the first attack period into three phases: November 20–21, November 22–29, and November 30–December 6. Note that this periodization depends on the changes in central bank policy. In the first phase the Central Bank of Turkey did not lend to problematic banks, while in the second one it did the opposite.[32] The sharp difference in the evolution of net domestic assets is noted in table 12. Though the domestic credit expansion helped to prevent interest rates from skyrocketing, at the same time, it increased the drain on international reserves. Note, further, that the magnitude of depletion of official reserves was greater than the magnitude of expansion in domestic credit creation, creating a reduction in base money. Hence the second phase witnessed a further rise in interest rates.

Mainly based on the drain on its international reserves and the reluctance of the regulation and supervision agency to address the root of the problem— that is, by taking over the system's bad banks—the Central Bank of Turkey announced on November 30 that it was going to keep its net domestic assets level constant. This marked the beginning of the third phase of the first attack period. Consequently, on that day the overnight rate jumped to 316 percent. This made life harder for state-owned banks, where there was a huge, accumulated interest rate risk potential. The next day's headline news was the middle-of-the-night negotiation with the IMF and the increased possibility of a new credit line. This news notwithstanding, the overnight rate jumped to 873 percent. Despite its announcement, on December 4 the central bank had to lend to a problematic bank to prevent that bank's default. Two days later, that problematic bank, Demirbank, was taken over, and the IMF made it clear that it was going to support the program by opening a new credit line. The

32. This asymmetric behavior was a matter of controversy. In the first phase Demirbank was the main problem. The reason behind such a policy was that the injection of liquidity would be a fruitless attempt, given the bank's nonviability. Moreover, one of the main pillars of the 2000–02 program was the preannounced crawling peg exchange rate regime. Such a move would have exacerbated the attack. The correct policy should have been to take over Demirbank immediately. However, the takeover did not occur until the late date of December 6. In the meantime, the difficulties of Demirbank turned into a systemic crisis, and the central bank had to change its policy.

new letter of intent was made public on December 18, and four days later the central bank announced its new monetary program. Despite the fact that the former limits put on the central bank's balance sheet by the IMF were changed, the path of the rate of depreciation of Turkish lira was not. Because of the agreement with the IMF, the reserve decline came to an end. Moreover, with the IMF's support facility, official reserves jumped to a level of $28.2 billion from a low of $18.3 billion (see figure 4). These events helped to calm the markets.

Final Eruption: February 19, 2001

A new problem emerged in the aftermath of the November crisis: the inconsistency between the interest rate level and the preannounced rate of depreciation of the Turkish lira. This was related to questions regarding the Treasury's ability to rollover debt, as the major market maker of government debt instruments was no longer in the picture. The upper limit of the annual rate of depreciation of the lira against a basket of euros and dollars was announced as 12 percent in 2001. But throughout the auctions in January 2001, the Treasury was not able to borrow below 57 percent in annual compounded terms. In the first auction of February, the interest rate increased to 70 percent. That was clearly an unsustainable situation. Either the interest rate should have declined to a level compatible with the rate of depreciation or the exchange rate regime should have collapsed.

On February 19, after a National Security Council meeting, the prime minister declared that he and the president were in deep disagreement, without naming a specific cause. He added that the disagreement amounted to a very important political crisis. The prime minister's announcement caused the overnight rate to skyrocket to 2,058 percent on February 20, followed by 4,019 percent on the following day (see table 12). On the date the announcement was made, the banking sector rushed to foreign currency. Since the U.S. markets were closed on that specific date, the banking sector foreign currency demand was not fully met by the central bank, which prevented a loss of $7.5 billion of reserves.[33] However, the depletion of reserves in the next two days and the interest rate level forced the government to accept the collapse of the crawling peg system on the night of February 21. Following the announcement that the lira would be allowed to float freely, the dollar exchange rate jumped to 958,000 liras from a level of 685,000 liras. The undersecretary of

33. On this issue see Central Bank of Turkey (2001, p. 94).

Table 12. Balance Sheet of the Central Bank, Interest and Exchange Rates, November–December 2000 and February 2001

Date	Net domestic assets[a] (trillions of lira)	Net foreign assets[b] (trillions of lira)	Base money[c] (trillions of lira)	Reserves[d] (millions of dollars)	Overnight rate[e] (percent)	Bond rate[f] (percent)	Exchange rate (dollar/lira)
First attack period, 2000							
November 15	−1,828	7,092	5,264	24,161	81.5	40.8	681,799
16	−1,873	7,334	5,461	24,520	73.7	38.5	682,942
17	−1,866	7,273	5,407	24,433	34.4	40.1	683,645
First phase							
November 20	−2,035	7,108	5,073	24,185	45.5	42.1	686,461
21	−1,992	6,959	4,967	23,842	66.5	46.1	687,009
Second phase							
November 22	−362	5,909	5,547	22,263	110.8	52.0	688,360
23	−1,357	5,950	4,593	22,284	85.5	49.4	688,849
24	−498	5,475	4,977	21,583	115.1	53.5	689,042
27	−523	5,258	4,735	21,291	80.5	50.3	689,213
28	233	4,336	4,569	20,080	184.5	67.7	685,762
29	1,162	3,649	4,811	19,161	160.8	79.0	682,883
Third phase							
November 30	1,172	3,348	4,520	18,820	315.9	97.6	682,101
December 1	1,094	3,422	4,516	18,942	873.1	84.1	681,032
4	1,832	2,958	4,790	18,299	782.5	131.4	676,239
5	1,707	2,812	4,519	18,285	363.2	71.3	679,404
6	1,597	3,134	4,731	18,633	182.7	73.9	678,875
7	1,096	3,608	4,704	19,267	119.6	74.7	675,379
8	1,045	3,762	4,807	19,624	94.7	88.9	677,108

Second attack period, 2001

February	15	−1,754	6,680	4,927	28,217	39.2	61.9	685,998
	16	−1,547	6,649	5,102	27,943	40.3	63.4	685,039
	19	−1,626	6,708	5,082	28,105	43.7	67.9	683,074
	20	−1,300	5,687	4,387	26,739	2,057.7	25,514.7	688,001
February	21	868	3,417	4,286	23,207	4,018.6	150.2	685,391
	22	2,070	3,373	5,443	23,267	1,195.3	147.7	957,879
	23	1,560	4,198	5,758	22,581	568.0	195.8	1,072,988
	26	1,205	4,046	5,251	21,988	102.1	145.3	946,306
	27	1,659	3,311	4,970	21,699	100.2	168.7	906,164
	28	2,156	2,915	5,071	21,432	100.1	245.3	920,678

Source: Central Bank of Turkey, Electronic Data Delivery System, www.tcmb.gov.tr.

a. Net domestic assets = credit to public sector + government securities + credit to banking sector − public sector deposits + other.

b. Net foreign assets = foreign assets − foreign exchange liabilities to nonresidents − foreign exchange liabilities to banking sector.

c. Base money = net domestic assets + net foreign assets

d. Reserves are international reserves.

e. Overnight rate is the weighted average uncompounded rate.

f. Bond rate is the compounded average secondary market rate.

the Treasury and the governor of the central bank resigned, which was followed by the replacement of the economy minister.

Conclusions

Analyzing the 2000 data in isolation, one would immediately observe poor macroeconomic performance. The public sector borrowing requirement, ratio of public debt to GNP, current account deficit, inflation level, and the ratio of the liabilities of the financial sector to official reserves were all high. Moreover, the lira was appreciated in real terms. However, this analysis would be a misleading picture of the Turkish economy. Turkey started to implement an IMF-supported program at the beginning of 2000. This program addressed macroeconomic imbalances and succeeded (to some extent) in reversing the negative trend. Relative to 1999, there was a sharp decline in both inflation and real interest rates as well as a significant increase in primary surplus. Consequently, the ratio of debt to GNP and the public sector borrowing requirement decreased.

It is true that the rising current account deficit and real appreciation of the lira was a source of increasing concern. However, an important part of the current account deficit was due to external shocks—rising oil prices and appreciation of the U.S. dollar against major European currencies. And, there was a built-in exit strategy from the crawling peg system, which was the main factor behind appreciation. Moreover, the program envisaged a further fiscal tightening for 2001 that would have been one of the remedies for the current account problem.

This paper argues that without a fragile banking system and triggering factors, the high current account deficit and real appreciation of the lira would not have been enough on their own to precipitate the 2000–01 crisis. There was risk accumulation in the banking system in the period preceding the crisis. For example, there was an increase in currency and maturity mismatches as well as a rise in nonperforming loans. Hence the banking system was highly vulnerable to capital reversals. However, risk accumulation was not homogenous throughout the system. There were two different types of dichotomization: private versus state banks and within the private banks. While the state banks were more open to interest rate risk, private ones were more prone to exchange rate risk. Within the private banking system there were some midsize banks that were heavily concentrated in government debt instrument business. Moreover, they were carrying these instruments by borrowing in the extreme short term.

Given the weakness in the banking system, it is no surprise that the crisis triggering factors were closely related to the banking sector and its practice of carrying government debt instrument portfolios. Main igniting factors were the delays in reforming the banking sector and the actions that caused the dichotomy in the banking sector to come to the surface. This environment made things extremely difficult for those banks that had desperately chosen to borrow in short-term maturity and lend to the government in relatively longer terms. Things were also difficult for state banks, which were suffering from duty losses. These banks that had been heavily dependent on overnight funds found themselves in a position not to be able to do business as usual.

Finally, one should note that the root cause of the banking system fragility was the high public sector borrowing requirement and the way it was financed. There was no close link between rising deficits and inflation, beginning as early as the 1990s. The main reason was that budget deficits were primarily financed through government securities. However, the sustainability of this financing mechanism was conditional on the continuation of demand for government securities. In the absence of a program that would have reduced borrowing requirements, a halt in demand would have forced authorities to monetize and hence would have caused a jump in both the exchange rate and the inflation rate. This led economic policymakers to try to prevent a decline in the demand for government securities. These policies, coupled with the upward trend in banks' government debt instrument portfolios, increased the vulnerability of the banking system. The role of monetary policy in risk accumulation in the period preceding the crisis is a topic for an upcoming paper.

Appendix A: Postcrisis Period

Both the Turkish banking system and corporate sector were severely affected by the 2000–01 crisis. The immediate recapitalization needs of the state-owned banks and the banks taken over by the Saving Deposits Insurance Fund led to a jump in the domestic debt stock, which was already too high. Meanwhile, rapid depreciation of the exchange rate had the potential of starting a new inflationary process. Additionally, policymakers lost their credibility. The undersecretary of the Treasury resigned, as did the central bank's governor. To overcome these problems, Turkey announced a new, IMF-supported pro-

Table A–1. Macroeconomic Indicators of the January 2001–July 2002 Period[a]

Date	Average exchange rate (lira/dollar)	Average secondary market interest rate (percent)	Average Treasury borrowing rate (percent)	Eurobond spread (end of period, basis points)	Annual inflation rate (CPI, percent)	Expected year-end inflation rate (CPI, percent)	Annual industrial production growth rate (percent)
January 2001	672,240	60.1	65.0	729	35.9	n.a.	7.5
February	739,889	103.1	122.5	936	33.4	n.a.	–4.9
March	968,299	154.8	193.8	990	37.5	n.a.	–7.6
April	1,209,865	127.0	130.5	864	48.3	n.a.	–9.6
May	1,132,510	85.1	82.0	833	52.4	n.a.	–9.4
June	1,215,605	83.2	88.4	848	56.1	n.a.	–10.1
July	1,320,506	95.2	91.9	1,021	56.3	n.a.	–11.0
August	1,400,947	89.1	92.7	904	57.5	63.7	–10.8
September	1,469,858	87.9	87.6	929	61.8	64.8	–9.2
October	1,600,157	87.7	86.4	884	66.5	68.4	–13.6
November	1,521,208	77.6	79.3	755	67.3	72.0	–14.4
December	1,452,198	72.6	74.1	678	68.5	69.8	–8.1
January 2002	1,369,182	70.8	71.4	641	73.2	47.3	–2.2
February	1,349,975	69.6	70.0	640	73.1	47.5	–5.0
March	1,356,993	65.2	68.5	591	65.1	43.6	19.2
April	1,317,739	56.6	58.7	577	52.7	37.0	14.8
May	1,389,555	57.0	55.3	629	46.2	36.7	11.1
June	1,523,940	69.1	72.3	847	42.6	35.2	7.1
July	1,649,121	75.4	72.6	912	41.3	35.7	12.4

Source: Central Bank of Turkey.

n.a. Not available.

a. Average figures are the monthly averages of daily data. Eurobond spread is the spread between the thirty-year Turkish Treasury eurobond yield and thirty-year U.S. bond yield. Annual figures denote annualized values for the monthly data, that is they are calculated as $[(X(t)/X(t-12)) - 1]*100$. Expected inflation data come from the biweekly survey of the Central Bank of Turkey.

gram in May 2001. The new program had three pillars: fiscal and monetary discipline, structural reforms, and a substantial amount of external financial support.

Based on the 2001–03 program, economic fundamentals continuously improved. However, up to October 2001 the markets' reaction was not in line with fundamentals. The situation was reversed in the October 2001–May 2002 period. The nominal exchange rate, inflation rate, interest rate, and Turkish eurobonds spreads all followed a significant downward trend. With the surge in political uncertainty at the beginning of May 2002, which was perceived by market participants as policy uncertainty, this positive stance began to change (table A-1).

The key to understanding these contrasting phenomena is the high ratio of domestic public debt to GDP and the issue of its sustainability. The imposed fiscal and monetary discipline of the program and the accompanying structural reforms notwithstanding, reducing the debt-to-GDP ratio to manageable levels requires a considerable time period. In the interim period, such an economy is vulnerable to changes in market sentiment, which increases concerns about the debt sustainability. Such a high level of debt raises the possibility of multiple equilibria. Given the macroeconomic fundamentals, the type of equilibrium in which the economy is in, or approaching, is mainly determined by expectations.[34] Negative expectations can lead an economy to a "bad" equilibrium, at which the rates of inflation, interest, and exchange are all high. Positive expectations will yield a "good" equilibrium. Based on this possibility, one should look at both fundamentals and expectations.

Fundamentals and Expectations: May 2001–October 2001

Right after the twin crises, Turkey took key structural reform measures:
—"Bad" banks were taken over by the SDIF and excluded from the banking system.
—The overnight borrowing of these excluded banks was significantly reduced, and some of the banks were recapitalized or merged, or both, while some were actually sold.
—There was a dramatic change in the governance structure of state-owned banks. Accumulated debts of the Treasury to these banks were paid and the state banks were recapitalized.

---

34. See, for example, Calvo (1988).

—A politically independent board of directors was appointed. The board's mandate was specified as protecting the interests of depositors.

—A new management for these state banks was appointed, and the number of branches and employees were significantly reduced according to an operational restructuring plan.

—In May 2001 the central bank law was changed and the bank gained "tool independence." The law explicitly stated that the main goal of the bank is price stability.

—In addition to structural reforms, both the fiscal and monetary policies remained on track.

However, excluding a few weeks from prior to the September 11 terrorist attack in the United States and up to mid-October, market expectations were not in line with the improvement in fundamentals. The interest rate stayed at a high level. The exchange rate followed an upward trend. The spread of the Turkish Treasury bond stayed at high levels (see table A-1). That is, the Turkish economy was at a bad equilibrium. But why?

There were at least four factors hampering gains in policy credibility: First, some political developments—that is, disputes among the coalition parties regarding some of the structural reforms—increased doubts about the continuation of the program and raised the tensions in the market. Second, as documented in this paper, the financial sector had a significant amount of open foreign exchange position before the crisis—that is, the sharp depreciation of Turkish lira did have an adverse impact on the balance sheets of the entire banking system. Third, there were external shocks, namely, negative developments in Argentina were thought to have the potential for a contagion effect on Turkey. Fourth, the exchange rate regime was radically altered and economic agents were not familiar with a floating exchange rate regime environment.

These developments led to negative expectations by the markets, as the sustainability of public debt was continuously questioned. There was a vicious cycle: despite improving macroeconomic fundamentals, negative expectations were pushing the economy to a bad equilibrium. That bad equilibrium, in turn, was validating negative expectations. In early August the exchange rate volatility started to decline, and this was seen as a positive sign for gains in policy credibility. However, the tragic events of September 11 reversed market sentiment. In just a few days time, interest rates increased by some fifteen percentage points and the Turkish lira depreciated considerably. Once again, the sustainability of the program began to be questioned.

Changing Market Sentiment: October 2001–May 2002

This worsening trend halted as it became evident that Turkey was going to further strengthen the ongoing program by additional structural fiscal measures and a banking sector recapitalization program aiming for a quick recovery of sound banks. Also, there was the additional credit line from the IMF. The government announced its primary surplus target for 2002 as 6.5 percent of GDP. This announcement was found credible by market participants, since it became evident that the ambitious primary budget surplus target of 6.5 percent of GNP for 2001 was, in fact, going to be met. In addition, developments in the central bank's balance sheet were in line with the constraints agreed to by the IMF. One should also add to these positive developments the fact that the political disputes among the coalition parties were finally out of the picture. There were other contributing factors as well, listed below:

—First, the fundamental differences between the Argentine and Turkish economies, such as the exchange rate regimes and the fiscal policies, became more apparent.

—Second, it was understood that the Turkish economy was going to register an important amount of current account surplus.

—Third, banks started to partially roll over their foreign credits.

—Fourth, the economic agents began to get used to the mechanics of the floating exchange rate regime and, since the beginning of August, the central bank's intervention in the foreign exchange market had been almost nil.

—Fifth, the structural reforms in the public sector were continued.

—Sixth, to finalize the restructuring of the financial sector, in February 2002 a recapitalization law was passed. In May 2002 all capital-deficient private banks presented their detailed capital strengthening plans to the Banking Regulation and Supervision Agency.

—Seventh, at the beginning of 2002, a debt management law, designed like a fiscal responsibility act, was enacted by parliament. All these measures helped the market understand that the authorities maintained a disinflation objective.

Consequently, the nominal exchange rate followed an almost continuously declining trend from mid-October up to the beginning of May 2002. A similar phenomenon was also observed in the interest rates. In March 2002, for the first time since the eruption of the crisis, the industrial production index showed positive growth. This growth stance continued in the following months, indicating that a significant output recovery process was under way. Inflation that was 68 percent at the end of 2001 started to decline and reached a level of 41 percent in annualized terms in July. Moreover, the gap between the inflationary expectations and the year-end target for 2002 continuously narrowed, also indicating a build-up of confidence and policy credibility. A similar phenomenon was also observed in the Turkish Treasury eurobond spreads (see table A-1).

Political and Policy Uncertainty

From the beginning of May, two negative developments occurred in the political arena. First, the prime minister was hospitalized and there were widespread rumors about his health. This was considered lethal to political stability, as it led to the possibility of a meltdown in his party—the party with the largest representation in a three-party coalition government. Second, discussions about the necessary steps that should be taken to meet the Copenhagen criteria—which would start the negotiation process for possible European Union accession—started to undermine the unity of the coalition government. The resulting political uncertainty led to an environment of policy uncertainty. Although there was no change in the fiscal and monetary policy stance, as of the beginning of May 2002, interest rate, exchange rate, and Treasury spreads once again started to deteriorate, demonstrating the importance and the fragility of market expectations once again.

Comments
and Discussion

Peter Garber: When Brookings asked for a comment on Özatay and Sak's paper, I tried to remember how we were thinking about Turkey going into the crisis. Our analysis of the Turkish situation was not unusual. We thought about the issues in Turkey in the standard way, considering economic fundamentals, debt dynamic issues, and financial sector problems.

First we looked at the fundamentals, which were seen as weak at the time, with low growth, bad fiscal picture, bad external picture, and high (though declining) inflation. Though we had held this view for a couple of years before the crisis, we thought that fundamentals were moving in the right direction.

After reviewing fundamentals, of course, we had to overlay confidence in the sustainability of the debt, since debt was still growing and the real interest rate was high. So we wrote the debt dynamic equation, which is the standard method of doing things when analyzing a country's economic condition. We often modify our descriptions of this methodology, calling it the "mindless debt dynamic equation," because one has to plug in several parameters that are assumptions about the growth rate of the economy—inflation rate, real interest rate, and primary surplus—to get whatever result one wants. Only in horrendous cases will this methodology imply an obvious unsustainability, as Morris Goldstein describes in this volume. The rest of the time, arbitrary assumptions will imply either debt explosion or convergence, according to one's prior preference.

Together, these methods would provide some indication about whether the situation was going to blow up. In our view, Turkey was not obviously going to blow up with certainty.

Finally, one adds what one knows about the financial sector. As a relatively large foreign player lending into the banking sector, we knew that there was a set of weak banks.

As the crisis unfolded there was sudden information about the magnitude of banking system losses. That tells one more about what will happen to debt dynamics and sustainability.

The official sectors' response to the crisis tells where the various imbalances in the system are going to blow up. For instance, is it going to be strictly an interest rate crisis? It would have been if the central bank had stuck to the limits on the net domestic asset position. That will hit the banking system in a particular way: some banks will win if they are liquid, others will bleed, and others will be cut off in a liquidity crisis.

Or, will it be a foreign exchange crisis? As Turkey's central bank managed the November crisis, it provided domestic credit to the banks. This threatened the foreign exchange policy and meant that the foreign exchange imbalances in the banking system were going to be important.

So, one immediately starts to analyze who is going to get hit under a particular crisis policy and who is not going to get hit.

These considerations require a detailed look at the financial system. I am glad that Özatay and Sak's presentation basically centered on the financial system. Of course, we knew, and as everyone did, that there were some rarified players in the system, of the sort that can exist only in high inflation. That is, in an environment of high inflation, financial institutions emerge that have no reason for existing at all in a relatively stable, noninflationary environment. The business of these institutions is simply to offer the public ways of avoiding the inflation tax or to speculate on the direction of the inflation.

Anyone with Latin American experience knows about these institutions. When the system starts to move toward a more stable situation—and we were theoretically in a disinflationary policy environment—such institutions are going to be swept from the scene as their profitability evaporates. They exist purely on spreads that will be eliminated in a more stable environment.

Demirbank was exactly one of these institutions, a purely prop-trading, speculative operation. But the bank effectively had a deposit guarantee from the government. Demirbank started to take on more risk and became a major player in the bond market. The bank acted as if it was not going to live much longer and had no franchise value, so it started betting. That is the classic path—if a bank has a guarantee on its deposits and nothing to lose, it takes higher risks.

Why would the regulator allow Demirbank to take those risks? That was already outlined. The regulator, that is, the government, needed to sell its bonds because it was running a terrible fiscal imbalance. But nobody wanted to buy the bonds at the interest rates that the government wanted to pay—especially for longer-term bonds.

Why would the government want to offer long-term bonds instead of short-term bonds? Because everyone knows, or has been told, that it is good to have a long-term debt profile. But if a government does not want to pay the interest rate that will get real lenders to hold this profile, then it dumps the debt into what is effectively a government bank. Any bank that is holding only government paper for assets should be viewed as a government bank.

The guarantee converts the longer-term paper into short-term debt of the government. More specifically, Demirbank financed its holdings of government paper through repos, which are overnight credit. What looked like longer-term government debt was really overnight credit to the government, and in the collapse the government quickly had to find funds to pay for it.

Demirbank (along with some other Turkish banks) in particular was the marginal buyer of government debt in the system. Now, we always try to identify who is the marginal buyer or seller of a security. Our strategists keep track of such information because it is crucial to know if there is only one buyer or if there is a lot of remaining buying interest. If there is only one, weak buyer who may suddenly be removed from the market, then instantly that market will collapse, and everybody holding that paper will collapse as well, through mark-to-market accounting. That is exactly what happened when Demirbank was forced out of the system.

Foreign lenders did not lend directly to Demirbank. They would happily lend dollars to the stronger banks in the system for an attractive spread. Then the stronger banks just played the carry trade by on-lending the funds overnight in lira to Demirbank through repos on the government debt.

Effectively, a chunk of the government debt was being financed by foreign lending through the strong banks to weak banks. This was a good deal for the foreign lenders, because in the end they had the capital of the stronger banks between them and the collapse. There was some belief that the government might restructure the domestic debt, but there was less fear that the foreign debt would be restructured.

In the event, foreign exchange reserves were expended to cover the outflow of foreign funds in November. In addition, there was confidence that there would be an International Monetary Fund (IMF) program with real money in it, because in the end Turkey was important to the United States.

All of these expectations materialized. Foreign lenders entering into the domestic banking system got their funds out of the country in November. That left the problem of financial reconstruction as a Turkish affair.

Özatay and Sak's paper is organized around the three generations of speculative attack models, but this was not really its central focus. The main point of the paper is the primary weight given to the banking system in the unfolding of the crisis. Whether the crisis fits into the framework of one theoretical crisis model or another is problematic. In fact, these models all boil down to pretty much the same thing in the Turkish context.

First-generation models are observationally equivalent to second-generation models. One can explain the crisis as driven by inevitable monetization of inexorably growing debt or a bad equilibrium driven by lack of confidence in the convergence of the debt dynamics. In the Turkish case, a third-generation model is basically a subset of a first-generation model because there is going to be an explosion of government debt to fill the hole in the banking system, and this debt will be monetized. The hole in the system itself was generated by public debt management policy.

Admittedly, I have a vested interest, but my own view is that the finance problem led to a classic domestic credit driven collapse, with a little bit of a detour through expanding the banking system with net foreign assets in the central bank because of the restriction on net domestic assets. But that restriction on net domestic assets was only temporary. Once the collapse was imminent, that restriction was lifted, foreign assets fled, and domestic assets exploded. In the end there was an anticipated future explosion in money to cover a financial hole, and that is a classic, standard first-generation model.

However, it does not really matter which generation model one wants to use to classify this episode. The important contribution of Özatay and Sak's paper is the attention paid to the step-by-step details of what happened to the financial system rather than the taxonomy of crisis.

There were several detailed issues in the paper that could use a little more explanation. For instance, structured products were referred to casually, but by now the details must be in hand. A description of the types and magnitudes of these products and how they were distributed around the system would be very helpful.

Basically, the situation in Turkey was similar to the one in Mexico in 1994. There was a large amount of swaps or repos as well as structured notes that thoroughly disguised and converted the banks' true positions. Once the off balance sheet items were added, the bank's picture could change dramatically. For instance, structured notes looked like dollar assets in the banking system, but in fact they were highly leveraged dollar liabilities playing off the carry trade, which would cause a tremendous hole in the system once the exchange rate was let go.

Another issue is what explicitly was the interconnection across the banks and size of the losses from the foreign exchange positions and interest rate positions? During the course of this crisis, there were many published papers that tried to figure out the distribution of the losses and estimate the overall imbalance in foreign exchange and interest rates in order to calculate the hole in the system.

While Özatay and Sak's paper alludes to that, it does not really give the numbers, which would be very helpful. The paper argues that there was no central bank expansion of net domestic assets going into the crisis, so that the expansion in central bank liabilities must have been driven by the inflow of reserves in the years before the crisis. It would be helpful to have the actual dynamics, the actual time series of these subcategories in the central bank balance sheet.

One final point concerns the issue of why the commercial banks were unconstrained. There must have been a lot of memo traffic between the regulator, minister of finance, central bank, and insurer about the banking system's positions. These must be fairly sensitive issues. But there must be some dynamic of that interaction where it becomes quite clear that the finance minister was getting a little desperate about where he was going to market his debt. Such a record would be what is needed to distinguish whether the financial system was sacrificed as an instrument of fiscal policy or the speculative behavior was an independent disturbance from the financial sector.

Atish Ghosh: It is always a pleasure to read a paper written by people who were clearly close to, and well informed about, the events being discussed. There is much in Özatay and Sak's paper with which one can agree, some points with which one may disagree, and as always, there are a couple of points with which one can quibble.

Özatay and Sak focus on the November 2000–February 2001 currency crisis. Their central thesis is that the crisis cannot be readily explained in terms of standard first-generation or second-generation crisis models, but rather that it is mostly rooted in weaknesses in the banking sector.

On first-generation models, the authors note that—in contrast to the Krugman model—central bank financing of the budget deficit was nil. While I agree that the crisis was not of the first-generation type, their claim that nil central bank advances to the budget means that there was no central bank financing brings me to my first quibble. It is true that since 1997 central bank advances to the government were zero. However, the central bank was still financing the government indirectly, by financing credit to the banks, which in turn bought large amounts of Treasury bills. Indeed, it was customary practice for the Central Bank of Turkey to look at Treasury bill redemptions and expected Treasury bill sales to calculate how much the market was short of liquidity, which the central bank would then generally accommodate. The reason that this did not result in a Krugman first-generation crisis was that Turkey maintained a more or less floating exchange rate until end-1999, so that the monetary expansion, rather than being manifested in a loss of reserves, simply showed up as high inflation (between 50 and 100 percent a year).

However, in late 1999 the Central Bank of Turkey moved to a (crawling but predetermined) pegged regime, with strict currency board rules (that is, full coverage of more than base money, plus zero change in net domestic assets of the central bank). As such, money financing of the deficit—direct or indirect—stopped as well.

I will return to some of the other elements of the first-generation crises—the large budget deficit, overvaluation of the currency, and widening current account deficit. As the authors note, by its very nature a second-generation crisis is more difficult to dismiss. Although Turkey did not go on an expansionary policy binge following the crisis (thereby fulfilling the speculative expectations), it did incur significant financial sector restructuring costs. Moreover, there is nothing in the second-generation models that rules out the possibility that the authorities are unlucky or lack credibility—that is, that they face an (*ex post*) unjustified speculative attack.

This brings the authors to their third explanation: weaknesses of the banking system. They provide ample evidence of this, in the public banks on account of the so-called duty losses (mostly agricultural credit subsidies), and in the private banks due to open foreign exchange positions and exposure to various other risks. There is not—or was not—much disagreement that the banking system was vulnerable, all the more so in a disinflationary environment in which the previous practice of earning high interest rates on Treasury bills (through the repo market) would be coming to an end, and many private banks would need to learn (or relearn) how to make regular commercial loans and assess risks.

According to the authors, it was these weaknesses, together with some slippages in structural reforms (most notably the long delay in making the new banking supervision board operational), and political uncertainties that caused the crisis.

Now, of course, as someone who was at least peripherally involved in the design of the 1999 stabilization program, I find this is a very comfortable thesis. It puts the blame squarely outside the macroeconomic arena and mostly on political uncertainties and structural vulnerabilities that—while being addressed under the program—could not be expected to be corrected overnight.

Yet one wonders whether the authors are being too generous in their interpretation. In particular, by 2000 the stabilization program was displaying many of the classic symptoms of exchange rate–based stabilization (ERBS) syndrome. Pegging the exchange rate had been remarkably successful in lowering real interest rates, leading to a consumption boom, real exchange rate appreciation, and widening current account deficit. By mid-2000 it was clear that the economy was overheating. Real demand rose by some 10 percent, the current account deficit was headed toward 5 percent of gross domestic product (against a program expectation of 2 to 3 percent of GDP), and the real exchange rate was appreciating by significantly more than the 10 percent undervaluation margin estimated at the start of the program. Yet the government was unable—or unwilling—to undertake additional fiscal tightening despite the rising risks to the stabilization program.

Most likely it is impossible to establish definitively whether the crisis resulted from weaknesses in the financial sector or whether it was a classic ERBS syndrome crisis. One indication is the pattern of capital flows around the time of the crisis: these were general portfolio flows, not outflows from the banking system.

Perhaps the most that can be said is that the ERBS program made the country more vulnerable to a currency crisis.

The Turkish experience raises two questions. First, should one conclude that an ERBS is inherently risky and prone to failure? Second, and related, was embarking upon an ERBS a sensible strategy for Turkey in 1999?

On the first question, there is indeed a popular perception that ERBS programs are prone to failure. But this may reflect nothing more than the often spectacular collapses of the exchange rate peg when ERBS fails. Indeed, one only notices a crisis when it involves the collapse of an exchange rate peg. Actually, the Turkish economy had been in crisis long before the November 2000 or February 2001 crises. With inflation rates of 50 to 100 percent, real interest rates reaching 20 to 40 percent, and highly volatile and often negative real GDP growth, it is hard to argue that the economy was not in crisis at least as far back as 1997. But because the exchange rate was not pegged, this period is usually not referred to as a crisis.

In fact a more systematic look at the cross-country evidence shows that a pegged ERBS is no more likely to fail than one based on floating rates. Using a large data set of IMF member countries, Ghosh, Gulde, and Wolf find that 44 percent of ERBS programs succeeded (in terms of achieving a durable fall in inflation), compared with 26 to 29 percent of stabilization programs based on floating or intermediate exchange rate regimes.[1]

On the second question, whether the ERBS strategy made sense for Turkey in 1999: on balance, it did (notwithstanding the outcome). In particular, it is not clear that there were many viable alternatives. In 1998 the government had tried a money-based program—without pegging the exchange rate—which succeeded in lowering inflation, but the cost of this incredible disinflation was extremely high real interest rates that made both growth and the public debt dynamics unsustainable. Would greater financing have helped the 1999 program (as, indeed, the International Monetary Fund and World Bank ended up providing)? Constraints on financing availability aside, there were also economic limits to how much foreign financing could be used. Simply put, Turkey faced a budgetary—not a balance of payments—gap. (Indeed, in 1999 the balance of payments was actually in surplus.) Trying to plug that budget gap with foreign financing would have entailed a massive sterilization problem, that most likely would have resulted in the balance of payments crisis that it was intended to avoid. The only ways to solve the budgetary problem were through fiscal adjustment, or by generating lower real interest rates—as the ERBS program promised (and delivered)—or through a debt restructuring.

In summary, Özatay and Sak's paper provides a useful account of the events surrounding the 2000–01 currency crisis in Turkey. One can agree with much of the paper, although the authors downplay too much the classic ERBS syndrome aspects of the crisis. In 1999 Turkey embarked on an exchange rate–based stabilization program mostly because there were few viable alternatives. It was a risky strategy—as was recognized at the time—and the program had more than its fair share of bad luck—a sharp oil price increase that widened the current account deficit by 1 percent of GDP, persistent inflationary dynamics that resulted in a larger than expected real appreciation, and the inability of the government to take additional fiscal measures when it became appar-

1. Ghosh, Gulde, and Wolf (2003).

ent that the economy was overheating. But equally, without the vulnerabilities in the banking sector, the slippage of structural reform, and the political uncertainties, the stabilization plan might have succeeded and the crisis been avoided.

Discussion: Michael Gavin thought it was peculiar that the Turkish stabilization program tried to convince holders of Turkish lira that the right exchange rate regime for Turkey in exactly eighteen months would be a floating exchange rate—but until then, the right exchange rate regime was going to be a very hard peg, not backed up by the institutional adaptations that a true currency board would require. Gavin said that had he been long on Turkish lira, he would have recognized that the downside risks at the moment of the float were greater than the upside risks. Three or four weeks before the start of the float, he would have wondered just how much the authorities would be willing to defend the currency for that last four weeks of the float. The answer is probably not much. And one could then ask: what about four weeks before that? Gavin did not see how this could not have unraveled in a speculative attack, even if it had not been triggered by political and banking system events.

The discussion then focused on whether the scheduled transition to a float created a one-way bet for speculators. Peter Garber pointed out that it is possible to have a transition from a fixed regime to floating regime, as long as the floating regime is no more inflationary than the fixed regime. Garber's question was whether that was credible. He argued that going into the crisis, there was not a one-way bet. The macroeconomic situation was bad, but getting better, and the same was true for underlying fundamentals. It had been a surprise when there was a sudden cutoff of financing to Demirbank from the better banks. There had not been an inevitability. Garber argued that the November crisis revealed information about how tough the authorities were going to be in maintaining the exchange rate regime. He thought that the exchange rate regime died in November because the authorities responded by expanding domestic credit.

John Williamson added that the switch to floating took the form of a widening band, and at the end of the period there was supposed to be a wide band. If the market thought the eventual rate was going to lie anywhere within that band at the period's end, there would not have been a crisis.

Steve Kamin shifted to another part of the paper. He pointed out that, in cumulative terms, Turkey has had continuously rising amounts of IMF lending. And that lending has been very important to promoting the country's stability. Turkey's public sector debt remains extremely high, in part because of the way in which the banking sector problems were resolved—the duty losses of the busted banks being added to the public debt. Kamin asked if the authorities had considered other options for resolving the financial problems of the banks if the IMF funding had not been forthcoming. He also asked why they had not chosen to redenominate all that debt in dollars, which would have significantly lowered the real interest rate.

Guven Sak responded by saying that Turkey still remained in the middle of a crisis, and the high public debt made the economy vulnerable to a confidence crisis. There was an enormous effort regarding fiscal discipline throughout 2001, as well as a lot of structural reform. The authorities have been successful until now, but the outcome still very much rests on growth expectations and the adjustment costs of the structural reform efforts.

References

Akyüz, Yilmaz, and Korbut Boratav. 2001. "The Making of the Turkish Financial Crisis." Paper prepared for Conference on Financialization of the Golabal Economy. University of Massachusetts, December 7–9.

Alper, C. Emre. 2001. "The Turkish Liquidity Crisis of 2000: What Went Wrong?" *Russian and East European Finance and Trade* 37 (6): 51–71.

Burnside, Craig, Martin Eichenbaum, and Sergio Rebelo. 2001. "Prospective Deficits and the Asian Currency Crisis." *Journal of Political Economy* 109 (6): 1155–97.

Calvo, Guillermo A. 1988. "Servicing the Public Debt: The Role of Expectations." *American Economic Review* 78 (4): 647–61.

———. 1994. "Comments on Dornbusch and Werner." *Brookings Papers on Economic Activity* 1: 298–300.

Calvo, Guillermo A., and Carlos A. Végh. 1999. "Inflation Stabilization and BOP Crises in Developing Countries." In *Handbook of Macroeconomics, Vol. 1C*, edited by John B. Taylor and Michael Woodford, 1531–614. Amsterdam: North-Holland.

Central Bank of Turkey. 2001. *Annual Report 2001*. Ankara (www.tcmb.gov.tr/new/evds/yayin/yay1eng.html).

Chang, Roberto, and Andres Velasco. 1998a. "The Asian Liquidity Crisis." Working Paper W67961. Cambridge, Mass.: National Bureau of Economic Research (November).

———. 1998b. "Financial Crisis in Emerging Markets: A Canonical Model." Working Paper 6606. Cambridge, Mass.: National Bureau of Economic Research (June).

Eichengreen, Barry. 2001. "Crisis Prevention and Management: Any New Lessons from Argentina and Turkey?" Background paper for the World Bank's *Global Development Finance 2002*.

Eichengreen, Barry, Andrew K. Rose, and Charles Wyplosz. 1995. "Exchange Market Mayhem: The Antecedents and Aftermath of Speculative Attacks." *Economic Policy* 21: 251–312.

Flood, Robert P., and Peter M. Garber. 1984. "Collapsing Exchange Rate Regimes: Some Linear Examples." *Journal of International Economics* 17: 1–13.

Flood, Robert P., and Nancy. P. Marion. 2000. "Self-Fulfilling Risk Predictions: An Application to Speculative Attacks." *Journal of International Economics* 50: 245–68.

Frankel, Jeffrey A., and Andrew K. Rose. 1996. "Currency Crashes in Emerging Markets: An Empirical Treatment." *Journal of International Economics* 41: 351–66.

Ghosh, Atish R., Anne-Marie Gulde, and Holger C. Wolf. 2003. *Exchange Rate Regimes: Choices and Consequences*. MIT Press.

Goldfajn, Ilan, and Roberto Rigobon. 2000. "Hard Currency and Financial Development." Working Paper 438. Pontifical Catholic University of Rio de Janerio.

Johnson, Simon, and others. 2000. "Tunneling." *American Economic Review, Papers and Proceedings* 90: 22–27.

Krugman, Paul. 1979. "A Model of Balance-of-Payments Crises." *Journal of Money, Credit, and Banking* 11: 311–25.

———. 1999a. "Balance Sheets, the Transfer Problem, and Financial Crises." In *International Finance and Financial Crisis*, edited by P. Isard, A. Razin, and Andrew Rose, 31–44. New York: Kluwer Academic Publishers.

———. 1999b. "Analytical Afterthoughts on the Asian Crisis." Mimeo. Massachusetts Institute of Technology.

Özatay, Fatih. 2000. "The 1994 Currency Crisis in Turkey." *Journal of Policy Reform* 3 (4): 327–52.

Sachs, Jeffrey, Aaron Tornell, and Andres Velasco. 1996a. "Financial Crisis in Emerging Markets: The Lessons from 1995." *Brookings Papers on Economic Activity* 1: 147–215.

———. 1996b. "The Collapse of the Mexican Peso: What Have We Learned?" *Economic Policy* 22: 15–63.

MORRIS GOLDSTEIN

Institute for International Economics

Lessons of Recent Currency Crises

Given all that has been written over the past half dozen years about the lessons of currency crises, I feel somewhat like Henry VIII's sixth wife on her wedding night: I know what is expected of me, but I am not sure I can make it that interesting. Nevertheless, let me try by focusing on lessons in two areas, namely, currency regimes and debt problems.

Currency Regimes

There is widespread dissatisfaction with the status quo on currency regimes for emerging economies on at least three counts.

First, the high vulnerability of adjustable pegs and simple crawls has been amply demonstrated during the past seven years. The crises of Mexico, Thailand, Indonesia, South Korea, Russia, Brazil, and Turkey speak loudly to the fragility of these regimes.

Adjustable peg regimes often led to complacency about currency risk and large currency mismatches. Few countries can defend a peg for long with a high interest rate defense, and a noncrisis exit to greater exchange rate flexibility has proved difficult to bring off.

The latest version of the crawl—namely the basket band crawl (or BBC regime), proposed by John Williamson (2000)—admittedly has some nontrivial advantages. Still, experience suggests that a BBC regime is not flexible enough to handle large and abrupt shifts in investor sentiment and private capital flows. When that happens, the band gets widened further and further until it is ultimately abandoned in favor of float. Moreover, recent empirical research suggests that intermediate regimes have historically yielded the highest aver-

173

age inflation rates and rates of monetary expansion; that is, they do not provide a good monetary anchor.[1]

Second, while less fragile than soft pegs, Argentina's experience documents that currency boards are by no means immune from speculative attacks. Just as important, currency boards do not offer a visible policy instrument to deal with recessions, since monetary policy is made abroad, concerns over debt sustainability often rule out countercyclical fiscal policy pump-priming, and the domestic economy is invariably not flexible enough to correct a large real exchange rate overvaluation without a change in the nominal exchange rate. Nor is a fiscal contraction likely to yield enough of a confidence boost (or decline in the risk premium) to be expansionary.

Dollarization, the hardest of the hard pegs, hardly looks like the solution. Yes, dollarization does away with currency mismatches. But if a dollarized emerging economy (with a debt problem) has an overvalued exchange rate, the correction will come via a decline in the domestic price level. This in turn means a higher real debt burden. In other words, dollarization does not do away with debt problems. Even more to the point, the most comprehensive review available of the performance of dollarized economies, undertaken by Sebastian Edwards (2001), concludes that dollarized economies show inferior growth performance relative to nondollarized economies, better inflation performance, and essentially no difference on either fiscal policy discipline or current-account behavior. No wonder, then, that Edwards concludes that most of the lofty claims for dollarization represent "misleading advertisement."

Third, it is known from the empirical work of Calvo and Reinhart (2000) as well as Hausmann and others (2000) that emerging economies do not float in the same way as large industrialized countries. Specifically, the former lean more heavily on interest rate policies and sterilized exchange market intervention to limit the movement in the nominal exchange rate. Moreover, this so-called fear of floating seems to be linked to the high incidence of dollar-denominated debt and large currency mismatches. In such an environment, a large depreciation could result in large-scale insolvencies and deep output losses. When floating is more *de jure* than *de facto*, emerging economies do not obtain the benefits associated with greater exchange rate flexibility. Moreover, a floating regime requires emerging economies to choose a nominal anchor for monetary policy, and the past performance of monetary targeting under (plain vanilla) floating has been found wanting.

1. See Levy-Yeyati and Sturzenegger (2000).

Emerging economies thus appear to be facing a no-win situation. If they opt for soft pegs or crawls, these regimes are likely eventually to blow up in costly collapse. Alternatively, they can reduce vulnerability by choosing a hard peg or a plain vanilla float, but these choices could well be accompanied by disappointing economic performance.

The main question, then, is whether there is another currency regime that will offer better overall prospects.

I submit there is. In my recent book, I call that regime "managed floating plus," where the "plus" is shorthand for a framework that includes inflation targeting (IT) and aggressive measures directed at reducing currency mismatching.[2]

If managed floating were enhanced in this way, it would retain the desirable features of a floating regime, namely greater monetary policy independence and better cushioning against large, external, real shocks. With its plus elements, however, it would also address the balance sheet problems and lack of monetary policy discipline that have contributed to a past fear of floating and to a weaker economic performance by emerging economies than could be the case.

This paper focuses on the currency mismatching problem because it appears to be the leading suspect in the large output declines observed in many emerging market currency crises of the 1990s.[3] In addition it is the currency mismatching problem that constrains emerging economies from lowering interest rates once a crisis occurs.

Significant progress in reducing currency mismatching can be obtained by:

—allowing nominal exchange rates to move enough to remind market participants of currency risk;

—having the International Monetary Fund (IMF) regularly publish and analyze data on currency mismatching at the economywide and sectoral levels;

—strengthening and rigorously enforcing prudential measures limiting currency mismatches on the part of banks and having banks monitor more carefully currency mismatches by their customers, especially those that do not generate dollar revenues; and

—encouraging the development of hedging instruments and domestic bond markets. In this latter connection, two of the factors hindering the development of domestic bond markets in the past, namely high inflation in Latin America and low government debt in Asia, are not now as relevant as they used to be.

2. Goldstein (2002).
3. See, for example, Cavallo and others (2001).

It should be clear that I am not a believer in the "original sin hypothesis," which postulates that currency mismatching in emerging economies is a market imperfection that is here to stay.[4]

As for the other part of the "plus," the record shows that the overall performance to date of IT in emerging economies has been impressive and represents a better nominal anchor than the leading alternatives, that is, exchange rate pegs or the targeting of monetary aggregates. Most analytical reviews conclude, *inter alia,* that countries adopting IT have been relatively successful in meeting their inflation targets; the track record on meeting inflation targets has been much better than that on meeting monetary growth targets; countries adopting IT still allow monetary policy to respond to falls in output; and a subsequent loss of fiscal discipline has rarely been associated with IT adoption.[5]

The three elements of managed floating plus should reinforce each other. The more currency mismatching is brought under control, the less should be the fear of floating. If the exchange rate is allowed to move, the greater will be the awareness of currency risk and the incentive to hedge against it. The less necessary it is to regard the exchange rate as a target, the more likely that inflation targeting will be successful, since the monetary authorities will then not have a competing nominal anchor with which to contend. The more successful the monetary authorities are in meeting their low inflation targets, the more willing should foreign lenders be to write financial contracts in the borrower's own currency and the more favorable should be the environment for developing local bond markets. And the greater the availability of domestic-currency-denominated financial instruments, the better the prospects for reducing currency mismatching.

To summarize, the lesson is that the currency regime matters a lot for crisis vulnerability, as well as for overall economic performance. The twenty or so larger emerging economies should opt for managed floating plus. It would give them a deterrent against currency mismatching and balance-sheet vulnerability, enough monetary independence to engage in gross tuning of monetary policy to counter recessions, enough "flex" in the exchange rate to deal with large shifts in capital flows, and a workable nominal anchor.

This is not pie in the sky. Chile, Brazil, and Mexico are already implementing much of the managed floating plus agenda with good effect, a group of other

4. See Eichengreen and Hausmann (1999).

5. See IMF (2001), Corbo, Moreno, and Schmidt-Hebbel (2001), Mishkin (2000), Truman (2003), and other material discussed in Goldstein (2002).

emerging economies (ranging from South Africa to Thailand) are moving in that direction, and still others (including some like China and India, both of which still maintain capital controls) are good candidates for such a framework in the medium term. In contrast, what has been seen in Argentina since the collapse of the currency board is "managed floating minus," with no anchor for monetary and fiscal policy and an asymmetric "pesification" plan that made the banking system much weaker in a myopic effort to curry political support from bank depositors.

If not managed floating plus for large emerging economies with heavy capital market involvement, you tell me what would be a better regime choice.

Debt Problems

When looking at the three largest recent crisis economies—Argentina, Brazil, and Turkey—one observes that they have a serious weakness in common: too much debt.

In Argentina and Brazil, external debt has not been so large relative to gross domestic product (GDP), but it is huge relative to merchandise exports—about 500 percent and 400 percent, respectively.[6] In Turkey, reflecting the enormous costs of recapitalizing the banking sector, the ratio of public debt to GDP is now near 100 percent.

With a stock of debt that large, the outbreak of a debt crisis is a constant threat, even with sharply improved budgetary behavior.

The standard kind of debt sustainability analysis that is often done—looking at the difference between real growth rates and real interest rates and calculating the primary surplus needed to stabilize the ratio of public debt to GDP—often turns out to be unduly optimistic for at least three reasons.

First, for emerging economies whose debt is denominated predominately in dollars, one wants to get a fix on their ability to generate dollar revenues. The implicit assumption when comparing debt to GDP is that resources can easily be redirected from the rest of the economy to the tradable goods sector (to earn foreign exchange). But history suggests that countries like Argentina and Brazil, with export sectors accounting for only about 10 percent of GDP,

6. In 2001 the ratio of external debt to GDP was roughly 55 percent in Argentina and 45 percent in Brazil. Reflecting the sharp downturn in the economy, the large depreciation of the exchange rate, and large projected fiscal costs of recapitalizing the banking system, debt ratios are expected to rise sharply in Argentina in 2002. Most of Brazil's government debt is domestic debt. See Deutsche Bank, *Emerging Markets Monthly* (April 2002).

do not fit comfortably with that assumption—certainly much less so than the export-oriented emerging economies of Asia. The amount of foreign-currency-denominated debt an emerging economy can carry is different when exports are one-quarter or more of GDP than when they are one-tenth of GDP.

If experience shows us that it is extremely rare for an emerging economy with a ratio of external debt to exports of 400 to 500 percent (and a ratio of total debt service to exports of 70 to 100 percent) to move to a more moderate ratio (say, 200 percent) without large-scale debt restructuring, then one can find little comfort in the calculation that a net public debt–to-GDP ratio of 45 percent could be sustainable. If no emerging economy other than Chile has escaped from that kind of high debt-to-exports situation since the early 1980s without a restructuring, it smells unsustainable.[7]

Second, even staying within a GDP framework, one worries about the negative feedback effects of very high real interest rates and of a much tighter fiscal position on economic growth. When an emerging economy is hit with negative shocks, is losing credibility, and sees its real interest rate rising sharply to 10 to 15 percent or more, it is very hard to envisage that economy growing at all. It is one thing if sky-high real interest rates last for a month. But it is another if they last for three months, six months, a year, or more. Likewise, tightening fiscal policy in an environment where the economy is already in recession or in a severe slowdown, where monetary policy is made abroad because of the exchange rate commitment, and where the debt-to-GDP ratio has been on a rising trend, is not likely to leave growth unaffected. Hence, you can get into a vicious cycle, with economic growth, tax receipts, and interest rate spreads interacting in ways that are difficult to capture in the standard debt sustainability formula.

Third, the interest rate that is observed in the market while an emerging economy is operating under an IMF program, or negotiating for an extension or enlargement of a program, does not tell what the (interest rate) spread will be when the country comes off the official feeding tube. For example, Turkey is now the recipient of one of the largest IMF programs in history. The country has been performing quite well under its IMF program, but its access to IMF financing is also being boosted by its geopolitical position—especially post–September 11. But look down the road two years, for example, and assume that official financing is less assured. Then ask what spread the market will require to meet the financing requirements of a country with a ratio of government debt to GDP of perhaps 90 percent? How long will that coun-

7. Deutsche Bank, *Emerging Markets Monthly* (April 2002).

try be willing to run large primary surpluses if the postprogram real interest rate is still quite a bit higher than the postprogram real growth rate?

In a similar vein, ask what might happen to Brazil's interest rate spread (already at 850 basis points and rising) if economic growth continues to be weak, if FDI comes in this year at only about half its 2000 level, and if the likely winner of the October 2002 presidential election offers some policy views that make international investors nervous.

All of this suggests that one should be more conservative in analyzing debt sustainability for emerging economies that operate in a volatile international capital market and that do not have the big export machines commonly found in East Asia. More stress testing is needed to get a better handle on who is likely to make it without debt restructuring and who is not. It is not the mean of the distribution of real interest rates and growth rates that gets you, it's the variance.

The same line of argument also lends support to recent initiatives to make debt restructuring by emerging economies more orderly and timely. These initiatives include collective action clauses (CACs) in bond contracts as suggested by U.S. Treasury Under-Secretary John Taylor (2002), the sovereign debt restructuring mechanism (SDRM) recently put forward by IMF First Deputy Managing Director Anne Krueger (2002), and tighter rules on access limits for IMF lending as proposed by, among others, reports by a Council on Foreign Relation Task Force (1999) and the Bank of Canada and the Bank of England (for example, see Haldane and Kruger, 2002).

These three initiatives would complement one another.

If there were wider use of CACs and the Krueger SDRM were in place, it would be easier for the IMF to stick to agreed access limits because the prospect of a disorderly debt restructuring would be lower.

The SDRM would alleviate the coordination problems that can arise in a world with many types of bonds, it would address existing debt overhang problems for bonds without CACs, and it would encourage more timely agreements between debtors and creditors in the "shadow of the court." The decentralized, market-driven nature of CACs would allow this branch of reform to move ahead quickly if incentives were right, while the more lengthy process of working out the details and securing international agreement on the SDRM was being attended to. And the likelihood that IMF loans in the future would be smaller would provide the incentive to adopt CACs more widely. This is particularly relevant since some of the other incentives proposed to promote CACs are apt to be too weak or nonoperational. For example, one doubts that the IMF membership will agree to disqualify a country from getting an IMF loan just because its bonds do not contain CACs. Recall that the Meltzer Commission in 2000 proposed a small set of "prequalification" conditions for IMF loans; these have gone nowhere.

To sum up, while only the naive recommend debt restructuring lightly, we need to pay greater attention to issues of debt sustainability at the time that IMF programs are agreed. Giving the borrowing country the benefit of the doubt that a very large stock of external or domestic debt is manageable may not be doing it much of a favor in terms of reducing its crisis vulnerability over the medium term. This is especially the case when extraordinary measures taken to avoid a default increase the probability of a financial-sector crisis by weakening the balance sheets of banks, pension funds, and others. Indeed, as the Argentina crisis has shown, it is possible to have not merely a twin crisis but rather a triple crisis, that is, the simultaneous occurrence of a currency, a banking, and a debt crisis. All the more reason, then, to heed the lesson of keeping the debt burden under control in the first place.

References

Calvo, Guillermo, and Carmen Reinhart. 2000. "Fear of Floating." Working Paper 7993. Cambridge, Mass.: National Bureau of Economic Research.

Cavallo, Michele, and others. 2001. "Exchange Rate Overshooting and the Costs of Floating." Mimeo. New York University.

Corbo, Vittorio, Oscar Moreno, and Klaus Schmidt-Hebbel. 2001. "Assessing Inflation Targeting after a Decade of World Experience." Mimeo. Santiago: Central Bank of Chile.

Council on Foreign Relations. 1999. "Safeguarding Prosperity in a Global Financial System: The Future International Financial Architecture." Task Force Report. New York.

Edwards, Sebastian. 2001. "Dollarization and Economic Performance." Working Paper 8274. Cambridge, Mass.: National Bureau of Economic Research.

Eichengreen, Barry, and Ricardo Hausmann. 1999. "Exchange Rates and Financial Fragility." In *New Challenges for Monetary Policy.* Federal Reserve Bank of Kansas City.

Goldstein, Morris. 2002. "Managed Floating Plus." *Policy Analysis in International Economics* 66. Washington: Institute for International Economics.

Haldane, Andy, and Mark Kruger. 2002. "Standstills: How to Do Them." Presentation prepared for Conference on Sovereign Debt Workouts. Institute for International Economics, Washington, April 1–2.

Hausmann, Ricardo, Ugo Panizza, and Ernesto Stein. 2000. "Why Do Countries Float the Way They Float?" Working Paper 418. Washington: Inter-American Development Bank.

International Monetary Fund. 2001. *World Economic Outlook*. Washington (May).

Krueger, Anne. 2002. "New Approaches to Sovereign Debt Restructuring: An Update on Our Thinking." Mimeo. International Monetary Fund.

Levy-Yeyati, Eduardo, and Federico Sturzenegger. 2000. "Exchange Rate Regimes and Economic Performance." Paper prepared for the First Annual International Monetary Fund Research Conference. Washington, November 9–10.

Mishkin, Frederic. 2000. "Inflation Targeting in Emerging-Market Countries." *American Economic Review* 90 (May): 105–09.

Taylor, John. 2002. "Sovereign Debt Restructuring: A U.S. Perspective." Mimeo. U.S. Department of the Treasury.

Truman, Edwin. 2003. "Inflation Targeting and the International Financial System." Washington: Institute for International Economics (forthcoming).

Williamson, John. 2000. *Exchange Rate Regimes for Emerging Markets: Reviving the Intermediate Option.* Policy Analysis in International Economics 60. Washington: Institute for International Economics.

JOSE LUIS MACHINEA
Inter-American Development Bank

Currency Crises:
A Practitioner's View

The growing frequency and magnitude of currency crises during the last decades can be partially explained by the abandonment of the Bretton Woods system and increasing importance of international capital flows. It is even tempting to say that the magnitude and frequency of these crises have reached unknown levels. However, evidence shows that the impact of currency crises on the level of economic activity during the 1973–98 period was similar to the level experienced during the heyday of the gold standard and capital flows mobility, between 1880 and 1914.[1] Nonetheless, this same evidence indicates that the frequency of currency crises has doubled since 1973 compared to the gold standard period. The higher frequency, magnitude of the devaluations linked to these crises, and contagion among emerging countries, and in some cases the developed world, have generated a considerable amount of research. Scholars, practitioners, and policymakers try to explain the causes of these crises. Most important, they attempt to extract valuable lessons for economic policy at the national and global level.

Since the seminal work of Paul Krugman, the growing body of literature that has tried to explain currency crises has been divided into three generations of models.[2] Thus the explanations have varied among these different types of models, ranging from economic fundamentals to nonlinearities in government behavior that lead to multiple equilibria and, therefore, to problems associated with self-fulfilling speculation (herd behavior), information cascades, and the like, as well as to financial fragility in the banking sector, usually associated with short-term liabilities and poor regulatory policies. The

---

1. Eichengreen and Bordo (2002)
2. Krugman (1979). See Krugman (1999) for a discussion of the models.

explanations include several relevant variables such as the prospective deficits associated with financial system rescue packages, short-term public debt, political uncertainty, and—especially after the Asian crisis—lack of transparency, cronyism, investment subsidies, and so on.

The different explanations generate a variety of recommendations in terms of economic policy. These range from relatively obvious ones, like pursuing consistent monetary and fiscal policies, to those associated with the choice of the exchange rate regime or with the health of the financial system. On the other hand, in much the same way as the discussion on the financial system has emphasized not only solvency but also liquidity-related matters, the recommendations related to currency crises have stressed the importance not just of the amount of debt (solvency) but also of its maturity. Additionally, in the same way in which problems of liquidity and self-fulfilling prophecies have generated a now century-old discussion on the need for a lender of last resort and related moral hazard issues in the case of financial crises, a similar discussion has developed in relation to currency crises at the international level.

This paper reviews some of the lessons of recent currency crises, with special emphasis on the Argentine collapse. A discussion of details from the Argentine case follows, drawing from my personal experience as a policymaker who made key choices on the verge of the country's currency crisis. The paper concludes with a synthesis of the lessons learned.

Lessons from Previous Crises

An important characteristic of currency crises is that frequently the significance of old lessons increases with each new episode. To illustrate this point, this paper reviews some lessons that were learned with the currency and financial crises of the Southern Cone countries at the beginning of the 1980s. Among them:[3]

—the attempts to stabilize the economy by reducing inflation through the use of the exchange rate as a nominal anchor usually result in an appreciation of the exchange rate;

—fixed exchange rates with considerable fiscal disequilibria do not just increase the current account deficit, they also create a perverse debt dynamic or, alternatively, a monetary expansion that precipitates the crisis;

3. See Díaz-Alejandro (1988).

—a similar effect on the current account deficit may be generated by an incorrect evaluation of the growth of future income by the private sector, which may contract too much debt and spend beyond equilibrium levels. This possibility is more likely in a context of capital account liberalization without an adequate supervision of the financial system, which leads to lending booms;

—a high current account deficit, in the context of a strong currency appreciation, has high probabilities of ending in a currency crisis;

—a currency crisis generates a financial crisis if the currency mismatch has been intermediated by the financial system. This, in turn, implies considerable fiscal costs.[4]

These features were also present in many of the later crises. In the case of Mexico in 1994, there was an additional issue of particular importance: the short-term liabilities of the public sector. From then on it was clear that the liquidity problems associated with short-term indebtedness, besides the total amount of debt itself, can be of special relevance to explain a currency crisis. Another relatively new feature of the tequila crisis was that it occurred in the context of highly globalized financial markets. Therefore, issues like the cost and availability of information, herd behavior, and coordination problems began to gain more relevance and gave birth to a still growing literature on contagion.

The Asian crisis was probably the least expected in light of previous experiences. Impressive growth rates, high levels of savings and investment, and a controlled fiscal situation did not seem to constitute the environment of a currency and banking crisis of such magnitude, despite the large current account deficit and currency appreciation, which in fact was substantially lower than in other crises. What went wrong in Asia? Different studies point toward the weaknesses of the financial system, both in terms of liquidity and solvency, as the main problem. The solvency issues created the feeling that at some point it would be necessary to use a strong monetary expansion to finance the fiscal deficit associated with the restructuring of the system.[5] In some way, this problem could be considered among the issues analyzed by first-generation models. At the same time, short-term obligations generated (at the first sign of uncertainty) a run of foreign creditors on loans in general and the financial system in particular. A central bank with few reserves could not act as a lender

4 . Although there are different estimations, in none is the fiscal cost of the currency and financial crisis in the Southern Cone less than 10 percent of gross domestic product.

5. See Corsetti, Pesenti, and Roubini (1998).

of last resort to the financial system for its foreign-denominated loans and at the same time generate the feeling that it was in a position to maintain the exchange rate parity. Somehow illiquidity produced self-fulfilling currency crises.[6]

Unlike Mexico, where the public sector had been the "bad guy," the salient element in the Asian crisis was the private sector's short-term indebtedness. It is nonetheless clear now, as evidence and experience show, that when the financial system is involved, the situation eventually ends up being a problem for the public sector. Therefore, an additional lesson derived from this crisis is that no matter who is the debtor, it is necessary to control short-term debt. However, it is still difficult to understand the magnitude of the crises if contagion elements are not incorporated into the analysis along with some wrong choices of economic policy.[7] In particular, the massive shutdown of financial institutions in a context of panic led to a deepening of the financial crisis, and with it, to a currency crisis. Note that financial panics remind us of the existence of multiple equilibria in capital markets.

What can be said regarding the current account deficit in relation to the Asian crisis? Until then, the common belief had been that a big current account deficit was a problem as long as it was the consequence of a high fiscal deficit or excessive optimism of the private sector, which leads to a rise in consumption to unsustainable levels.[8] This was not the case in the Asian countries, and thus a new explanation—related to the quality of investment—emerged. Fingers pointed to investment subsidies, corruption, and cronyism as the main factors behind the lack of profitability of investment and, therefore, behind the financial system's solvency problems. Although there is some evidence in this respect, this paper contends that placing an excessive responsibility of these factors on the currency crises is, at the least, stretching the argument too much. The advantages and disadvantages of institutional arrangements and subsidy mechanisms in the Asian countries were well known by everyone, so it is hard to believe that they were responsible for generating a crisis of such proportions. Maybe the lesson is that although there are "better" and "worse" types of current account deficits, depending on the amount of private investment and the way in which they are financed, the size of the deficit is *per se* a sign of vulnerability in times of great volatility in capital movements.

6. See Chang and Velasco (1999) for a theoretical discussion of liquidity crises.

7. Sachs and Radelet (1998).

8. On the impact of consumer misperceptions regarding the business cycle, see Heymann and Sanguinetti (1998). A different interpretation of the increase in consumption is related to expectations of the unsustainability of the exchange system. See Calvo and Végh (1999).

In this sense the Russian crisis made one thing clear: contagion was a major issue in the new, liberalized, global capital markets. It also became clear that from then onward, the international financial community would not be willing to rescue all countries in distress. At the time of this paper's writing, the declarations of government officials from developed countries as well as of multilateral credit agencies—if not their actions—seem to show that the moral hazard argument is gaining momentum, which is another way of saying that the Russian crisis did not leave many lessons. Some people seem not to be aware of the existence of systemic risks. Many people (the same people in fact), do not seem to understand that after the Russian crisis it has become quite difficult to argue that moral hazard is a highly relevant issue in explaining the lending process to emerging economies. (Of course, after the Argentine crisis it is not relevant at all.) Perhaps, paraphrasing Díaz Alejandro (1988), this is a situation where, in a short period of time, one will be able to say "goodbye moral hazard, hello meltdown risk."

Contagion effects, in fact, do have sizable consequences. Brazil's economy, for instance, was the most affected by the Russian crisis. Some problems with its fundamentals, an important appreciation of the exchange rate (due to an exchange rate–based stabilization process) and a large short-term public debt were some of the factors behind the country's contagion. These problems were similar to those faced by Mexico at the time of the tequila crisis. The main difference seemed to be that in Brazil the short-term debt was mainly denominated in the domestic currency. However, the attempt to increase interest rates in order to stop the speculative attack was self-defeating in terms of the solvency of the public sector. It was quite clear that the increase in interest rates was transforming a liquidity problem into a solvency one, and domestic debt is as important as external debt when solvency issues are at stake.

An additional conclusion was extracted from the Brazilian experience at the time: since the Argentine economy was able to resist the speculative attack without too many problems, some concluded that not only were hard pegs a better option than soft pegs in terms of exchange rate regimes, but hard pegs could be the solution to currency crises and economic distress associated with them.

To synthesize this discussion, empirical evidence on new crises supports some of the conclusions deriving from the experience of the 1980s. The new literature not only refines many of the arguments and proves them, but also introduce new elements into the discussion.

Short-term deadlines for the private and public sectors—almost independent of the total amount or dynamic of debt—are a very important factor for explaining currency crises. For example:

—Not only do currency crises generate financial crises (mainly through the mismatch of currencies), but weak financial systems could, in turn, lead to a currency crisis through liquidity issues and expected fiscal costs associated with rescue programs.

—Contagion in financial markets is a phenomenon far greater than in the crises of the past. Thus issues such as lack of information or information costs, leverage and margin calls, trade links, and so on are especially relevant and deserve additional research.

—The existence of multiple equilibria in financial markets increases the importance of policy actions and coordination, and therefore the role of multilateral institutions, at the onset of currency crises.

Recent Currency Crises: Argentina's Case

What lessons can be drawn from recent currency crises, namely those occurring in Turkey and Argentina? In the case of Turkey, there are few doubts that the problem originated in bad fundamentals. This, at least, is what one can deduce from the behavior of the ratio of debt to gross domestic product (GDP), which increased from 41 percent to 98 percent between 1998 and 2001. Although Fatih Özatay and Güven Sak have made a subtle analysis, differentiating the elements encompassed by each of the crises of the last two years, it cannot be ignored that high interest rates generated increasingly unmanageable debt arithmetic—despite the efforts to achieve a primary deficit.[9] The increase of public debt held by the banks worsened the already fragile situation of the financial sector and, therefore, generated expectations of a greater public deficit in the future. Additionally, the system's liquidity problems were magnified as a consequence of short-term liabilities funding long-term lending to the public sector.

Somehow, the Turkish crisis does not add new elements to what was already known from previous crises, that is, high fiscal deficits and weak financial systems are not compatible with a fixed exchange rate. However, there is an element that is relatively new and, in some way, appears also in the Argentine case. When an important share of financial system assets are public sector lia-

9. Özatay and Sak, this volume.

bilities, two types of problems emerge: 1) liquidity difficulties, given the different maturities of liabilities and assets; and 2) solvency problems, which arise as a result of the uncertainty linked to debt payments by insolvent governments. When, on top of this situation, there are political difficulties and announcements that the government will move to a more flexible exchange rate regime (as was the case in Turkey), the almost inevitable consequence is a currency crisis.

The Argentine case is somewhat more novel. After all, Argentina had not only been the star pupil of the Washington consensus, but it had also learned some of the lessons from previous episodes of international turmoil. In particular after the financial crisis of 1995, the country had built a banking system that, according to different standards, was among the most solid in the world.[10] In fact it was the second-most solid banking system after Singapore. Additionally, the debt maturity had been rising for many years, and toward the end of 2000 its average half-life was 7.3 years.[11] Also by the end of 2000, short-term debt represented 78 percent of international reserves, compared with a simple average of 96 percent in the countries of the East Asian crisis. However, when the principal on long-term debt due in 2001 is added, the ratio of debt service obligations to international reserves amounts to 149 percent. Finally, the ratio of M2 to reserves was 2.8, compared with values that stood at between 3.7 and 7.2 in the East Asian countries at the onset of the crisis, and a value of 5.1 for Brazil in December 1998.[12]

What exactly went wrong in Argentina? This question is addressed by the papers presented in this volume and some others that have been published recently.[13] The answer is not simple. It is enough to mention that while one of these papers (Hausmann and Velasco) emphasizes the problems of an excessive fiscal adjustment, another contribution (Powell) points to the absence of a greater adjustment as the main difficulty. Conventional wisdom has pointed to three possible—and very arguable—lessons related to what went wrong. The arguable lessons are:

—Convertibility is not an adequate hard peg. If a hard peg is to be chosen, the hardest of hard pegs—dollarization—should be selected.

—Convertibility was not sustainable because Argentina did not follow adequate macroeconomic policies.

10. See World Bank (1998), app. A, pp. 39–61, for a cross-country analysis of financial standards.

11. Data provided by the Ministry of Economy of Argentina.

12. Author's own calculations based on Central Bank of Argentina, Corsetti, Pesenti, and Roubini (1998), and World Bank, *World Development Indicators* (WDI) (2002), respectively.

13. Calvo, Izquierdo, and Talvi (2002); Perry and Servén (2002).

—Convertibility generates problems that in general terms are similar to those generated by other pegs, for instance, overvalued exchange rates and high current account deficits. A detailed discussion of these three points follows.

Dollarization

It is commonly argued that the advantages of hard pegs are: 1) they generate a greater fiscal discipline than other exchange rate systems; and 2) they reduce the risks of distress associated with large devaluations and therefore reduce borrowing costs. This latter effect should be especially relevant in economies with a large share of dollarized liabilities, where devaluation increases the risk of default. The question is whether dollarization can contribute in a greater way than convertibility to the achievement of both these goals, considering that there are costs of switching from one system to the other, especially in the form of seigniorage loss.[14]

With respect to fiscal discipline, there is no reason to believe that dollarization can make things better when compared to a system of convertibility. There is some evidence indicating that hard peg systems introduce a greater amount of discipline on the fiscal front.[15] However, the true question is whether these systems increase fiscal discipline in relative terms with respect to the demands and rigidities they impose. For example, Argentina is a case in which fiscal discipline improved considerably in the 1990s, but not enough to make the convertibility regime sustainable. In the extreme, when credit was not available in the second half of 2001, many provinces did not adjust expenditures but relied on printing "pseudo-money"—to be precise, provincial bonds circulating as a means of payment. Convertibility, or dollarization *per se,* would not prevent provinces from inflationary finance.

Regarding the benefits that a hard peg has on the perception of the markets in general—and on the risk of default in particular—it is evident that dollarization should generate, when compared to a system of convertibility, some reduction in the country risk. However, it is extremely difficult to assess the importance of this effect, which would seem to be positively correlated with

14. Other costs include the permanent loss of monetary policy, and the possible political costs associated with the loss of a symbol of sovereignty, such as a country's own currency.

15. See Goldstein (2002) for a synthesis of the evidence on this subject. Counterexamples abound. Of these, Chile is the most relevant, having been the Latin American country that exercised the highest degree of fiscal discipline during the last fifteen years, and doing so in the context of a soft peg.

Figure 1. Country and Devaluation Risks, 1994–2001ᵃ

Index, 1994 = 100

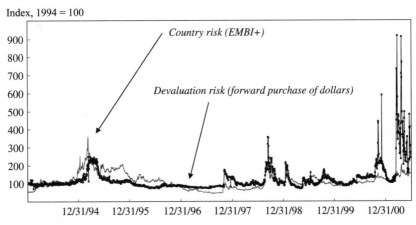

Souce: JP Morgan (2002).

the degree of dollarization of the economy.[16] Figure 1 shows the evolution of both the devaluation risk and country risk (or default risk) for Argentina. The devaluation risk is measured by using the forward rate for the future purchase of dollars (one-year period). The country risk was taken from the JP Morgan Emerging Markets Bond Index Plus (EMBI+) for Argentina. Figure 1 shows the significant relation existing between both variables (correlation coefficient of 0.82), which is an indicator that good and bad news affect both markets in a similar way. On the other hand, that is fairly obvious: could anyone think that Argentina would abandon convertibility without defaulting on its debt or, inversely, that given the magnitude of its dollar-denominated debt, the country could fulfill its obligations after devaluing? In any case, different tests have been carried out trying to find a behavioral pattern by which one series follows the other without obtaining any conclusive results, as was in fact expected.[17]

16. Powell and Sturzenneger (2000) find only partial evidence of this relationship when using a sample of Latin American countries. The evidence is more conclusive when a sample of European countries is considered.

17. Among other tests, this paper has looked at all the important variations experienced by country risk or devaluation risk between January 1994 and October 2001. In order to do this, a series was constructed using a moving average for five working days of both series, and defined "important variation" as a one percentage point change in one or both series, in the rate of the bonds composing the EMBI, and in the forward exchange rate that measures devaluation risk. The variation was measured with respect to the series value in a ten-day period. To avoid considering changes that originate in a common cause, all the variations that occurred within the twenty days following an important variation were eliminated. Forty-one cases were detected,

In any case, it is evident that the benefits of switching to a dollarization system should be evaluated in relation to the costs of losing seigniorage revenues. The net benefits should be positive if one can reach an agreement with the country whose currency is adopted in order to obtain some recognition of the aforementioned seigniorage.[18] In the absence of such an agreement, it would seem that convertibility is a better system in the middle run, that is, in a period of time long enough to gain reputation while collecting seigniorage revenue. In the short run, dollarization is a faster way to purchase reputation, and therefore it carries greater net relative benefits with respect to other types of regimes. Be that as it may, the question of whether dollarization is preferable to convertibility (once it has been decided to establish a hard peg) does not have a clear answer, although it could be argued that the former exhibits some short-term benefits linked to greater credibility.

The relationship existing between the benefits of each exchange rate system and period of time that is considered for the analysis leads to a more general consideration. In trying to purchase credibility in the short run, many countries give up instruments of economic policy that could be used in the future or sources of income, such as seigniorage, when switching from a convertibility regime to dollarization. Obviously, the discount rate used to assess this trade-off will be larger the greater the prevailing instability, which leads one to conclude that these decisions should not be made in times of crisis. Unfortunately, this is what usually happens.

Consistency

The argument that convertibility was unsustainable because of the inconsistency of macroeconomic and microeconomic policies is somewhat true, but it does not add much from the point of view of the lessons to be learned. The reason is that no fixed exchange rate regime is sustainable if the rest of economic policy is not consistent with it. One of the supposed advantages of convertibility is that *per se* it could introduce a sufficient degree of discipline in the fiscal and other areas (wage and price flexibility).

In any case, the most important question is whether a consistent macroeconomic policy would have made convertibility sustainable or if, in any case,

---

out of which thirty show variations of the same sign in both series. Of the eleven cases in which both series exhibit different signs, seven correspond to important changes in the devaluation risk and four correspond to the country risk. Using another approach, Powell and Sturzenneger (2000) define *a priori* certain events as "devaluation risk" and try to see if that affects the country risk, finding that such a relationship exists in the Argentine case.

18. Fisher (2001).

Figure 2. Public Sector Expenditures, National and Provincial Governments, 1990–2000[a]

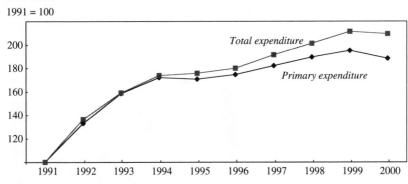

Source: Ministry of Economy of Argentina (2001).
a. Measured in current dollars.

the system would have experienced the problems that are common to all fixed exchange rate regimes. Before going into this discussion, one should consider three points on the idea that in the Argentine case public expenditure and the deficit were excessive during a substantial part of the 1990s, and that this impacted the regime's sustainability. First, total public expenditure in dollar terms increased by 101 percent between 1991 and 1999 (primary expenditures increased by 85 percent), as is shown in figure 2.[19] On the other hand, figures 3 and 4 show, respectively, the relatively high public sector deficit and the strong increase of the public debt, which went from 31 to 47 percent between 1993 and 1999, a period of relatively high growth of the economy.[20]

Second, greater public expenditure and a greater fiscal deficit might have exerted upward pressure on the price of nontradable goods and therefore contributed to the currency overvaluation. However, this last issue is not straightforward: the argument that an increase in public expenditure increases the price of nontradable goods rests on the assumption that the public sector spends relatively more on this type of goods, usually public works. In Argentina there was no significant increase in public works, but there was an increase

19. When deflated by the rate of U.S. inflation, the increase was 65 percent. However, when the deflator is the rate of international inflation relevant to Argentina, average of export and import prices, the increase in real terms was 121 percent. This increase is the result of the fall in both prices from 1991 to 1999. All calculations are based on data from the Ministry of Economy of Argentina and International Monetary Fund, *International Financial Statistics* (IFS) (2002), as noted in the respective figures.

20. The increase in debt is greater than the recorded deficit due to the existence of non-budgetary items, but mainly because of the recognition of old debts that were paid by issuing bonds (see Powell's data in this volume).

Figure 3. Public Sector Deficit, Total and Primary, 1993–2001

Percent of GDP

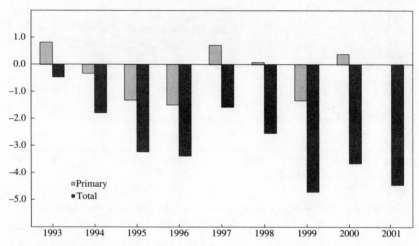

Source: Ministry of Economy of Argentina (2001).

Figure 4. Total Public Debt, 1993–2001

Percent of GDP

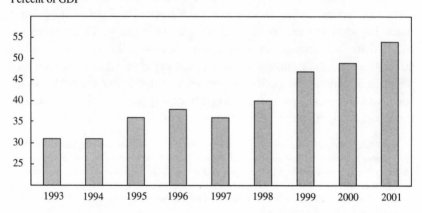

Source: Ministry of Economy of Argentina (2002).

in provincial wages, which generated some upward pressure on private wages.[21] However, it is also true that a large percentage of the increase in expenditure was due to higher pensions, meaning that it was mainly an income transfer, which did not necessarily add to the demand for nontradables.

Although the lower internal demand associated with a more restrictive fiscal policy—that is, a lower fiscal deficit—could have contributed to diminishing the appreciation of the exchange rate, it is also valid to ask whether a more virtuous fiscal policy would have generated greater confidence, and with it, a greater inflow of private capital, with the obvious effects on the price of nontradables.[22]

Third, a lower fiscal deficit would have helped to keep the debt at reasonable levels, and would have therefore made it easier to go through the recessive and deflationary adjustment without generating the feeling that the debt was becoming too hard to pay back.

Therefore, beyond the fact the fiscal loosening may have contributed somewhat to the currency appreciation, the more negative effect resulted from the increase of debt during the ascending phase of the cycle, which created the need for a strongly procyclical policy in the recessive phase and generated a feeling of debt fatigue.

Exchange Rate Appreciation

The other conclusion that can be drawn from this situation is that convertibility, like any other fixed exchange rate regime, generates a currency appreciation. This is especially the case if the regime in question is used to stabilize the economy and coincides with a great inflow of capital to emerging countries. Experience shows that what usually happens is that in the two years following either convertibility or dollarization, consumer prices increase, by 230 percent in Estonia, 93 percent in Lithuania, 46 percent in Argentina, 134 percent in Ecuador, and only 4 percent in El Salvador (note that data for El Salvador is for a fifteen-month period).[23] Beyond these observations, and

21. The increase in provincial wages may have affected private wages until 1994. From that point onward, average unemployment above 15 percent and a public sector that ceased to absorb employment seem to suggest that the public sector was not an important element for explaining the low flexibility observed in nominal wages. On the other hand, lower public spending would have allowed for lower taxes and a corresponding increase in competitiveness.

22. Hausmann and Velasco's paper in this volume claims that a more expansive fiscal policy always increases demand, but this result is basically obtained by assuming that capital inflows are not linked to the size of the fiscal deficit and public debt.

23. Author's own calculations based on IFS (2002). The two-year period was estimated

from a conceptual point of view, there are two relevant issues that must be analyzed to see whether convertibility could generate different behaviors than those arising from soft pegs, namely its impact on capital flows and effect on private and public sector discipline. Regarding the first point, one can expect that convertibility, being a more credible exchange rate regime, will increase the flow of capital into the country and thus contribute to a greater appreciation of the local currency. With respect to the disciplinary effect of convertibility, this paper has already mentioned the increase in public spending in Argentina, and in the private sector nominal wages increased by 36 percent during the first two years of convertibility. Therefore, there is no reason to believe that convertibility induces a lower exchange rate appreciation than soft pegs. On the other hand, there are reasons to think that deflation can be somewhat easier, since companies will be more aware that an increase in competitiveness can only come through a decrease in costs. This does not mean that convertibility will not face all the difficulties linked to price and wage rigidity. It took a flexible economy like that of Hong Kong four years (from May 1998 to May 2002) to achieve a price deflation of 11.2 percent,[24] while in the case of Argentina deflation was just 3.1 percent between 1997 and 2001.[25] Besides, deflation generates well-known credit market problems that affect the stability of the financial market.

Which of these lessons is more valid in the Argentine case? There is no doubt that the fiscal policy of the 1990s was not consistent with convertibility in the medium and long runs. But it is also true that even with consistent macroeconomic policies, a hard peg does not preclude an exchange rate appreciation. While it makes deflation in a later period less difficult, it is probable that it does not do so to such an extent as to conclude that the system is always sustainable, let alone to think that it is preferable to other forms of exchange rate arrangements that allow for greater flexibility. The best exchange rate regime crucially depends on the level of openness of the economy, the degree of dependency of the current account on the country to which the currency is tied, the magnitude and frequency of external shocks, and the degree of dol-

using the accumulated inflation rate of the twenty-four-month period immediately following the month when the currency board or dollarization was implemented, that is, when the nominal exchange rate was fixed.

24. Author's own calculations based on data from the Hong Kong Monetary Authority (www.info.gov.hk/hkma/eng/statistics).

25. Compared with the U.S. inflation rate from 1995 to 2001, the Argentine consumer price index (CPI) underperformed the U.S. CPI by 20.5 percent. The evolution of the Argentine CPI showed during this period a downward trend relative to the evolution of the U.S. CPI. Author's own calculations based on IFS (2002).

larization of existing liabilities. Note that Argentina is a very closed economy, with weak trade links to the United States and prone to large external shocks—in particular of financial nature. It does not fulfill the conditions for a hard peg.[26] However, it has a very high level of liabilities dollarization.

Finally, this paper concurs with the belief that dollarization—putting aside all political considerations for the time being—is a more efficient system than convertibility only in the short run. In any case, dollarization would not have avoided the appreciation of the exchange rate and consequently the difficult task of gaining competitiveness through deflation. It is obvious that convertibility would have experienced fewer problems if macroeconomic policies had been more consistent, but there are few doubts that an appreciation of the exchange rate and a difficult adjustment process would have nonetheless followed the strong external shocks suffered by the economy. In this context is hard to understand how dollarization could have helped to reduce substantially the costs of adjustment.

The discussion above seems to suggest that the adoption of a convertibility system was a mistake. However, this is not necessarily the case. As usual in economics, the costs and benefits of any system must be evaluated, taking into account the alternatives. It is evident that convertibility contributed to the stabilization of the economy and was therefore initially necessary, if it is considered within the context of Argentina's inflationary history. The question is a rather different one and related to whether convertibility should have been abandoned in the good times. The answer is that it would have been the best thing to do, but one must agree on the fact that the political economy of this process is a very complex one. Can one imagine a minister of economy trying to convince the president that convertibility should be abandoned while the economy is growing at 6 percent a year? However, the truth is that none of Argentina's ministers of economy even attempted to convince the president to switch exchange rate regimes. While the political economy of such a move is clearly very complicated, it is still valid to look for an explanation of why this was not done in December 1999, when President de la Rua took over from Carlos Menem. What were the options at the time? What can be said about

---

26. According to author's calculations, which are based on data from WDI (2002) and International Monetary Fund, *Direction of Trade Statistics* (2002), between 1990 and 1999 the average openness coefficient of Argentina was 14.4; exports to the United States in the same period only represented 10 percent of total exports. During these years, around 40 percent of annual observations presented variations in private capital flows higher than 3 percent of GDP, (author's own estimations based on IMF, *World Economic Outlook,* 2002).

the choices that where made, from both *ex ante* and *ex post* perspectives? The following section of this paper attempts to shed some light on these issues.

Argentine Policy Options in December 1999

In order to evaluate (from a policymaker's perspective) what the alternatives were in December 1999, it is necessary to understand the prevailing situation at that time. The main issues were:

—Lack of competitiveness as a consequence of an increase in the equilibrium exchange rate. This increase was in turn a consequence of several external shocks, including the drastic reduction of capital flows (figure 5); a fall in exports prices of around 23 percent between 1996 and 1999;[27] the devaluation of the currency of the main trade partner (Brazil); and the appreciation of the dollar. The last two factors account for an appreciation of the real effective exchange rate of around 15 percent between December 1997 and December 1999 (figure 6).

—Recession during the previous eighteen months.

—Large fiscal deficit (4.7 percent of GDP in 1999) and perverse debt dynamic (an increase of GDP to 47 from 31 percent in the previous six years in spite of the peso appreciation—that is, the debt at the equilibrium exchange rate was even higher).[28]

—Long history of high inflation, two episodes of hyperinflation, and therefore the expectation of a high pass-through from the exchange rate to prices.

—Appearance that the sudden stop of capital flows would continue for a while.

Considering all these factors from a purely economic point of view, the textbook recipe in this case clearly indicates that the most reasonable policy action would have been to devalue the currency and reduce the fiscal deficit. However, there were some additional factors:

—Liabilities of the private and public sectors were totally dollarized (85 percent of total credit to the private sector, 96 percent of the public sector debt, 65 percent of total private deposits, and 78 percent of time deposits).[29]

—Contracts with public utilities companies were dollarized and indexed to the U.S inflation rate, as were most of the contracts among the private sector.

27. Based on data from Argentina's Ministry of Economy.
28. See figures 3 and 4.
29. Data provided by the Central Bank of Argentina.

Figure 5. Private Capital Flows, Fourth Quarter 1994–First Quarter 2002[a]

Net as percent of GDP

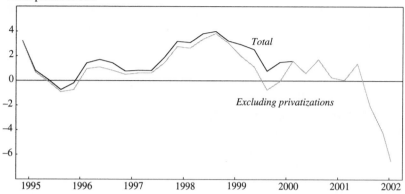

a. Four-quarter moving average.

Figure 6. Real Effective Exchange Rate, April 1991–April 2001

1991 M4 = 100

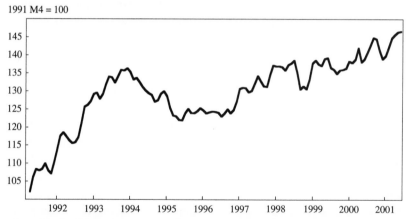

Source: International Monetary Fund, *International Financial Statistics* (2002).

—The established convertibility regime was a binding social contract with the population (according to opinion polls, a large majority of the population wanted to maintain the convertibility regime).[30]

—There was a consensus among analysts against devaluation; some were even in favor of full dollarization.[31]

30. For example, a national poll by Mora y Araujo & Asociados showed that as late as December 2001, 62 percent of the population was against devaluation.

31. See, for example, Hausmann (1999).

—There were positive prospects regarding external factors, such as the weakening of the dollar (due mainly to the large current account deficit of the United States and a higher rate of growth in Europe), the revaluation of the main trade partner's currency (after a large devaluation), and an increase in the world's rate of growth (expected increase in export prices).

Taking into account these additional factors, the evaluation of the economic team was that the most reasonable policy action was to maintain the convertibility regime. At the same time, of course, fiscal tightening was seen as fundamental to obtaining external support—that is, external financing. In order to improve competitiveness, it was necessary to introduce more flexibility in the economy, and this objective was pursued through labor reform and the deregulation of several sectors, mainly telecommunications. The economic measures designed to reduce the fiscal deficit should not aggravate the competitiveness problem, meaning that they should be mainly aimed at reducing expenditures (1 percent of GDP) and increasing taxes on personal income and consumption (0.6 percent of GDP). One alternative was to go for an additional reduction in expenditures. This was the best alternative, but the only way to do it was through less transfer to the provinces. This was discussed at a cabinet meeting and everybody agreed that it was not politically feasible. At that time the opposition controlled the Senate and two-thirds of the provincial governments.

It was expected that these measures were going to restore growth, or at least could prevent a worse scenario. Better international prices and the depreciation of the dollar, together with more flexibility of prices and wages, could help to improve competitiveness. In the meantime, fiscal tightening and structural reforms could help to soften financing restrictions and allow a reduction in interest rates. But what were the alternatives to the measures discussed above? Some options included:

—Maintaining or increasing the fiscal deficit. Considering the negative debt dynamic and that Argentina (unlike the developed world) faced some restrictions in financial markets, the question simply was, who was going to finance such a deficit? Of course, this is a consequence of not saving in the good times. Anyway, this alternative does not deserve a more lengthy discussion simply because it was beyond the budget constraint.[32]

—Making a larger adjustment to the fiscal deficit in order to improve credibility and reduce interest rates. This was a more reasonable alternative. Given

32. The only possibility would have been a jumbo package from the IMF, but that was not feasible at the time.

the fact that a fiscal tightening was necessary to convince the markets to provide further financing, it could be convenient to turn necessity into virtue and attempt a greater fiscal adjustment. The idea would have been to get a larger reduction in interest rates that could have compensated for the additional reduction in demand; but this was not granted, especially considering the sudden stop of capital flows to emerging markets at that time. This alternative was evaluated, but there was no political support for it, especially considering that the additional reduction in expenditures should have come mainly from the provinces. As mentioned above, the opposition controlled the Senate and provinces. Other alternatives, such as a general reduction of wages and pensions, were unthinkable at that time.[33]

—Full dollarization. The reason would have been the elimination of the risk of devaluation, hoping it could have helped to change expectations. As has been argued in this paper, the impact of such a measure on capital inflows was not clear. It is even possible that some of the market agents would have argued that as the result of the measure, fiscal deficit would have increased by 0.3 percent of GDP, given the loss of seigniorage revenue, and therefore additional adjustment were needed. Besides these considerations, the political resistance to dollarization would have resulted in political turmoil and lack of legislative support for any kind of initiative.

—Devaluation. As argued above, a successful exit from a hard peg should be done in good times, that is, with an appreciation of the exchange rate. Of course, those were not good times, and therefore exiting the convertibility clearly implied devaluation. There were two ways to devalue. The first alternative would have been to devalue the currency and, in order to avoid the balance sheet problem, convert all dollar contracts (including deposits, domestic credit, and external debt, as well as private and public debt) into domestic currency. This solution would have broken all contracts and would have triggered a default on the external debt. After that the question would have been how to finance a current account deficit of 4 percent of GDP and a fiscal deficit of a similar magnitude.[34] Moreover, it is quite difficult to imagine that a financial crisis could have been avoided after such extreme measures. A run on deposits would have been the most likely result.

---

33. Later in the year, at the end of May, wages of public employees were reduced on average by 10 percent; this saved 0.2 percent of GDP. A similar reduction of pensions would have saved additionally 0.6 percent of GDP (calculations based on data from the Ministry of Economy of Argentina).

34. Of course, the economic collapse would have ended with a current account deficit.

The second alternative would have been to devalue while trying to maintain the contracts in their original currency. This in turn would have been almost impossible. Among other things, a real devaluation of 40 percent would have increased the debt to around 70 percent of GDP. The renegotiation process among the private sector would have been extremely complicated, and it would have paralyzed the contracts for a long period of time.

In any case, to abandon the convertibility would have most likely resulted in a large devaluation, debt default, and financial crisis.

Having been responsible for the country's economic policy, I still think that the economic policies implemented then were the best options possible, given the data that were available at that time. Maintaining the convertibility had some costs, but abandoning it would have had even larger costs, among them a financial crisis. From that experience, it is clear that the cost of exiting the convertibility increases as time goes by, as both the volume of dollar-denominated contracts and the currency mismatch in the financial system increase. The only doubt still remaining concerns the alternative of a larger fiscal adjustment. However, considering the "sudden stop" of capital flows, there was the risk of an additional demand contraction. Besides that, I have no doubt that the government coalition was not prepared for such a move. In any case, if the idea was to have a big impact on the markets, a reduction of total expenditures of around 10 percent was necessary. Is any political party in the world prepared for such an extreme measure? I do not know of any example since the Great Depression, and everybody knows how that experience ended. Even with the intention of gaining the financial market's confidence, this decision would have produced such political turmoil that the investors would have taken, in the best possible scenario, a wait-and-see attitude.

Unfortunately, external factors did not behave as expected. The dollar appreciated even more and the real failed to appreciate after the initial large devaluation. Moreover, the Federal Reserve increased interest rates. Although country risk declined during the first quarter of 2000, the level of economic activity did not recover. The response to the country risk increase in April was to deepen the fiscal adjustment through a reduction in nominal wages in the public sector. Other bad news included the weakening of the government's political coalition, which finally led to the vice president resigning his post. The country risk increased by 300 points in the thirty days following the resignation.

The only way to try to restore credibility in such a context was through a jumbo package. We negotiated it with the IMF. At the time, we were able to obtain external financing, while avoiding additional fiscal restrictions in the short run; moreover, some tax reductions for enterprises were announced in order to improve competitiveness. However, the agreement with the IMF included a long-term fiscal adjustment that was necessary to assure debt sustainability—such as a reform of Social Security to reduce future expenditures—and an agreement with the provinces in order to avoid additional transfers if tax revenues increased. Finally, additional structural reforms were announced, with the aim of reducing costs and improving people's well-being, such as the *obras sociales* reform and more deregulation.

Contrary to what has been said, the market reaction to the new program was positive.[35] Two months after the jumbo package was approved, there was a 300-point reduction in country risk, a reduction in interest rates, as well as an impressive improvement in consumer confidence. However, the long-term measures agreed on with the IMF were not approved by the Congress, and there was a series of bad news and external factors that damaged this improved confidence, including that:

—the government's political coalition was falling apart;

—tax revenues were not increasing;

—the independent central bank had increased the reserve requirement by two points (back to around 24 percent of total deposits);

—the president of the central bank was accused of money laundering and there were plans to impeach him; and

—Turkey, the other country receiving a jumbo package from the IMF, had moved to a floating exchange rate regime.

This was too much bad news for an economic minister who was already worn out by fifteen months in office and the economic recession.[36] At that time, March 2, 2001, the political situation was even worse than at the beginning of de la Rua's administration, because the government's political coalition was extremely fragile. Deposits and reserves, however, were at their highest levels ever. At that time, there was not a currency or banking crisis (see figures 7a and 7b).[37]

35. Calvo, Izquierdo, and Talvi (2002) argued that the fiscal loosening generated a negative reaction from markets. However, the markets reacted well because more of the financing of that deficit was granted. The negative reaction from February onward was related to bad news (mentioned earlier in this paper) and basically to doubts related to the fulfillment of the IMF targets and, therefore, the disbursement of money by the IMF.

36. Powell mentions in this volume that he does not know why I resigned and presents different interpretations of my personal behavior on the matter. Let me just say that it was the result of not having the president's confidence and support. I think it is a satisfactory reason.

37. By the end of February, financial system reserves reached around $33 billion, while total deposits amounted to more than $75 billion.

Figure 7a. Private Sector Deposits, June 1, 2000–January 1, 2002

Millions of dollars

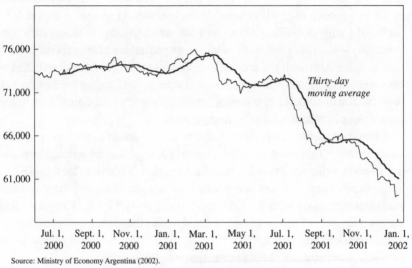

Source: Ministry of Economy Argentina (2002).

Figure 7b. International Reserves, June 1, 2000–January 1, 2002

Millions of dollars

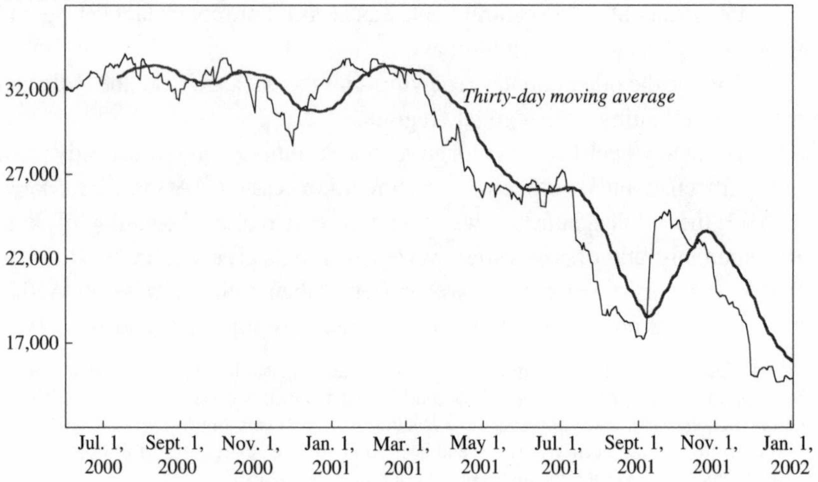

Source: Ministry of Economy Argentina (2002).

The new economic minister, Ricardo Lopez-Murphy, decided to pursue an additional adjustment in government expenditures equivalent to 0.7 percent of GDP.[38] Demonstrating how fragile political support for the government was, his measures were quickly dismissed and he was forced to resign after only fifteen days in office. After this failure of the orthodox approach of cutting expenditures to regain market confidence, the next economic minister, Domingo Cavallo, attempted a more heterodox approach. Perhaps this is one of the reasons why he initially received strong political support. He decided not to pursue a fiscal tightening and argued in public with the president of the central bank about the need for monetary expansion. After a month, the central bank's president was dismissed and the central bank, under pressure, reduced reserve requirements. Besides that, Cavallo decided to modify the convertibility regime, tying the peso to a basket of currencies (euro and dollar). This was perhaps the worst error. There was no improvement at all in competitiveness, but this measure raised expectations that additional movements away from convertibility were to come. Cavallo also implemented a huge debt swap that extended the debt maturity, thus avoiding the default in the short run, but at the cost of an increase of interest rates on the swapped debt. In trying to avoid a liquidity problem, the solvency difficulties were exacerbated. From July onward, deposits and international reserves kept falling most of the time (see figures 7a and 7b). Later, when the level of economic activity was falling at a rate of 4.9 percent year-to-year in the third quarter of 2001,[39] Cavallo tried to achieve a zero fiscal deficit rule, but he did not have the same political support as he had at the beginning of his administration. From this point, currency and financial crises moved together; there was not another possibility in an economy that was almost completely dollarized.

I conclude the story here. Other papers on Argentina illustrate what followed. This paper tries to show that there were no easy solutions in 2000, after the seeds of Argentina's economic problems had been planted during the 1990s. I still believe that there were no better economic policy alternatives in 2000. The crisis that followed during the second half of 2001 had its roots in these decade-long problems, but it could have been avoided. The collapse was the direct consequence of a strong wave of self-fulfilling pessimism, fed by mismanagement of economic policy and the collapse of the government coalition.

Of course, this brief story of Argentina under the de la Rua presidency was written by one of its participants, and therefore it is probably biased. In

38. *Clarin,* March 16, 2001.
39. According to estimates by Ministry of Economy of Argentina (www.indec.gov.ar).

any case, it has tried to show the main factors behind the Argentine drama. A detailed political analysis is needed to have a better understanding of what really happened, although one thing is quite clear: most of the political leaders never understood the magnitude of the economic problems that Argentina was facing. It should be recognized, however, that the economic developments were not appealing for any politician. To mention just a few, the reduction of nominal wages and pensions along with lack of growth are hardly a politician's dream context. Should they be the only ones to blame for the depth and extension of the crisis? Is it not true that most economists never expressed too much concern on the main problems of Argentine economy during the 1990s? Is it not true that the IMF supported the Argentine programs through all that period?

What followed de la Rua's resignation is well known. With a financial crisis and *de facto* default on the debt, it was almost impossible to avoid the abandonment of convertibility. As mentioned earlier, a financial crisis and debt default go together with moving away from convertibility. While the change of exchange rate regime implied breaking most of the contracts in the economy, it is almost impossible to imagine a worse way to do it. Moreover, is difficult to understand why, at the time of this writing, Argentina has not been able to reestablish the rule of law. The consequence has been the deepening of the depression that began in July 2002.

What Has Been Learned?

There are some key lessons to be drawn from the 1990s currency crisis, and particularly from the Argentine crisis.

—To peg the exchange rate (even a hard peg) in a world plagued with large external shocks is usually a problem, except for very open and already dollarized economies that have a close trade relation (and even better, a similar business cycle) with the anchor country. Therefore, if there is no alternative to a convertibility regime to stabilize the economy, it should be abandoned in good times. Similar lessons have been learned many times in the last twenty years. The good performance of the economy at the initial stages of fixed exchange rate systems is usually the main reason underlying a government's reluctance to abandon this type of exchange rate arrangement.

—A convertibility regime is not a substitute for the required political consensus to maintain fiscal discipline.

—When a dollarized economy with a hard peg suffers an external shock, there are no easy solutions. Things are even worse if the country is running a relatively large fiscal deficit and does not have enough wage and price flexibility. To abandon convertibility at that time will prompt a financial crisis and insecurity about the rule of law; to maintain it could result in recession and deflation. Therefore, if convertibility was not abandoned in good times, it is not clear what the best solution is in bad times, although one of the variables crucial for this decision is the level of dollarization.

—Massive dollarization of the financial system should be discouraged, even if it reduces the rate of growth in the short run. One way to do that is allowing indexation clauses, establishing different reserve requirements and increasing the provisions for dollar loans to nontradable activities. Besides that, a managed floating exchange rate would eliminate the free insurance implicit in a hard peg. Once the economy is fully dollarized is almost impossible to abandon a hard peg without a financial crisis.

—In an emerging country with a convertibility regime, a fiscal surplus should be the target when the economy is growing. It should be achieved through fiscal expenditure restraint. The Argentine debt had increased by 16 percent of GDP in six years, while the economy was growing at an average rate of almost 5 percent.

These recommendations are not easily followed. In a highly dollarized economy, introducing restrictions on financial contracts in dollars will reduce the financial system deepening and slow growth in the short run. At the same time, it will be very difficult to maintain control over fiscal expenditures when the economy is growing at the rate of 6 percent on an annual basis. It will be even more difficult if the president is seeking reelection.

—The Argentine crisis was not caused by a weak financial system or a liquidity problem. The financial system was healthy, and average debt maturity was more than seven years. In any case, a prolonged crisis at the end became a liquidity crisis—and then turned into a financial crisis.

—A very liquid and solvent financial system helps to manage the transition when the country faces adverse external shocks. For instance, in Argentina the deposits kept increasing during 2000 in spite of the economic and political problems. However, there is no way to build a bulletproof financial system. The financial system in Argentina withstood a drop in deposits of 21.3 percent from the end of February 2001 to the end of December 2001 (see figure 7-B). Building a more liquid financial system is impossible, unless one opts for a narrow banking system, but such a system would not be useful in terms of financial intermediation.

—If there is a weakness in the financial system or a liquidity problem, it is quite difficult to solve it using market instruments in the middle of a crisis. The Argentine mega swap is a good example of how a liquidity problem could be transformed into a solvency problem. Attempts to close banks during a financial crisis without paying deposits would be a way to feed on financial panic (East Asia and Argentina in 1995).

—If all contracts have been broken, restoring credibility will be a very hard task. It is impossible if one does not have either a program or an agreement with the international community. That is what happened in Argentina, and the country probably will suffer the consequences for a long time.

—What about the role of the IMF? First of all, I do not think that moral hazard has been a major issue in most of the last currency crisis. Besides that, of course, there is always some kind of moral hazard with rescue packages, but it seems that most of the last financial packages avoided meltdown risks. I think Argentina had a reasonable possibility with the 2000 jumbo package. The IMF should not be blamed for the Argentine failure to deliver. However, the IMF should be blamed for supporting inconsistent policies during the 1990s.

References

Calvo, Guillermo, and Carlos Végh. 1999. "Inflation Stabilization and BOP Crises in Developing Countries." In *Handbook of Macroeconomics,* vol. 16, edited by John Taylor and Michael Woodford. Amsterdam: Elsevier Science.

Calvo, Guillermo, Alejandro Izquierdo, and Ernesto Talvi. 2002. "Sudden Stops, the Real Exchange Rate, and Fiscal Sustainability: Argentina's Lessons." Working Paper 469. Washington: Inter-American Development Bank.

Chang, Roberto, and Andrés Velasco. 1999. "Liquidity Crises in Emerging Markets: Theory and Policy." Working Paper W7272. Cambridge, Mass.: National Bureau of Economic Research.

Corsetti, Giancarlo, Paolo Pesenti, and Nouriel Roubini. 1998. "Fundamental Determinants of the Asian Crisis: A Preliminary Empirical Assessment." Paper prepared for the JIMF–Fordham University Conference on Perspectives on the Financial Crisis in Asia.

Díaz-Alejandro, Carlos. 1988. "Good-bye Financial Repression, Hello Financial Crash." In *Trade, Development and the World Economy: Selected Essays of Carlos Diaz-Alejandro,* edited by Andrés Velasco. New York: Blackwell.

Eichengreen, Barry, and Michael D. Bordo. 2002. "Crises Now and Then: What Lessons from the Last Era of Financial Globalization?" Working Paper W8716. Cambridge, Mass.: National Bureau of Economic Research.

Fischer, Stanley. 2001. "Exchange Rate Regimes: Is the Bipolar View Correct?" Paper prepared for the annual meeting of the American Economic Association, New Orleans, January 6.

Goldstein, Morris. 2002. "Managed Floating Plus." *Policy Analyses in International Economics* 66. Washington: Institute for International Economics (March).

Hausmann, Ricardo. 1999. "After Ten Years of Convertibility: Should Argentina Move to Greener Pastures?" Paper prepared for the Conference on the Tenth Anniversary of the Convertibility Law, organized by the Banco Central de la Republica Argentina, Buenos Aires, April 5–6.

Heymann, Daniel, and Pablo Sanguinetti. 1998. "Business Cycles from Misperceived Trends." *Economic Notes* 27 (2): 205–32.

Krugman, Paul. 1979. "A Model of Balance-of-Payments Crises." *Journal of Money, Credit, and Banking* 11: 311–25.

——— 1999. "Balance Sheets, the Transfer Problem, and Financial Crises." In *International Finance and Financial Crises,* edited by Robert Flood and others. Kluwer Academic Publishers.

Perry, Guillermo, and Luis Servén. 2002. "The Anatomy of a Multiple Crisis: Why Was Argentina Special and What Can We Learn from It?" Mimeo. World Bank.

Powell, Andrew, and Federico Sturzenegger. 2000. "Dollarization: The Link between Devaluation and Default Risk." Mimeo. Central Bank of Argentina and Universidad Torcuato Di Tella.

Sachs, Jeffrey, and Steven Radelet. 1998. "The East Asian Financial Crisis: Diagnosis, Remedies, Prospects." *Brookings Papers on Economic Activity* 1: 1–90.

World Bank. 1998. "Argentina: Financial Sector Review." Report 17864-AR. September.

Y U N G   C H U L   P A R K

Korea University

Does East Asia Need
a New Development Paradigm?

Viewing the twentieth century as a competition of economic models, many observers claim that capitalism proved its superiority in the semifinals of the 1980s. And Frankel and Roubini describe how some claim that the American brand of capitalism beat the Japanese brand of capitalism in the finals of the 1990s.[1] In an opposing view, Stiglitz argues that despite the financial crisis that devastated East Asia, many of the alleged institutional weaknesses blamed for the collapse may well have only played a minute role.[2] East Asia was not any more vulnerable to the crisis than other regions, and East Asia may remain the best model of development the world has seen to date. Stiglitz adds that the East Asian miracle was real and based on a set of sound fundamentals and public policies.[3]

Between these two opposing views there is a third—that increasing demands for economic governance reforms and unwavering commitment to open trade and financial regimes, together with strong fundamentals under more transparent and democratic auspices, provide the basis for substantial optimism for the future of the East Asian development paradigm.[4]

Supporters of Stiglitz's view would point out that structural vulnerabilities of the East Asian countries, which are long-standing problems, did not impede the rapid growth process for almost three decades before the crisis. Then why did they suddenly wreak havoc on these countries? Opponents of Stiglitz's view would then retort that these countries were adding new risk factors to an

---

This paper is derived from Park (2002).
1. Frankel and Roubini (2000).
2. Stiglitz (1998).
3. Stiglitz (1998).
4. Haggard (2000, pp. 236–37).

211

already large set of vulnerabilities, thereby increasing their propensity to financial crisis. The debate on the causes of the East Asian crisis in 1997, whether the crisis countries were suffering from short-term liquidity problems or cumulative effects of old as well as new structural weaknesses, is not likely to end anytime soon.

The International Monetary Fund (IMF) and the World Bank invariably point to the structural problems in the public, financial, and corporate sectors as major causes of the crisis and assert that only a decisive and fast structural reform will ensure recovery and medium-term durable growth.[5] A number of recent studies on the East Asian crisis, while recognizing structural vulnerabilities, put more blame on distortions in international financial markets, in particular, panic and herding of market participants. To many advocates of the liquidity-panic view of the crisis, the rapid pace of recovery in 1999 and 2000 in East Asia was hardly surprising and was vindication that the region did not, in fact, need the IMF reform to stabilize its financial markets by restoring its access to international capital markets.

Five years after the crisis, East Asia is at a crossroads. If Frankel and Roubini are correct in their description, East Asian countries should not hesitate to replace entirely the precrisis model of development with an Anglo-American system of capitalism.[6] On the other hand, if the problems associated with the imperfections of international financial markets are more to blame as the causes of the crisis, East Asia would be better off by staying with the traditional East Asian model and at most reforming it to be compatible with changes in the domestic and global economic environments.

This paper searches for a new development paradigm that could help East Asian countries adapt to societal and political changes taking place in the region while retaining their precrisis vitality and competitiveness for durable growth in integrating into the global economy. Is the East Asian development model, as it was described by the World Bank study of the East Asian miracle, so outdated and out of touch with the realities of a new global economy that it should be repudiated in favor of an alternative model, such as Anglo-American capitalism?[7] If it is not, can the model be reformed in a way that will make it as viable for postcrisis development as it was in the past in East Asia?

At the outset, it should be emphasized that East Asia covers a huge territory, is home to almost 2 billion people, and in 2000 accounted for 23 percent

5. World Bank (2000), Fisher (1999), and Lane and others (1999).
6. Frankel and Roubini (2000).
7. World Bank (1993).

of the total world gross domestic product. It indeed would be presumptuous to talk about a new paradigm for all of East Asia, just as it would be to define the East Asian development model as if it applied to all East Asian countries. This paper analyzes some of the structural weaknesses of the precrisis East Asian model and asks whether the general features of the model would survive the global economy of the twenty-first century, driven by information and communication technological innovation. A discussion of some of the reforms of the financial, corporate, and public sectors necessary to rejuvenate the model as a new paradigm for postcrisis development in East Asia and concluding remarks follow.

Weaknesses of the Precrisis East Asian Model

Even before the outbreak of the crisis, the East Asian system had been showing many structural cracks. During the five-year period preceding the crisis, the system had been unable to moderate the asset boom and associated current account deterioration, which were caused by a massive increase in capital inflows. When much of East Asia came under speculative attack as a result of a contagion effect of Thailand's crisis, the system simply broke down.

The three decades of rapid growth embedded many institutional weaknesses and rigidities in the system, which in turn bred resistance to changes that were necessary to facilitate societal and economic adjustments to political democratization, economic liberalization, and globalization of the world economy. More specifically, the East Asian countries failed to restructure their systems in line with democratization and market liberalization, and to be credible at their interfaces with global markets. This paper identifies four critical failures.

The first failure was the inherent conflict between East Asia's governance mechanism, on the one hand, and democratic polity and market liberalization on the other. East Asian countries were slow in developing a democratic governance mechanism at various levels of the economy to replace the system of "consultative polities" that, as described by Campos and Root, characterized these authoritarian regimes.[8] By the early 1990s it was clear, at least in some East Asian countries, that the consultative mechanisms of coordination and cooperation between the government and private sector—and between the dif-

---

8. See Campos and Root (1996) for the consultative mechanisms of coordination.

ferent groups within the private sector—were crumbling and degenerating into collusion, political cronyism, and corruption.

The collapse of consultative polities bared serious coordination problems at the national, industry, and enterprise levels. Large, family-owned firms or industrial groups were growing more politically powerful, to the point of dictating national economic policy. Their predatory pursuit for a large share in many markets, including financial ones, brought on a further concentration of both economic power and industrial structure. Yet many of the East Asian governments literally did not care to know what the large, family-owned enterprises and their main banks were doing. Governments acted as if they should not be involved in monitoring the behavior of banks and corporations, lest it could be misunderstood as unnecessary intervention in a market economy. In addition banks did not seem to know what their client firms were doing. Labor movements became more militant, disrupting not only workplaces but at times entire national economies, yet governments could no longer mediate disputes between labor and management.

The East Asian model's second failure arose from the delay in developing a financial infrastructure as well as legal and regulatory systems that could support a market-oriented and open financial system. During the early 1990s, the bulk of foreign capital inflows were channeled to domestic firms through a poorly managed and inefficient banking system. Banks should have improved their asset-liability and risk management. However, ensconced in a closed and regulated market environment, the banks, which were placed under the direct control of the government in many East Asian countries, did not have incentives to foster risk management capabilities required in a deregulated financial environment. The banks were slow or negligent in complying with global standards on capital adequacy, loan classification, loan loss provisioning, and lending restrictions, including those on investments in stocks and bonds. They certainly did not care to monitor their client firms—not nearly as much as privately owned and deregulated banks would do. The "control syndrome" meant that the government did not realize either the need or the urgency for building an effective supervisory and regulatory system that would buttress a market-oriented and liberalized financial system, although the banks were increasingly exposed to new and greater risks. In the relationship banking that characterized the East Asian financial system, banks were supposed to play an important role in governing corporations, but it was unclear who was to monitor the banks. In the end, it was the government.

East Asian policymakers embarked on financial market deregulation and opening toward the latter part of the 1980s. Financial deregulation sought to diversify financial instruments and markets. Due in part to this effort, banks, nonbank financial institutions, and capital markets all grew quickly and became more active in the 1990s. However, the financial deregulation was not accompanied by institutional reform for strengthening regulatory, governance, legal, and judiciary systems that would improve accounting, auditing, and disclosure requirements of financial institutions and firms. The deregulation also failed to include reform for infrastructure development.

Advanced market infrastructures, such as competent accounting and securities law firms, investment banking, credit rating agencies, corporate restructuring specialists, and fund managers were understandably slow to develop. In the absence of these market supporting institutions, it is questionable whether incipient capital markets could have been buffered against speculation and served as stable sources of investment financing. As far as the financial system is concerned, the failure of the East Asian development model did not lie in bank domination, but was instead rooted in poor management and regulation of the banking sector. Why were the East Asian policymakers not attentive to these institutional problems? As long as the economies were growing as rapidly as they did in the 1970s and 1980s, these problems were not a cause for concern.

While most of the East Asian economies chose an adjustable dollar peg system for their exchange rate management, in many cases the system was controlled, and as a result prone to overvaluation. Beginning in the early 1990s, despite the apparent structural weaknesses and overvalued currencies, the East Asian economies were forced to open their financial intermediation industries and liberalize capital account transactions, thereby setting them up as easy targets for speculative attacks. Even if these countries were inclined to shift to free floating, they could not easily do so because they failed to develop market infrastructures such as hedging facilities that would have eased the difficulties of the regime shift. Here again, the adjustable peg system itself should not be faulted so much for the crisis, as it was mismanagement that kept the nominal exchange rate out of line with market developments.[9]

A third failure of the system is found in the closed and nontransparent corporate sector, which did not fare well with market liberalization and opening. In the early 1990s, major corporations from East Asia were beginning to borrow heavily from international financial markets and expanding their direct

9. On this point, see Williamson (2000).

investment throughout East Asia, and even in Europe and North America, as part of their globalization strategy. Although these corporations were becoming more active on the global scene, they were slow in reforming themselves to accept global norms and practices in accounting, disclosure, and corporate governance. Western investors were attracted to the growing economies of East Asia and to owning a stake in these large corporations that looked invincible with a global reach. Up close, however, these corporations were riddled with poor accounting and auditing irregularities, nontransparent management, and little protection of minority stockholders. Once again, East Asian economies failed to build a modern corporate sector that was transparent and accessible to foreign investors.

It has been shown that export-led development strategy was the most conspicuous, as well as successful, feature of the East Asian development model.[10] However, it was liable to a number of serious domestic risks, which were overlooked or improperly addressed, resulting in market distortions, concentrated industrial organization and private economic power, an inflexible exchange rate system prone to overvaluation, and, in some cases, perpetuation of government control of markets and the financial system. This is the fourth failure of the East Asian model.

When East Asian economies were embarking on the export push—Korea in the early 1960s and Southeast Asian countries a decade later—they had to cope with a formidable array of structural and institutional problems. There was no pool of entrepreneurs, managers, and traders who could initiate and lead development of export-oriented industries. The small and unstable financial systems could not direct resources to these industries, because the risks in lending to exporting firms were perceived to be too high. In many cases, efficiency of export industries required adoption of increasing-return technologies. These constraints, together with the limited availability of domestic and foreign resources, forced policymakers in the East Asian economies to support a small number of large producers—in some cases one or two—in each of the industries promoted for exports.

These firms grew to become successful exporters. With the growth of the economy, they developed into industrial groups such as the *chaebol* in Korea. The expansion and increase in the number of industrial groups created a monopolistic and oligopolistic market structure in many industries and resulted in concentration of private economic power. With a protected trade regime and closed financial system, the pricing and supply behavior of these groups

10. World Bank (1993).

in domestic markets had to be regulated. And East Asian policymakers attempted to rein in these powerful groups indirectly through the banking system, which they controlled with dubious success.

The emergence of powerful industrial groups also built barriers to financial deregulation and market opening. Although ownership of banks, and in some cases nonbank financial institutions, by any single shareholder was limited to adhere to the principle of separating commerce from banking, the industrial groups could easily dominate the management of banks and other nonbank financial intermediaries through cross-ownership and taking advantage of regulatory loopholes. Short of direct government control, it was often argued there were no adequate measures to prevent the industrial groups from dominating the banking industry. Insofar as the industrial groups held dominant market shares in many industries, it was also argued that domestic financial deregulation *per se* would not improve allocative efficiency of the financial system, while it was bound to increase concentration of power in the hands of a few family-owned industrial groups.

Reform Agenda

Although the crisis exposed a number of structural problems and damaged the universal applicability of the model, East Asia's experience with the crisis by no means proves that the East Asian system was surpassed by the Anglo-American model, as Frankel and Roubini describe.[11] A review of the characteristics and evolution of the East Asian model suggests that despite its structural weaknesses and failures to fend off financial crises, some of the main features of the system remain intact. These main features could serve well for postcrisis development of East Asia, although as a whole the model is in need of a major structural repair.[12] However, one must hasten to add that this conclusion does not mean that East Asia can remain content with its vintage 1960s–70s model, placing the blame for the 1997 crisis on foreign speculators. In fact, except for the basic building blocks of economic fundamentals, all aspects of the model, in particular institutions governing the financial system, the corporate sector, and the labor market, will have to be reformed. This need for reform is not surprising in view of the fact that the model, summarized by the World Bank miracle study, had evolved as a development paradigm

11. Frankel and Roubini (2000).
12. Park (2002).

designed to serve the interests of nondemocratic or authoritarian regimes during an era characterized by tightly controlled and closed markets, as well as protectionist trade practices.[13] What, then, are the necessary reforms and how could they be implemented to make the model as effective in a new East Asian and global environment as it was before?

Although the liberal policies of the Washington consensus still find many proponents, the virtues of the mixed economy are now better appreciated than before. As Rodrik points out, "the idea of a mixed economy is possibly the most valuable heritage the twentieth century bequeaths to the twenty-first century in the realm of economic policy."[14] Reflecting on this heritage, a new paradigm is most likely to be one of a large variety of mixed economy models that combine the state and market (*laissez faire* and intervention), as was the case in the old East Asian development model. The major challenge facing East Asian economies in the coming decades, therefore, is to nurture evolution of their own specific models of a mixed economy. In this evolutionary process, East Asian policymakers will come to realize that democratization has imposed a different participatory mechanism for consensus building. Economic liberalization has reduced the scope of industrial policies and other types of market intervention. It has also required the creation of a new set of institutions for financial regulation and supervision, corporate governance, and the management of industrial relations for the efficiency and stability of the market.

East Asia may not have to embrace Anglo-American capitalism. However, the global realities leave the region with no choice but to conform to international standards of transparency, disclosure, corporate governance, and banking, all established by the advanced countries in Europe and North America. Cultivating compatibility between the new East Asian system, on the one hand, and global standards and codes on the other will be important, because most of the East Asian countries will continue to rely on North American and European markets for their exports and will integrate themselves into a new global economy, which is likely to be dominated by the United States and European Union.

These two economies will dictate the rules governing international trade, foreign direct investment, and international financial transactions. At the same time, viability of the new East Asian model would require consistency with the rules of the World Trade Organization and the capacity to accommodate

13. World Bank (1993).
14. Rodrik (2000).

the global activities of multinational companies. It would also require the flexibility needed to adjust to the ongoing revolution in information technology. The scope and speed of the overall economic reform will have to be adjusted to the quality of government, institutional capacity to reform, and the other political and societal constraints to which East Asian emerging and developing economies are subject.

What type of a new model could satisfy all these old and new conditions and specifications? There would be little disagreement that the fundamentally sound development policies of the earlier periods will survive political as well as economic liberalization in East Asia. Indeed East Asian countries would be better off if they continued to adhere to the sound policies from which they benefited during the rapid growth period. These policies include:

—incentive schemes for promoting high rates of saving and investment;

—ensuring large investments in education in general, and research and development in particular;

—sustaining macroeconomic stability;

—maintaining market openness to acquire foreign technology and exposure to foreign competition;

—complementing social welfare policies with the growth-with-equity strategy.

As for the restructuring of the precrisis model, the discussion of the failures of the system in the preceding section leads one to identify the following areas where fundamental reform is required.

Governance

One of the priorities of reform falls on building a new governance system by embracing a set of new democratic institutions, rules, and norms, and complementing it with a host of new institutions for conflict management, social insurance, and regulations so that the market system can function better. In particular regulatory and judicial mechanisms for enforcing investor and creditor rights need to be improved by reforming securities, commercial, and bankruptcy laws. Many of these institutions are Western concepts and will have to be transplanted on an inhospitable East Asian cultural terrain. Unless this transplantation is carefully managed, with due consideration of the capacity and constraints of the reforming economies, the reform may not succeed. Specifically, the legal and judiciary reform will be met by strong political obstacles set up by bureaucracies and large, family-owned enterprises, the two principal groups of architects of the East Asian paradigm of development. Instead of blindly introducing an ideal set of institutions and rules borrowed from the West, East Asian countries would be better advised to enact rules that they can enforce within the existing legal and judicial framework.

East Asian countries will also be struggling with the question of why democracies have not been effective in moderating social conflict and political instability, improving government effectiveness, and establishing the rule of law. The following agenda includes East Asia's priorities for institutional reform for more effective governance:

—Establishing and enforcing procedural and constitutional rules for the democratic system and market-supporting institutions.

—Improving the quality, effectiveness, and efficiency of the delivery of public services.

—Enhancing the effectiveness of the judiciary and regulatory system.

—Reducing the incidence of corruption.

Role of Government

While accelerating their plan for building democratic and market institutions is critical, most East Asian governments cannot ignore the fact that their role has been undergoing a fundamental change from leading economic development to leading social development. However, less-developed East Asian countries may have a better chance of making a smooth transition to a democratic and market-oriented regime if they first succeeded in developing a strong but limited government. And within this framework of governance, these economies may be able to design industrial policies, consistent with the World Trade Organization, to facilitate technology transfers and manage limited intervention in the market when market failures dictate stronger actions. To these countries, the priorities of public sector reform are likely to be directed to establishing rules and norms that could provide government officials with incentives to act in the collective interest, while controlling corruption and arbitrary actions.

Social Protection

There is widespread consensus that East Asian countries, even after recovering from the crisis, may not be able to return to the high growth path of the precrisis period. This deceleration of economic growth has undermined the viability of the growth-with-equity strategy for social welfare. However, this does not necessarily mean that the European welfare system is an alternative mechanism for social protection for East Asia. To the extent that targeting the poor is the objective of social welfare policy, one can make a strong case for East Asia's social contract, which places emphasis on investment in people and communities.

Individual countries in East Asia will find it increasingly difficult to produce public goods for social welfare on their own as a result of economic globalization. This difficulty suggests the need for collective Social Security and harmonization of the tax system through economic integration at the regional level.

Industrial Relations

The region will be searching for ways to accommodate labor's growing demand for political participation. In managing industrial relations, East Asia's task would be to weigh the relative advantages of the Anglo-American system favoring labor market flexibility to the European "corporatist" approach, which places more emphasis on labor's participation in economic and social choices. After many years of suppressive labor policies, East Asian countries will benefit from making room for labor's political participation without compromising labor market flexibility. As far as labor participation is concerned, unlike in other areas of economic management, there cannot be a single approach acceptable to all of East Asia. Each country is expected to fashion its own mechanism of participation and bargaining with labor, compatible with its political system.

Financial Reform

Despite the structural problems that crippled the functioning of the financial system when it fell victim to a speculative attack, East Asia may have to depend on a bank-oriented financial system for an extended period of time in the future. This system would remain until a legal and regulatory structure is established that provides adequate protection to outside investors as a foundation for efficient securities markets.

Theory and experience do not prove that a capital market–oriented financial system is more effective in promoting economic development and financial market stability in emerging market economies. In fact in many East Asian countries, particularly those at earlier stages of development, the sequencing of financial reform would begin with improving efficiency and stability of the banking system before setting out to develop money and capital markets, because they have not established an efficient and stable payment system and the legal and regulatory system capable of supporting securities markets.

If there is one lesson to be learned from the crisis, it is that East Asian corporations will not be able to maintain robust growth unless they reduce their leverage by going directly to capital markets, rather than to banks, for their investment financing. In this regard, the backwardness of capital markets could serve as one of the major constraints on future growth in East Asia. Therefore, more developed East Asian countries may attempt to develop simultaneously both market-based and bank-based financial systems. Both require a set of prudential regulation, supervision, and administrative rules, although the development of capital markets requires a more elaborate system of regulations and legal infrastructure. Development of the regulatory and legal infrastructure may in turn require a medium-term strategy in which reforms involving capital adequacy, loan classification, loan-loss provisioning, and risk management and corporate governance introduce and enforce international codes and standards.

Reform of Industrial Organization

East Asian countries will gain little by dismantling large, family-owned businesses. What is needed at this stage of development is the strengthening of bank-based corporate governance and other legal and judiciary reform that will improve the transparency and accountability of these enterprises and provide better protection of minority stockholders.

Despite their problems of inefficiency, nontransparency, and inadequate governance, the breakup of East Asian family-owned industrial groups may cause more harm than good. The experiences of Western economies also suggest that the building of market institutions, better governance, transparency, and the protection of minority stockholders over time will strengthen market discipline to which the East Asian industrial groups will be subjected and which will weed out the inefficient groups. Increased competition from domestic market liberalization and integration into the global system will also weaken the traditional advantages of a large, family-owned group. In particular, the growth of knowledge-based industries could accelerate the breakup of these groups.[15] It is also worth nothing that East Asian industrial groups are not so much products of Asian values as they are of a certain stage of economic development.

15. World Bank (2000).

Some of today's industrial icons, such as Ford, Thyssens, and Siemens, started out as family businesses. Over time, they have become modern, transparent, and shareholder-friendly corporations.[16]

Exchange Rate System

In the aftermath of the East Asian crisis, emerging market economies have been given two alternatives choices for their exchange rate regimes: a free-floating or a currency-board system. The experiences of East Asian and other emerging market economies do not support viability of the two corner solutions. Instead they suggest that the policymakers of the East Asian countries may be justified in operating a managed floating system, which allows intervention in the foreign exchange market to smooth high-frequency movements in nominal exchange rates.[17]

Regional Integration and Cooperation

During the last decade, more advanced East Asian economies have gone so far into Western reform based on the Anglo-American capitalism that they cannot, and in fact should not, turn back the clock to return to the old East Asian development model. However, in a Washington consensus milieu, other less-developed countries in the region could be thrown into a disorderly and confusing process of market deregulation and opening without adequate preparations. East Asian countries may desire to determine an appropriate scope, and control the speed, of economic reform that will facilitate their gradual and smooth integration into the global economy. However, unless they are prepared to coordinate their policies and pool resources to guard against future crises through forming regional cooperative arrangements, there is the concern that their institution building reforms and future policies regarding market opening are likely to be dictated by international financial institutions and advanced economies in Europe and North America.

Small East Asian countries have found it increasingly difficult to provide many of the important public goods such as social protection, combating corruption, securing financial stability, and resolving the conflict between domestic politics and global economics. These public goods may be more efficiently produced at a regional level. Recognizing this reality, combined with the need for solidifying regional defenses against future crises, they have

16. "The End of the Tycoons," *Economist,* April 29–May 5, 2000, pp. 67–69.
17. Dooley, Dornbusch, and Park (2002); Goldstein (2001).

initiated serious discussions of the need and modality of regional integration in East Asia through trade liberalization and financial cooperation at various intergovernmental forums. These efforts have resulted in a number of regional agreements for integration, such as the Chiang Mai Initiative in 2000. In this initiative, ten members of the Association of Southeast Asian Nations (ASEAN), along with China, Japan, and South Korea (known as ASEAN plus Three), agreed to establish a system of bilateral swaps, which is a facility for liquidity support for those participating countries suffering from short-run balance of payments problems. However, receding fear of another crisis has combined with Japan's deepening recession to dampen considerably the initial enthusiasm for regional cooperation and integration. The China-Japan rivalry on political and economic leadership in East Asia and other regional disputes on trade, territory, and historical issues have also been formidable barriers to advancing the regional movement for integration.

Conclusion

With the growing acceptance of the liberal ideology of the Washington consensus throughout East Asia since the early 1990s, many countries in the region embarked on liberal reform, deregulating and opening their markets for goods and services as well as financial assets. Democratic transition and economic globalization accelerated the reform process even before the crisis. Unable to manage the speculative attack on their own, the three crisis-hit East Asian countries—Indonesia, Korea, and Thailand—had to seek IMF rescue financing, and with it to accept a structural reform program aimed at transplanting Anglo-American free market capitalism in place of a development system that had served them well for three decades before the crisis. Many detractors of the IMF were critical about the reform programs, arguing that these programs were so misguided and out of touch with the realities of these countries that they could not work. Although the jury is still out, growing evidence suggests that the IMF-directed reforms covering the financial, corporate, and public sectors have not been as successful as initially expected, and in many instances resulted in little more than cosmetic changes.

Over the last three years, the rapid recovery has renewed a reevaluation of the East Asian miracle and a search for the kinds of institutional reforms East Asia cannot avoid or delay to regain its precrisis dynamism and strength. The rethinking centers on the question of whether the East Asian model in the old structure still provides a better framework for development than an American free capitalism model for emerging market and developing economies in the region. This question arises because many of the structural problems in East Asia may not have been any worse than those faced by other countries (including advanced countries) and may not have been directly responsible for the crisis.[18] Nevertheless, the crisis itself, and the subsequent revelation of the weaknesses in the crisis-hit countries, provide good reason to think about whether East Asian countries can stay with the old regime, reform it while keeping major elements intact, or eschew it altogether in favor of an Anglo-American model of free capitalism.

The discussion of the failures of the precrisis East Asian model leaves little doubt that it will have to undergo an extensive overhaul to be credible as a development paradigm, not because it was susceptible to crises, but because it may have become too outdated to cope with the changes taking place in both domestic and global economies.[19] For example, many of the policies, such as the export push that worked well at early stages of development, may no longer be relied on, and the old governance system that befits authoritarian governments has become irrelevant to democratic regimes. The East Asian development model is not a static concept, but rather path dependent in the sense that its formation has been greatly influenced by cultural, historic, and political factors. A new system will also evolve over time with societal, political, and economic changes taking place in East Asia and throughout the global economy. But without proper reform, it may not be a viable one.

Although the precrisis East Asian development model is outdated in many respects, neither the crisis itself nor the structural failures have necessarily rendered the model dysfunctional. Certainly, the structural weaknesses of the model do not support the view that East Asian countries will find it in their interest to emulate Anglo-American free capitalism, and that institutions and policies should be likewise reformed to support the indigenization of such an Anglo-American model. The real challenge in developing a new East Asian paradigm for postcrisis development is not to graft the Anglo-American model on East Asia, but to reform the existing system to make it better suited for, and more flexible to adjust to, the new realities of East Asia and the rest of the world.

18. Stiglitz (1998).
19. Park (2002).

References

Campos, Jose Edgardo, and Hilton L. Root. 1996. *The Key to the Asian Miracle: Making Shared Growth Credible*. Brookings.

Dooley, Michael, Rudiger Dornbusch, and Yung Chul Park. 2002. "A Framework for Exchange Rate Policy in Korea." In *Korean Crisis and Recovery*, edited by David T. Coe and Se-jik Kim, 483–521. International Monetary Fund and Korea Institute for International Economic Policy.

Frankel, Jeffrey, and Nouriel Roubini. 2000. "The Role of Industrial Country Policies in Emerging Market Crises." Paper prepared for the Conference on Economic and Financial Crises in Emerging Market Economies. National Bureau of Economic Research, October 19–21.

Fischer, Stanley. 1999. "The Road to a Sustainable Recovery in Asia." International Monetary Fund. October 18 (www.imf.org/external/np/speeches/1999/101899.htm).

Goldstein, Morris. 2001. "Managed Floating Plus and the Great Currency Regime Debate." Paper prepared for G-20 Workshop on Exchange Rate Regimes. Ottawa, June.

Haggard, Stephan. 2000. *The Political Economy of the Asian Financial Crisis*. Washington: Institute for International Economics.

Lane, Timothy, and others. 1999. "IMF-Supported Programs in Indonesia, Korea, and Thailand: A Preliminary Assessment." *Occasional Paper* 178. Washington: International Monetary Fund (June).

Park, Yung Chul. 2002. "A Post-Crisis Paradigm of Development for East Asia: Governance, Markets, and Institution." Paper prepared as a background study for the paradigm project of the Asian Development Bank Institute. Tokyo, June.

Rodrik, Dani. 2000. "Development Strategies for the Next Century." Paper prepared for conference on Developing Economies in the Twenty-first Century, Institute for Developing Economies, Japan External Trade Organization. Chiba, Japan, January 26–27.

Stiglitz, Joseph. 1998. "Toward a New Paradigm for Development: Policies and Process." Prebisch Lecture, United Nations Conference on Trade and Development. Geneva, October 19 (www.worldbank.org/html/extdr/extome/jssp101998.htm).

Williamson, John. 2000. "Exchange-Rate Regimes for East Asia: Reviving the Intermediate Option." Washington: Institute for International Economics (forthcoming).

World Bank. 1993. *The East Asian Miracle: Economic Growth and Public Policy*. Policy Research Report. Oxford University Press.

———. 2000. *East Asia: Recovery and Beyond*. May.

Discussion

The discussion focused on questions of political economy and the role of financial markets. Dani Rodrik echoed the concerns raised by Yung Chul Park by asking whether the global financial architecture being constructed is actually compatible with the kind of institutional diversity that Park presented. Rodrik also questioned whether developing countries were getting more investable resources out of enhanced capital mobility. Morris Goldstein's comments raised the possibility that the good old-fashioned debt-dynamics equations yield answers on sustainable debt stocks that are too generous.

Martin Evans asked why the political economy in these countries does not allow for changes in policy when times are good. Alternatively, Evans said, it could be that it is the financial markets that get it wrong by not assessing the risk correctly. If that is the real question, he continued, then the discussion's policy focus ought to be directed on why the markets are incorrectly assessing the risk—a completely different set of policy issues from the traditional international macroeconomic issues.

Susan Collins raised the market flexibility issue. That topic did not get a lot of play in this discussion. But in many other discussions about the restructurings that are needed when countries are recovering from crises, market flexibility plays a key role. Labor market flexibility was an important issue in the Argentina discussion, but not in the discussion about Asian countries, Korea in particular. Collins also wondered about the role of exchange rate regimes in setting off vicious and virtuous cycles. It remained unclear to her whether the choice of an exchange rate regime can allow a country that is in a vicious cycle to somehow jump-start a virtuous cycle. Managed flexibility with inflation targeting, of the sort Goldstein discussed, can help avoid crises,

227

but it is not obvious that it is necessarily part of the package that shifts a country to the virtuous growth cycle.

Sidney Weintraub asked Park whether the argument that East Asian countries need reserves, and hence export promotion, as their safety valve implies that they should have complex input protection in order to be able to have trade surpluses and undervalued exchange rates. Park responded that most of the countries are still on International Monetary Fund (IMF) programs, and they are not allowed to impose any kind of input restrictions whatsoever, so that is neither a policy or an option they can entertain. Direct export promotion is out of the question. But these countries will have to maintain some kind of export competitiveness, and that is a major reason why they continue to intervene in foreign exchange markets.

Barry Bosworth said that Argentina was not a good example of a political economy problem. The problem in Argentina was that the economists did not agree. There was a lot more uncertainty at the time among economists about what was the optimal policy to follow. Bosworth echoed Rodrik's concern that if there are not going to be large capital flows to these countries, what is the benefit of having a very open capital system? Rodrik added that the situation is even worse, as many countries are putting a dollar in reserves for every dollar they are borrowing, which in view of the interest differential implies making an outward resource transfer.

Kristin Forbes brought up the presentations' contrasts on financial and banking systems. Park focused on the weakness of the financial systems in Asia. One of the lessons of the Asian crisis was how important it was to have strong financial systems in order to better respond to crises and alleviate the impact of an initial crisis. But Argentina has very well-capitalized banks and strong financial systems—and that did not help alleviate the crisis. It raises the question whether it was right to draw the lesson from the Asian crisis that a strong financial system is critically important in dealing with financial crises. Forbes pointed out that Goldstein did not spend very much time talking about the banking system, and asked whether he viewed building a strong financial system as a second-tier issue, to be dealt with after the issues of exchange rate and monetary policy.

Goldstein clarified that he thought the banking system was important. He has written a book on the banking business and core standards. But establishing appropriate currency regimes and maintaining debt sustainability were also key elements of crisis prevention. That did not imply a change in priorities.

Panel: Views on Currency Crises

In his response, Jose Luis Machinea pointed out that, at the end of the day, there was a trade-off with respect to the financial system. You can have a very strong financial system with very high liquidity ratios, like the 22 percent in Argentina, but then the system does not serve for financial intermediation. The legal requirement was 11 percent. With regard to the financial markets' responsibility in setting off the crisis, Machinea thought that the markets were quite myopic; there are a lot of information problems and imperfections in the financial markets. During the 1990s, the markets did not worry about the increase in government expenditure or the fiscal deficit—the financial markets kept lending to Argentina. The same thing happened in 1999, when the fiscal deficit was almost 5 percent of the gross domestic product (GDP). The government was still able to raise money in the financial market and we were also able to raise money in the financial market in 2000.

Machinea agreed that economists also vacillated about convertibility—it was not just the politicians. He meant the term "political economy" to apply to the views of economists as well. On the issue of market flexibility, he clarified that his focus was on the macroeconomic side of things. With convertibility, one cannot have deflation if one does not have flexibility. Machinea agreed that while in the long run capital flows should increase the level of economic activity and rate of growth in developing countries, during the last ten years the noise that they have been introducing into the system has produced perhaps more costs than benefits. But the time to discuss restrictions on capital flows is when the current account deficit is close to zero. It is not the time to discuss putting any kind of restrictions on capital flows when the current account deficit is 4 or 5 percent of GDP.

Morris Goldstein clarified that he was not saying that you could not borrow. What he was saying is that a ratio of total debt to exports, or external debt to exports, of 400 to 500 percent is a lot. So is a ratio of 100 percent of public debt to GDP. A country wants to stay out of those ranges if possible. It does not mean that you cannot do any borrowing. It just means that a country cannot overdo it. With regard to the question of how to switch policies when growth is 6 percent, Goldstein thought the answer is that most countries do not. So you do not want to get into a system that you are likely to have to change. That is why Goldstein liked the floating plus scheme, because you do not get as easily into an overvaluation problem and a transition problem.

On the architectural diversity question, Goldstein thought there are some aspects of architecture reform, such as in banking and financial system, that are relatively uncontroversial. It is very hard to find cases where state-owned banks do very well. It is probably very hard to find instances where very lax procedures, lack of classification of nonperforming loans, and restrictions on foreign entry of banks are desirable. Diversity could well be desirable in capital controls, family-owned businesses, and some other things. It is true that there is a lot of disagreement among economists, even though there is a little less disagreement now, after the crash of the currency board. But who knows how long that will last?

Goldstein said he did not get much into capital controls, even though he thought that is a very relevant issue. To some extent, if you regulate capital flows, then the case for flexibility to deal with large shifts becomes less pressing. As another option, he cited the example of India, a country that has some elements of managed floating plus, but also has some capital controls. India's method was not the way Goldstein would choose to go, but it was another option.

On the moral hazard issue, Goldstein said that the discussion was distorted. Some people think there is no such thing as borrower moral hazard. He asked why Asia is accumulating reserves and doing regional monetary arrangements. Goldstein thought that the reason was that Asian countries found out in the Asian crisis that the IMF did not respond in the way that countries hoped. So now countries are relying more on themselves. On the lender side, the best evidence comes from looking directly into the workings of Japanese and Korean financial systems. One finds a big web of implicit and explicit guarantees at the domestic level. Those guarantee systems produce a lot of excessive risk taking. The question becomes: if lender moral hazard is prevalent domestically, why should it not be prevalent internationally?